	JUN	2004
	JUN 09	
	JUL	X X 2015

Twayne's United States Authors Series

Sylvia E. Bowman, *Editor*

INDIANA UNIVERSITY

Francis Marion Crawford

FRANCIS MARION CRAWFORD

by **JOHN PILKINGTON, Jr.**

University of Mississippi

 67

Twayne Publishers, Inc. :: New York

MANUFACTURED IN THE UNITED STATES OF AMERICA BY
UNITED PRINTING SERVICES, INC.
NEW HAVEN, CONN.

To

L.K.P. AND C.K.P.

Preface

THE VERDICT of this generation on the esthetic qualities of American writers in the decades before and just after the turn of the twentieth century has been rendered with such finality that protest or appeal is no longer possible. Everyone knows that the judgment has favored William Dean Howells, Henry James, and perhaps Mark Twain; and no one wishes to challenge the rights of these men to positions of literary eminence. The very unanimity of critical opinion about this matter has demonstrated the extent to which these authors have satisfied our image of the past and affirmed the qualities which we approve in the literature of our own time. Against these judgments the present critical biography of Francis Marion Crawford is not entered as a document of dissent. The purpose of writing it is not to effect a Crawford revival, and the commonplace opinion that Crawford was not so brilliant a writer as Howells, James, or Mark Twain is neither contested nor questioned.

When so much has been conceded, what remains? Part of what remains is the extraordinary popularity of F. Marion Crawford as one of the central facts in the literary and intellectual history of three highly important decades in American life. In open competition, Americans preferred Crawford's novels to the fiction of Howells, James, and even Mark Twain. Americans liked Crawford's stories well enough to purchase each of his forty-four volumes by the tens of thousands and to support three collected editions of his works during his lifetime. If any proof were needed, a glance into the glass covered book shelves of any private library assembled by a book-lover between 1883 and 1909 would reveal volume after volume of F. Marion Crawford's novels; and even the most cursory survey of the elegant pages of America's leading literary periodicals would suffice to show that Crawford contributed far more to them than any of the acknowledged masters (excluding of course the material that Howells wrote as a literary columnist about other novelists).

Aside from his fiction, the American public recognized Crawford as a thoroughly acceptable lecturer, playwright, critic, and historian. The point is that, in his own day as a professional man of letters, Crawford competed for public recognition on better than even terms with Howells, James, and Mark Twain. Crawford had something to offer that Americans wanted and wanted badly, something that his now more famous contemporaries evidently did not have;

in other words, Crawford represented in the late nineteenth-century America a force with which the literary and intellectual historian must reckon if these decades are to be placed in an adequate perspective.

Although in Crawford's case the literary work cannot be separated from the biographical basis upon which it rested, Crawford's biography possesses an interest in itself for the historian of American culture. Crawford was a living example, fully recognized in his own day, of the American expatriate, of the American dream of romantic escape to the past and present of Italy, and of the American longing for the life of genteel culture. He was a kind of American Ulysses journeying through life on the kind of odyssey thousands of Americans longed to make themselves. He was a marvelous example of what culture, travel, and education could accomplish for a man. He appeared to prove the worth of the ideals of the genteel tradition in America. The verdict of his own generation upon his life was phrased in the customary allusion to him as the "magnificent Marion Crawford." As a literary celebrity and as a constant source of feature articles in newspapers and literary periodicals, he far surpassed both Howells and James and probably Mark Twain.

Although the more lofty mansions on the Parnassian mountain have been assigned by our generation to Howells, James, and Mark Twain, the literary critic should still remember not only that F. Marion Crawford gave classic expression to the theory of the literature of entertainment but also that during the 1890's he led the opposition to the critical manifestoes of Howells, Hamlin Garland, and Frank Norris. Despite the changes in literary fashions that have elevated others above him—Howells has certainly suffered along with Crawford—Crawford also delighted a generation of American readers with stories that compelled their attention to the very last page.

F. Marion Crawford's contribution to American letters must be stated in terms of both his life and his literary production. His books furnish examples of what Americans considered good fiction during the later part of the nineteenth century, and his life corresponds to what they believed was good living. In both respects Crawford was just as much a part of the stuff that made America as the poetry of Henry Wadsworth Longfellow. As a force and phenomenon of his time, Crawford must be included along with Howells, James, and Mark Twain in any historical assessment of the last half of the nineteenth century.

JOHN PILKINGTON, JR.

University of Mississippi
December 1, 1963

Acknowledgments

This critical study of the life and works of F. Marion Crawford has been written because a number of generous persons have demonstrated their interest in him by assisting me; and, although they are in no sense accountable for what I have written, without their help the volume could never have been finished. To the members of Crawford's family who have provided manuscripts for my use, answered my inquiries, and helped me with the research, I am deeply grateful. Crawford's daughters, Signora Eleanor Marion-Crawford Rocca and Mother Clare Marion-Crawford, have assisted me; and, although they may not have always completely agreed with my interpretation of their father's career, they have encouraged the project and made valuable suggestions about difficult problems. Mrs. Winthrop Chanler, Crawford's half-sister, kindly elaborated for me the reminiscences of Crawford which she had already published in her volumes of memoirs; and Mrs. Chanler obtained for me permission to see and use Crawford's letters to the Duchess of Sermoneta, whose generosity I also acknowledge. Miss Rosalind Richards and Mr. Lawrence Terry have graciously given me access to papers and manuscripts of their families. For comments and recollections about Crawford, I wish to thank Mr. Samuel Prescott Hall.

Although in the notes and references I have tried to record instances of specific indebtedness, there remain colleagues and friends whose contributions cannot be identified in that manner. I appreciate the many kindnesses of Professor Howard Mumford Jones whose lectures at Harvard initially interested me in Crawford's life and work. My colleague, Professor Clare L. Marquette, has carefully read the manuscript and made valuable suggestions. Mrs. Dudley R. Hutcherson and Mrs. John G. Douglas have helped in the preparation of the manuscript. Above all, I am grateful to my wife, Lillian, who with patience and understanding has read each page of the manuscript not once but many times. The skillful editing of Miss Sylvia Bowman has saved me from many an error.

For their generous cooperation and helpfulness I am indebted to Mr. William A. Jackson, director of the Houghton Library of Harvard University, and to Mr. George L. Stout, director of the Isabella Stewart Gardner Museum, and to Mr. William N. Mason, assistant director of the Isabella Stewart Gardner Museum. For assistance in solving many of the problems of Crawford's biography, I am grateful to the staffs of the Henry E. Huntington Library, the Boston Public Library, the Butler Library of Columbia University, and the Library of the University of Mississippi. I am indebted to Mr. Jacob Blanck, research editor of the Bibliographical Society of America, for assistance in the preparation of the bibliography of Crawford's works.

For permission to make use of their holdings of manuscript material by and about Crawford, I make acknowledgment to the Houghton Library of Harvard University; the Isabella Stewart Gardner Museum; the Yale University Library; and the Library of Congress.

Contents

Chronology

1854 Francis Marion Crawford born August 2 at Bagni di Lucca, Italy.

1866 Entered St. Paul's School, Concord, New Hampshire.

1869 Returned to Rome; began to participate in social life of the city.

1870 Went to Hatfield Broad Oak, Essex, to study for Cambridge.

1873 Admitted pensioner at Trinity College, Cambridge; remained one year.

1874 Enrolled in the Technische Hochschule at Karlsruhe, Germany.

1876- Studied at Karlsruhe and at the University of Heidelberg;
1877 returned to Rome early in the spring.

1879- Edited the *Indian Herald* in Allahabad, India; left in July,
1880 1880, to return to Rome.

1881 Came to the United States; began to seek literary employment with help of Samuel Ward; met Mrs. Isabella Stewart Gardner.

1882 Wrote *Mr. Isaacs* and *Doctor Claudius.*

1883 Completed *A Roman Singer;* wrote *To Leeward* in Sorrento; went to London with Sam Ward to secure additional publishing contracts.

1884 Married Elizabeth Christophers Berdan in Constantinople and returned to Rome for the winter; wrote *Zoroaster.*

1885 Wrote *An American Politician, A Tale of a Lonely Parish,* and *Saracinesca;* spent the summer in Sorrento; rented Villa de Renzis.

1886 Birth of daughter, Eleanor; wrote *With the Immortals* and *Paul Patoff.*

1887 Purchased Villa Crawford; wrote *Marzio's Crucifix;* leased Torre San Nicola; began *Sant' Ilario,* sequel to *Saracinesca.*

1888 Birth of son, Harold; completed *Sant' Ilario* and *Greifenstein.*

1889- Suffered from fainting spells and stomach trouble; wrote
1890 *A Cigarette-Maker's Romance* and *The Witch of Prague* in

Munich; birth of twins, Clare and Bertram; began long voyage to East and probably completed *Khaled*.

1891   Wrote *Don Orsino*, third part of *Saracinesca* series.

1892- Wrote *Pietro Ghisleri*; returned to the United States for
1893   the first of many annual visits; renewed friendship with Mrs. Gardner; read from his novels; published *The Novel: What It Is*; traveled in Europe during the summer and returned in the fall of 1893 to direct legal proceedings of Berdan Firearms Company; completed *Katharine Lauderdale* and *The Ralstons*.

1894   Wrote *Casa Braccio*; in August returned to Italy to write *Taquisara* and *Adam Johnstone's Son*.

1895   Cruised extensively in the Mediterranean; returned to the United States; wrote *A Rose of Yesterday*.

1896   Purchased yacht *Alda*; completed *Corleone*; began dramatization of *Doctor Claudius*.

1897- Began *In the Palace of the King*; lectured in America; com-
1898   pleted *Ave Roma Immortalis*; returned to Italy in May, 1898; wrote *Via Crucis*.

1899- Finished *In the Palace of the King*; toured with company
1900   to help with revisions of play; returned to Italy and completed *The Rulers of the South*.

1901   Wrote *Francesca da Rimini* for Sarah Bernhardt; completed *Marietta*.

1902- Completed *Cecilia* and *The Heart of Rome*.
1903

1904   Began research for multi-volume history of Rome in the middle ages; completed *Salve Venetia* and *Whosoever Shall Offend*.

1905- Finished *Fair Margaret*; worked in the Colonna library at
1906   Rome; wrote *Arethusa* and *A Lady of Rome* at Torre San Nicola; suffered from asthma; completed *The Primadonna* during the winter of 1906 at Rome.

1907- Visited United States for last time in April, 1907; completed
1908   *The Diva's Ruby, The Little City of Hope, The Undesirable Governess,* and *Stradella*.

1909   Finished *The White Sister*; died April 9.

Francis Marion Crawford

CHAPTER 1

An Expatriate Boyhood

I

FRANCIS MARION CRAWFORD was born August 2, 1854, in the ancient Italian resort of Bagni di Lucca. Had his birth taken place in the winter, he would most certainly have been born in Rome. There his parents made their home in the second story of "Villa Negroni" near where Nero was supposed to have watched Rome burn. There his father, Thomas Crawford, the most important American sculptor of the 1840's and 1850's, practiced his art among the twelve studios which had been built for him among the ruins of the Baths of Diocletian. There Louisa Crawford, a tall, aristocratic woman with dark hair and soft, delicate features, found sufficient leisure from the demands of her growing family to become one of the leaders of the social life of the Eternal City. The heat and the humidity of the Roman summer, thought to produce fevers and bronchial diseases, prompted the Crawfords to seek each year the resorts of the Italian mountains or the Swiss Alps. In 1854 their choice had been Bagni di Lucca, famous for its mineral springs and mountain coolness.

Artistic recognition had not come easily or quickly to Thomas Crawford. Although he was often described as a native of Ireland, he was probably born in New York City in 1813. Remarkably talented as a boy, at the age of fourteen he could carve wood with rare skill; at nineteen he became apprenticed to Frazer and Launitz, noted monument-makers in New York City; and at twenty-three he went to Rome to work under the noted Danish sculptor, Bertel Thorwaldsen. There Crawford worked for years in poverty and obscurity until the sale in 1840 of his "Orpheus and Cerberus" to the Boston Athenaeum resulted in widespread, public enthusiasm for his art. In a few years his success equaled that of his famous predecessors, Hiram Powers and Horatio Greenough.

Despite an outward manner that was variously described as cold, indifferent, or preoccupied, Thomas Crawford enjoyed the respect and admiration of his contemporaries. He produced in rapid succession such impressive pieces of sculpture as "Genius of Mirth," "Autumn," "Homer," "Adam and Eve," and "Eve Tempted." He was commissioned to sculpture the Washington Monument at Richmond, the pediment for the Senate building in Washington, the bronze door to the Senate wing of the Capitol, and the figure of "Liberty" (also called "Freedom") for the dome of the Capitol. With the help of his assistants, Thomas Crawford in a very brief period turned out an astonishing number of large statues, but after his death his reputation quickly declined. Critics complained of careless execution, too rapid work, and a lack of compelling ideas. To Americans of his generation, however, Thomas Crawford was an acknowledged genius, and at the time of his son's birth in 1854, he was at the summit of his fame. Seen in retrospect, Thomas Crawford's career was almost prophetic of the path his son would follow.

In 1843, Thomas Crawford had met Louisa Cutler Ward in Rome. A year later they were married. By the time Francis Marion was born, there were already three daughters in the family: Annie, born in 1846; Jennie (often called "Piccola"), born in 1847; and Mary ("Mimoli"), born in 1851. They were all very much aware of their American relatives. Annie and Jennie had been to America to visit their mother's sisters, Julia Ward Howe and Annie Ward Mailliard, and their uncle, Samuel Ward; and Mrs. Howe had been in Rome when Mary was born. The children knew something of the differences between Italy and America and may have vaguely felt the importance of the Ward family.

The Wards had been prominent in New England ever since the seventeenth century. John Ward, one of the first members of the family to emigrate from England, lived in Rhode Island until his death in 1689. His son, Thomas Ward, married the granddaughter of Roger Williams. Richard Ward, son of Thomas Ward, became governor of Rhode Island, an honor also achieved by Richard's son, Samuel Ward, who was the first of a distinguished line of Samuel Wards. Although Lt. Col. Samuel Ward kept the tradition of politics in the family intact by marrying the daughter of a governor, his son, Samuel Ward (1786-1839), found a new field of endeavor in banking. He married Julia Rush Cutler, who was descended from the sister of General Francis Marion. Julia Ward named one of her sons Francis Marion, and her daughter, Louisa Cutler Crawford, selected this distinguished name for her own son.[1]

Although Louisa Crawford was to live in Italy most of her life, she always maintained close relationships with America, exchanging frequent letters and visits with her family in New England. Early in 1856, when he was scarcely two years of age, Francis Marion accompanied his mother and sisters on one of these visits. Later in the summer Thomas Crawford, who was beginning to suffer from a serious eye disease, joined his family briefly at Newport and then returned to Italy.

Shortly after his return to Rome, pain and the impairment of his vision forced him to abandon his work. In 1857 his sister, Mrs. William S. Campbell, and his closest friend, Luther Terry, an American painter living in Rome, accompanied Crawford to Paris and then to London for treatment. Louisa Crawford joined them, leaving her children behind with her sister, Mrs. Annie Ward Mailliard, in Bordentown, New Jersey. No one had much hope for Crawford's recovery. After months of intense suffering, he died in London, on October 10, 1857, at the age of forty-three. His widow brought the body to America for burial at St. John's Church, New York City. Late in 1858 or early in 1859, Louisa Crawford returned with her children to Rome.

Although Thomas Crawford died when his son was only three years old, the sculptor exercised a profound influence upon the career of the future novelist. The boy's tall, handsome figure and his unusual manual dexterity were portions of his inheritance from his father. In later years Francis Marion was to exhibit the same capacity for rapid artistic creativity and sensitivity to popular taste that had marked his father's best years. From the Wards on his mother's side, Francis Marion received not only his name but also the aristocratic bearing, the charm of his personality, and the tendency toward a career in politics that had characterized the family for generations. But most of all, Thomas and Louisa Crawford gave their son the inheritance of a dual nationality that helped to fill his life with the romantic experiences that were to become the plots of his novels. From his very earliest years, Italy and America were to combine in his temperament and later in his art. The Roman background made a difference, a difference noted by his cousin as early as 1858:

My first meeting with Marion Crawford is the first thing I remember. I was three years old. He was four. . . . He wore a dress of blue broadcloth embroidered with black braid, starched pantalettes, patent leather ankle ties, and short white silk socks. Such raiment I had never seen! In our family [that is, Julia Ward Howe's] the children were plainly dressed. The purple and fine linen of this little Roman cousin impressed me as much as his beauty.[2]

II

The next eight years of Crawford's life were to be spent mainly in Rome. After his father's death, Louisa Crawford moved her family from the old "Villa Negroni" outside of Rome to an apartment at the Casa Dies, near the Pincian gardens. After several years her friendship with Luther Terry, who had known her husband well for fifteen years and had helped her in his final illness, deepened until, despite the difference in their ages, they were married on September 21, 1861, in Rome. Luther Terry had come to Rome from Connecticut two years before Thomas Crawford. As a painter Terry had not achieved spectacular success, but his work had been admired and sometimes purchased by discriminating collectors. His patience and understanding eventually won for him the admiration and respect of the Crawford children. Two children were born to this marriage: Louisa Margaret Terry, born August 6, 1862, and Arthur Noel Wurtz Terry, born December 25, 1864.

Much of Louisa's time was devoted to the educational problems of her children. Jennie and Mary were sent to a boarding school in England, but Frank, or Frankino, or Frankie, as he was variously called in the family, remained in Rome. Louisa Terry did not want him reared as an Italian. She insisted that English be his native language, that he not attend Italian schools, and that his playmates be English or American boys. She made good her intentions, for Francis Marion—though technically an expatriate like his mother, father, and step-father—never considered himself anything but an American and never relinquished his American citizenship. His mother's plans for her son's educational advancement, however, were not carried out without difficulties that exerted a distinct influence upon his character and temperament.

Her determination to keep her son as American as possible prompted her to rely heavily upon private tutors; but, whenever possible, she enrolled him in small classes conducted by foreign teachers who catered to the Anglo-American colony in Rome. In one of her letters to Jennie Crawford, Louisa commented on Crawford's activities in 1863:

> Frankie has just returned from school . . . [and] is studying faithfully to-morrow's lessons. After these are conned, . . . he will have his luncheon, dress and go to dancing-school in lilac kid gloves and patent leather pumps. Lessons and dancing are by no means my idea of keeping the feast, but the long holiday [at Christmas] has been most irksome to dear Frankie, and work is at

present his great desire, a more miserable boy I never saw than during these ten days, he has been. "What shall I do?" has been the perpetual cry.[3]

Crawford's desire for something with which to occupy himself seems more than a child's restlessness. It reflects the lack of playmates, and it begins what becomes a rather persistent note of loneliness in Crawford's boyhood.

The difficulty of finding proper tutors for Crawford was a source of constant trouble for his mother; and the resulting irregular schooling had in turn an effect upon the boy. On one occasion Louisa wrote that, when she thought she had found a person for French and English, the tutor, a certain "Mr. Appel," suddenly disappeared, leaving her "a distressed Mother looking for a teacher."[4] A few months later Louisa wrote that he was attending a class in French and German but concluded that "His little fellow student Mary Beck leaves to-morrow, so that this is the last day . . . and he must go on again by himself, for the next few months."[5]

Louisa's phrase, "go on again by himself," characterizes Crawford's childhood in Rome. She kept him out of the Italian schools and did her best to provide adequate private tutors, but she thereby tended to exclude him from the companionship of boys his own age. She recognized the problem and expressed her concern to her daughter:

> The two [Crawford and his step-father] had a hot walk to the Villa Medici . . . where Frank gets his only sight of boys' play life—the French priests making it a resort with their several classes. Not that he ever plays with them, but he is greatly interested in watching their goings and comings. . . . It is rather sorrowful for the dear fellow to grow up so without boys' companionship. . . . He is quite alone in his amusements, and gradually forgets how to do as other boys of his age.[6]

Louisa made similar statements in other letters to her daughters. The lack of continuous school experiences and the absence of playmates of his own age forced Crawford back upon adult associates and his own resources. His parents filled the gap where they could by taking Crawford with them on visits to the villas of their friends; the boy looked upon these excursions with great delight. Louisa's letters mention his walks to the important historical buildings of Rome and to many of the Italian villas owned by her friends. His mother knew, however, that her son's educational program contained grave deficiencies.

As Crawford became older, these deficiencies became increasingly evident. Louisa Terry must have been distressed by the fact that the regular discipline of educational routine was notably absent from his schooling. A long succession of teachers of strikingly different nationalities and educational methods was certainly not calculated to further a coherent program; and the periods between tutors, when the boy had to "go on again by himself," served only to underscore heavily the major problem. What was worse, Louisa Terry saw that she was being defeated in her efforts to bring him up as an American. It was not that he was becoming an Italian; rather, it was that the trend of his studies and his teachers was neither American nor Italian. One suspects that his mother knew already what her niece was to voice years later when she wrote: "My aunt's devotion to her children was proverbial. She gave them all the grace, glamour, polish, that it was possible to acquire, but she could not give them a country."[7]

III

Louisa's effort to give her son a country led her to seek a school for Crawford in America. She selected St. Paul's School at Concord, New Hampshire. It had recently been founded by George B. Shattuck who had been a schoolmate of Louisa's brother and a pupil of her former tutor, Dr. J. G. Cogswell. While Louisa was in America in 1856, Dr. Cogswell probably recommended St. Paul's and introduced Louisa to the Reverend Augustus Coit who had just been elected to the rectorship of the new school. In the ten years that followed, she had every reason to think highly of her selection. Coit obviously endeavored to make the school the American equivalent of the English public schools at Eton, Rugby, and Harrow. He was a staunch Episcopalian, and the Episcopalianism which he inculcated in his pupils was approved by Louisa. By 1866, when she made her final decision, she must have realized that her son would associate at St. Paul's with well-bred American boys whose fathers and mothers represented the wealth and social prominence of New England; and she could have taken comfort in the knowledge that her sister, Julia Ward Howe, lived only a few miles away in Boston.

Crawford was to spend three years at St. Paul's. On October 20, 1866, John Tyler Wheeler, the Latin instructor, recorded the new student's arrival in *The Rural Record*, a kind of school diary: "There is a new arrival at the school today, Master Francis Marion Crawford, 12 years of age, from Rome, Italy.... Francis is able to converse in both French and Italian, besides his English, and can read German well and speak it with considerable ease." Academically, Crawford's preparation for St. Paul's seems to have been good. His assignment to the Second Form meant that, in addition to the usual religious subjects, he studied English, Latin, French, Roman history, and arithmetic. In the second half of the year, Greek was added and geometry substituted for arithmetic. During his second year, he pursued a more advanced version of this program, reading Caesar in his Latin class and studying classical geography and English history. In the following year he advanced to Virgil, Xenophon, and algebra. There is every reason to believe that he did well in French, mathematics, history, and the classics. Crawford's troubles at St. Paul's were not academic.

Louisa Terry could have expected that her son would encounter problems. He had been brought up in well-to-do circumstances in a foreign land which to him was his native country and in an environment dominated by women. At St. Paul's he was suddenly projected into surroundings that were austere by comparison and populated chiefly by his own sex. Although Crawford was tall, handsome, and strong in appearance, he had had little association with other boys and knew nothing of boys' sports. Lack of skills consistent with his age and physique was a serious handicap, and in this respect he probably never caught up with his associates. When he arrived, he appeared to be older than the other boys; and he was distinctly different from them in speech, dress, and manners. There is little wonder that for months he was lonely and homesick. The death of his sister Jennie increased his depression. Letters from his family seem to have failed to lighten his gloom, but as the months passed he became less despondent. Probably the fact that he gradually came to be accepted by the other students helped his mental outlook; but at St. Paul's he was never popular in the sense of being a leader. Crawford never won any athletic distinctions; and, though afterwards remembered as a good scholar, he never received an academic prize. In the spring of 1869, he returned to Rome and persuaded his mother to permit him to remain in Italy.

Beyond his moderate academic achievement and additional maturity, the ultimate significance of Crawford's boarding-school experience is difficult to evaluate. His mother's willingness to allow him to stop short of finishing his preparation for Harvard suggests that he had no desire to continue at St. Paul's; and, certainly once he was back in Italy, he showed no wish to return. One is led to conjecture that the real trouble lay in the fact that the easy, irresponsible life he had led in Italy had already claimed him to such an extent that he could not willingly conform to the more exacting pattern of the American schoolboy's way of life. Louisa Terry had waited too long to send him to America.

IV

The winter after his return from America in July, 1869, was a kind of interlude for Crawford. He enrolled in no school and adhered to no established program; rather, he accepted many of the invitations urged upon him to attend the parties and dances of the Roman social season; and, for the first time in his life, he fell in love. The girl was Lily Conrad, tall, slight, with brown eyes and golden hair, the daughter of a Confederate army officer. Her father had died, and Mrs. Conrad, who had remarried, was in 1869 the wife of the Marchese Cavalletti of the Pope's Noble Guard. Lily had been educated at the Sacred Heart Convent of the Trinità dei Monti, and she was visiting the Terrys when Crawford arrived. Her background, which already included several years in the international social set in Rome, somewhat paralleled Crawford's. Although three years older than he, she became the object of his constant attention. He made no secret of his passion; and, even after she married another man, he may have continued for some time to believe himself in love with her.[8]

Crawford's education must have continued to be a vexing problem for Louisa Terry. When he refused to return to America to study for Harvard, she accepted England as the next best place. Accordingly, to prepare him for entrance examinations at Cambridge, she sent him to work under the direction of the Reverend George Burn at Hatfield Broad Oak, Essex. This little village had been in existence since the twelfth century, and in 1870 it was an agricultural community noted principally for the church of St. Mary. Very little is known of Crawford's life in the vicarage of this rural community where he lived for the next three years, but a fictional treatment of his experiences probably appears in *A Tale of a Lonely Parish* (1886). The setting of this novel reminds one of Hatfield Broad Oak, and the vicarage there may have been in his mind when he wrote that "the life at the vicarage of Billingsfield, Essex, was not remarkable for anything but its extreme regularity. Prayers, breakfast, work, lunch, a walk, work, dinner, work, prayers, bed. The programme never varied, save as the seasons introduced some change in the hours of the establishment."[9]

The dull life at the vicarage in Hatfield Broad Oak was interrupted occasionally by trips to London and by vacations on the Continent. Twice Sam Ward, his uncle, sent for him to come to London. During one of these meetings, Uncle Sam gave his nephew a "£5 tip," which, according to Ward, Crawford spent in the company of "a minor canon of Westminster who sent him home drunk, not with wine or stout but with the Divine melodies of a concert of ancient music."[10] Uncle Sam reported to Louisa Terry that he had given her son "a plain talk against smoking and in favor of grappling with the University" immediately.[11] On another occasion Crawford was called to London to see Julia Ward Howe who was then a delegate to the first International Congress of Women. In July, 1872, after a pleasant visit to Venice, he traveled northward with his family to Brescia and thence through the Maloja Pass to Pontresina in the upper Engadine valley of the Rhaetian Alps. Often he took long walks with his mother to St. Moritz and the Roseg and Morteratsch glaciers, and once he nearly lost his life in a fall while climbing the Piz Bernina, the highest peak in the Rhaetian Alps. Later he took a week's tour on foot through the Austrian Tyrol. [12]

The summer vacation exhilarated him, and when he returned to Hatfield Broad Oak in September, 1872, his mother wrote that "he intends to go up in January for his matriculation,"[13] but another year interposed before he "grappled" with the university. Not until October 8, 1873, was he admitted as a pensioner at Trinity College, Cambridge. Although his attention to academic matters was not noteworthy, he studied diligently enough to receive first-class honors in the general examination which he took in the Lent term of 1874; the subjects for it—elementary mathematics, divinity, Latin, and Greek—he had probably prepared at Hatfield Broad Oak. Years later, Crawford, speaking of his student days at Cambridge, was quoted as saying, "I distinguished myself there chiefly in two ways, I think—in pugilism and in tandem driving."[14]

Crawford was plainly sowing wild oats. He had made his first acquaintance with the pleasures of wine and excitement in Italy after his return from America. In the vicarage of Hatfield Broad Oak, there had been little chance for such indulgences, but at Cambridge the opportunities were limited only by one's funds or credit. When he joined his mother on the Continent in the summer of 1874, she observed his conduct with great alarm and hastened to ask her husband to investigate the possibilities of sending Crawford to "New Zealand or even the Far West, anywhere where he cannot get at more than an allowed sum of money and where severer out door life will work off this craving for excitement." The italics in her final comments emphasize her fears: "Make all possible enquiries about both sides of the world. It must be a place where *no* dissipations can reach him. Otherwise I am fully persuaded that he will drift not only to the bad but to the worst. We *must* devote all our energies to this question."[15]

Crawford had never been thrifty, and in his defense it could be said that there had never been any need for him to economize, nor had economy ever been urged upon him. While he was attending St. Paul's, Julia Ward Howe's protests to Louisa that Crawford was "a little too fond of spending money"[16] went unheeded; but in 1874, when Louisa learned that he had departed from Trinity leaving behind him a large number of unpaid accounts, she was thoroughly upset and frightened. When other bills that Crawford had not mentioned appeared later, she became desperate; although she knew that they must be paid "sooner or later," she hardly knew how. Looking back on the past, she blamed St. Paul's for permitting the boys "unlimited pocket money and no questions asked as to what was done with it."[17] Her criticism, however, may have been somewhat unfair, for Julia Ward Howe had warned her about Crawford's laxity in money matters. With more reason Louisa could have blamed the practice then in vogue among the Cambridge tradesmen of extending almost unlimited credit to undergraduates. This policy was certainly not designed to keep the undergraduates out of debt, and Crawford was neither the first nor the last to fall victim to it.

Under normal circumstances Louisa Terry might not have been greatly concerned about her son's seemingly lavish expenditures, but at the time she probably believed that she herself was facing financial disaster. Her expenses had been very heavy during the past year. While sending Crawford to Trinity, she had covered the very considerable expenses of the wedding of Annie to Erich von Rabé early in 1874 and a few months later the marriage of Mary to Hugh Fraser; and to each daughter she had promised to send a large annual allowance. Her own funds derived in large measure from a trust fund established by her uncle, John Ward, and administered by her cousin, Charles H. Ward. About this time the sudden financial failure of Charles H. Ward threatened to leave her with financial commitments far in excess of her income.

The crisis in Louisa Terry's financial affairs powerfully influenced the direction of Crawford's life. On the one hand, it emphasized the fact that sums which were sufficient for comfortable or even luxurious living on the Continent could not provide a comparable standard of living in England or in the United States. On the other hand, it dramatized for him the fact that he already possessed very strong theories about the standard of living suitable for a gentleman. Very likely Crawford had never openly voiced these notions and even more probably no one had ever questioned them, but now his ideas were evident from his actions and those actions and ideas were being questioned. Louisa Terry's losses raised an even more important question: If he was ever forced to rely upon his own efforts to support himself, what would he do? The answer could perhaps be delayed, but the question for the first time began to obtrude itself not only upon Crawford but also upon the other members of his family. For the next ten years it would continue to produce anxiety and tension in the minds of Crawford and his mother.

V

Crawford's first reaction to his mother's insistence upon economy was a stubborn refusal to return to the English university where, he said, his allowance of £300 could "never have been considered enough by any reasonable man."[18] His sisters and their husbands had suggested that he go to New Zealand or to California, and Crawford himself may have had some vague notion of going to California. Subsequent and cooler reflection convinced the family of the unreality of this solution; and, at the suggestion of Erich von Rabé, Annie's husband, they decided to send Crawford to the Technische Hochschule at Karlsruhe, Germany. Crawford obeyed, and with very little enthusiasm enrolled in the school on October 22, 1874; but the tension between him and his family, especially his mother, did not subside at once. He virtually ceased to communicate with his family. Once he went to Danzig on business for Louisa Terry, and afterwards she wrote her husband (December 13, 1874) that Crawford had seized the opportunity to have a "severe spree." Two months later she reviewed the situation:

> I have not heard from him [Crawford] for more than two months—indeed have had but one short note since he went to Carlsruhe. I scarcely know what to do. If I write to him it is encouraging him in disrespect—if I do not send money it encourages him in debts. We know that he is well, for Annie had the brilliant thought to write to a lady whom she knows there and through whom we have heard of him; but all our knowledge is hearsay. Erich has written three or four times without success, and is very indignant at his silence.[19]

Crawford's differences with his mother were not lasting. In a short time communication between them was as affectionate as ever. She continued to have moments of concern about his drinking and spending, but she must have been greatly encouraged by Crawford's evident liking for the school at Karlsruhe and by his comments about the proper conduct of life. His letter written during the winter of 1875, for example, was surely everything she could have desired and must have removed any doubts she might have had about her son's attitude:

I have just returned from a week's visit with a friend of mine, Graf Degenfeld-Shönberg [*sic*], I am glad to say in perfect health. I had a very delightful time with the old bachelor, at his castle of Schönberg, about half an hour from Heidelberg. You know I cannot shoot, but I try it. . . . I am having a very pleasant literary time of it, just at present. It sounds incredible in this century, but I am reading "My Novel" [presumably Bulwer Lytton's *My Novel; or, Varieties in English Life*] actually for the first time. I have not yet finished the first volume, but to form an adjective like "uxurious," I am very "firstvoluminous"; the book never leaves me. . . .

Idiot that I was not to understand your love for the German language, years and years ago; think what I might have read in that time. A people, a language and a literature, after my own heart. But there's no good crying over spilt milk, as the man said when he upset his full glass of champagne. N.B. This shews that the proverb existed before the Deluge and Noah's subsequent invention of wine, since spilt wine is a much more apt simile for the golden opportunities thrown away, than milk. Otherwise one might with equally fine expression say "There's no good crying over spilt arrowroot. . . ."

I am registered in the forest school as I proposed to be, and attend lectures with varying regularity.[20]

Because of its location in the great Black Forest region, Karlsruhe was an important center for forestry, but Crawford at twenty-one was still too immature to make a final choice of a vocation.

Within three months he had tired of forestry and had written his mother that the "die is cast," that he had made his "final choice," and that "all other accomplishments and tastes" would sink "into utter oblivion." He then announced his decision: "I have chosen Chemistry as a Career, not as leading to anything else but as a science." Much of his enthusiasm he had caught from a friend:

Harry [Howe], who is a sensible man, was extremely sanguine about it [chemistry], and assured me with the certainty of a man who knows what he is talking about, that it is *the* career of the future, and what is more of the present, inasmuch as it affords almost from the first, I mean as assistant in the laboratory, a salary ample even in America for one's own support. . . . My career will of course be in America, where I can profit by Harry's advice and worldly astuteness—he is himself an excellent chemist.[21]

After his mother expressed her sympathy with his latest ambitions, Crawford was ready to revise his entire academic program and to begin all over again in another country. Enthusiastically he wrote her that he had determined to attend the University of Lund in Sweden. He called this new decision "the final stroke which decides everything and in which I *must* not fail."[22] How long the excitement over the prospect of studying at the University of Lund sustained his interest in chemistry is a matter for conjecture. Certainly he never attended this university, and in the letters which have survived he never again mentioned chemistry as a possible vocation. What seems most likely is that Crawford finished out the term at Karlsruhe and the following year, 1876-77, went to the University of Heidelberg.

The German experience later proved valuable; but the gain came from experiences outside the classroom. While at Karlsruhe and at Heidelberg, Crawford absorbed a great deal of miscellaneous information about the country and the people. He used his holidays to visit the principal cities and museums of Germany. Ansbach, Nürnberg, Berlin, and Strassburg became familiar places. He learned to speak German fluently, and he read widely in German literature. Although he had not yet dreamed of becoming a novelist, he had unconsciously added to his potential literary equipment by sharpening his powers of observation and by increasing his ability to combine description and incident to produce an arresting anecdote.

Much of what Crawford learned and experienced in Germany was to be embedded in his novel *Greifenstein* (1889). This dramatic story of love and bigamy among two generations of the Greifenstein family has its setting in the Black Forest and in a German university town which appears to be a thinly disguised Karlsruhe. The castle of the Greifenstein family may owe a good deal to the Schloss of Graf Degenfeld-Schönberg. Crawford wrote in his novel, "The name of Greifenstein will not be found on any map of the district, but those who know that wild and unfrequented country will recognize the spot."[23] There can be little doubt that many of his German classmates would have recognized the description of the Black Forest, the discussion of German student life, the analysis of duelling and the famous German "Korps," and the portrayal of the German aristocrat, Hugo von Greifenstein, as products of Crawford's experiences at Karlsruhe. In 1875 and 1876, however, Crawford had not the slightest idea that he would one day write such a novel about a German student; indeed, the irony of his entire German education lies in his unconscious preparation for a vocation totally dissimilar from his conscious intentions.

VI

The problems which had begun to trouble Crawford and his family while he was in England and had continued to plague them throughout his schooling in Germany remained unsolved in 1877 when Crawford was back in Rome. The winter of 1876-77 was particularly difficult for Louisa Terry who faced an almost disastrous loss of income and consequent humiliation at the hands of the von Rabé family in West Prussia. In May, 1877, while on her way to spend what she probably suspected would be an unpleasant summer with Annie in Lesnian, Louisa wrote Crawford from Bozen a letter which reveals clearly the situation:

> The regret at having given you up so many weeks before the law of inevitable necessity would have obliged me to do so is still heavy upon me. And yet there was not after all much satisfaction in those capricious glimpses of you, caught by waking late at night, sometimes not even thus caught, only a great heart disappointment at hearing the click of your key in the door just as I had given you up and gone to bed. . . . You will find my loving blessing, a very oft repeated tale, tucked away in its last corner. Write when you can, if but ten words, my love to my "only joy."[24]

One infers that, although Crawford often left home early in the evening and returned very late, his mother's feelings toward him were both tender and sympathetic. But tension between them would mount again before the summer was over.

Crawford was then translating documents for a group of engineers and a book for George Perkins Marsh, the distinguished author and diplomat who since 1860 had been serving as the first United States minister to the new kingdom of Italy. For a few weeks after Crawford's mother departed, he worked steadily "at the office." About the middle of June he suddenly left Rome on a walking tour to Subiaco. When Louisa Terry heard about his actions, all of her former fears revived. "I don't want him to mistrust you," she wrote Luther Terry, "as he might if I speak of his being less steady at his work, and yet I must try and keep him up to it, by such influence as I have over him."[25] When Crawford wrote Luther Terry that he was working for the engineers at Olevano (about seven miles from Subiaco), he complained that his mother had been given a false impression of his movements. At this point, Louisa Terry, who was distressed and harassed from all sides, voiced her exasperation and disappointment to her husband:

> I know not what to say about Frank, so disappointed, wounded, astounded am I. The entire through and through unfaithfulness

is the greatest pain, added as it is to the extraordinary selfishness. That he has not written one word to me since I left is of smaller importance, but it is an added distress that all my devotion and patience should be so thrown away. I am seriously considering whether my wisest plan would not be to refuse to give him any further support and so oblige him to work for his living. I am so puzzled by the leaving his translating work all this time. . . . Have the engineers thrown him over for some misunderstanding or misconduct. It was a great liberty in him to take, to ask that I should furnish money for such a mere party of pleasure. When he spoke of going into the mountains [that is, the hills near Subiaco and Olevano] it was as one of a walking party with Dr. Nevin and Mr. Garland, and for this he was bound to furnish himself. What shall I do? For I *will* not keep him in Rome in idleness another Winter. The idea of cutting off the allowance to his sisters and maintaining him in his self indulgence. It is not to be thought of. I feel extremely inclined to take him at his word, for once he said, "I shall never really be worth anything until all other means fail me, but the labour of my own hands." What is the answer from Dr. Coit?[26]

An effort had been made to secure a place for Crawford with St. Paul's School, but Dr. Coit, the rector of the school, evidently had no position to offer.

Louisa Terry had some right to feel hurt at Crawford's indifference and to be despondent over his future; nevertheless, her impatience with him was doubtless increased by her financial difficulties with the von Rabé family over the promised allowance to her daughter Annie. The distance between herself and her son may have added to her fears. "What an anxiety he is to us!" she exclaimed to her husband, "and how passing strange it is, that withal his self love, he should be utterly without ambition, without one quality necessary to a career."[27] Yet if the summer of 1877 was distressing to Louisa, it most certainly was also a painful time for Crawford. Although his side of the matter has not survived in letters, there can be little doubt that he never forgot the unpleasantness of those months; and years later he wrote a fictional account of them in two of his finest novels, *Katharine Lauderdale* (1894) and *The Ralstons* (1895).[28]

The relationship between mother and son was never again so strained as it was in the summer of 1877. By the time she returned, Crawford had announced his intention of studying Sanskrit at the University of Rome. Curiously enough, it had been while he was at Subiaco and Olevano that he had chanced to read the shabby, brown Sanskrit grammar that had once belonged to his sister Mary and determined to master the language. Viewed in retrospect, the incident became one of the turning points in Crawford's life, but in the fall of 1877 it was merely another enthusiasm that might or might not last.

With his study of Sanskrit at the University of Rome, Crawford's formal education came to a close. His cousin described him at the age of twenty-three as "one of the handsomest men I have ever seen—tall, splendidly built, with a noble head, classic features, and hands and feet of sculpturesque beauty. His eyes were blue, dancing, full of light, real Irish eyes."[29] She thought him a charming companion, as indeed he had every reason to be; for, in addition to his inheritance of natural artistic talent from highly cultured persons, he had had one of the most remarkable educational experiences that the nineteenth century could have offered.

In a century which was committed to the concept of travel and humanistic studies as keys to a broad cultural outlook, Crawford would have seemed to many the living embodiment of its ideal. Americans like Henry James, Sr., who had time and money to lavish upon superlative educations for their children, sent them to Europe. Americans felt that they stood on the perimeter of the cultural circle and looked inward toward a center which was Italy. Crawford's was a reverse process, for he was born at the center and as he matured he began to look outward toward the rim. Few men of his day possessed the mastery of Italian, English, German, and French that Crawford obtained in his youth; and to them he added Latin, Greek, and Sanskrit. Among his American literary contemporaries, only William Dean Howells, Henry James, and Henry Adams even approached the breadth of Crawford's linguistic education; but none of them—not even the well-traveled Henry James—could match his knowledge of the European setting and character. Put beside his cosmopolitan contemporaries, Crawford stands as the true cosmopolite—the man without a country and the man without a national bias. The paradox of this assertion, of course, is the fact that Crawford would have denied it every day of his life.

Despite his marvelous education and the depth of his culture, Crawford seemed living proof of the assertion that culture by itself would never put food into man's mouth. Crawford might not have agreed with the comment, but neither would he have realized that for him the best way to make a living from the ingredients of his culture was to mix with them the elements of the market place. As the year 1877 came to a close, Crawford still thought he could see ahead of him a scholarly career. He guessed wrong, but his mistake ironically enough provided the final experience that would put him on the right track.

CHAPTER 2

Search for a Profession

I

UNTIL LOUISA TERRY'S financial reverses forced an appraisal of the problem, neither Crawford nor his mother had ever given more than a passing thought to his future. Throughout much of his youth the decisions affecting his education had been dictated by the exigencies of place and family ties. These matters had seemed more urgent than future goals. When the precariousness of the present made consideration of the future imperative, however, his mother turned, as indeed she always had turned, to America; but Crawford in every instance found some reason for preferring another direction. The inference is plain that he had no real desire to spend his life in America. His point of reference was Europe or, more specifically, Italy.

Louisa Terry would not abandon her desire to see her son established in America. In 1874 she had asked her husband to make inquiries about opportunities for her son in the United States. In the summer of 1877 Dr. Coit had actually been approached about a place for Crawford on the faculty of St. Paul's School; and, during the same summer, Luther Terry, with her approval, had reminded Crawford that, if he wished to secure a position in the United States, he must please George P. Marsh, whose recommendation, Terry felt, would weigh heavily with American employers.[1] Late in 1877 the arrival from Boston of several members of her family including Crawford's cousin, Maud Howe, strengthened Louisa's hand. The Wards joined her in emphasizing America as the land of opportunity for Crawford; they could see nothing ahead for him in Italy.

For a brief period Crawford yielded to the strong influence of Maud Howe, who persuaded him to accept temporarily the family's decision to send him to the United States. Possibly more than any other member of the family, Maud Howe recognized the immense capacities latent in her cousin, but she said she was "horrified" by the lack of purpose in his life. She felt the distinct charm of Crawford's personality and wondered how he could be content to live at home, idle and supported by his mother. America, she firmly believed, was the only place for him; and, in their long, earnest talks about his future, she urged him to seek his fortune there. Crawford caught some of her enthusiasm and seemed actually on the point of leaving for the United States; but the project failed to materialize. After Maud Howe left Italy a few weeks later, his enthusiasm waned quickly; but she had, as Crawford later remarked, "more than anyone else" encouraged him "to strike out and be independent."[2] She was good for Crawford; she had done what the negative pressure of financial necessity and repeated criticism of his inactivity had not been able to do: by giving him the sympathy, encouragement, and optimism of someone his own age, she had led him to desire his own independence.

II

The plan for Crawford to visit America in June, 1878, may have been abandoned because no certain employment could be found for him and because his intense interest in Sanskrit prompted him to prefer India. Shortly after he returned from his walking trip to Olevano and Subiaco in the fall of 1877, he met an Indian scholar, whom Crawford's sister later identified as Doctor d'Acunha; and, under his influence, Crawford continued his study of Sanskrit at the University of Rome. To perfect his knowledge of the language, Crawford determined to attend the University of Bombay; he may even have expected to be employed as an instructor at the university. Having borrowed a hundred pounds from a friend of the family, Crawford sailed for Bombay early in January, 1879; by the middle of March, he had already begun his linguistic studies.

Although the position at the University of Bombay failed to materialize, Crawford studied purposefully until the hundred pounds which had been advanced to him for the venture had been exhausted and until he had learned, as he said later, that the study of languages was "profitable intellectually but not otherwise."[3] As his funds dwindled, he endeavored to support himself by contributing articles to the *Bombay Gazette*, but he quickly perceived that only a regular salary would support him in India. As a last resort he prepared an application for enlistment in the British Army. Before the papers could be mailed, however, the editor of the *Bombay Gazette* offered him the editorship of the *Indian Herald* in the historic city of Allahabad on the Ganges River, more than six hundred miles inland. Crawford accepted the offer immediately, and for the first time in his life he had an important responsibility thrust upon him.

The *Indian Herald* was then owned by Ajoodhya Noth, a wealthy native merchant and a Cashmere Brahman. When Crawford arrived, he found the paper had been badly mismanaged. His reforms included the employment of an efficient staff and the enlargement of the daily edition. The work of editing and managing (Crawford performed both functions) proved to be congenial to his temperament and challenging to his imagination. Before he had been in charge three months, he wrote his mother with considerable pride: "My occupation becomes more and more absorbing—Everyone here is beginning to take a real interest in the paper, and people high in office contribute and criticize."[4] Because of the compulsion of responsibility, he rapidly developed a business acumen which neither his mother nor the Wards in America had believed possible.

The editorship proved a turning point in Crawford's career. It enabled him to become financially independent of his mother, to meet the challenge of manhood, and, above all, to learn how to work. Ultimately it changed him from an irresponsible dilettante to a dedicated, purposeful intellectual. The very nature of the job, requiring a specific amount of work to be accomplished by a given time, operated as a steadying force upon him. At the same time, it corresponded to his conception of the position which a man of his social and intellectual background should occupy. Although his daily life may have been, as he said, outwardly monotonous, this monotony was the kind which suited his intellectual tastes and temperament; for there was in Crawford's personality a strange combination of a strong desire for excitement and a compelling need for long periods of solitude. As he grew older, the streak of asceticism in his character became more and more pronounced and often seemed to overbalance his romantic eagerness for activity and adventure; but in his youth the two sides of his nature were evenly weighted and in Allahabad particularly the circumstances of his work presented opportunities for satisfying both cravings.

Two events which took place during Crawford's residence in India permanently influenced his later life. One occurred during the late summer of 1879 when he was forced to make an exhausting journey to Simla on business connected with the *Indian Herald's* relations with the English government. Simla, located in the Himalayan Mountains and almost a thousand miles from Allahabad, became the seat of the government during the hot season. At Simla, Crawford met Alexander M. Jacob whose name and adventures Crawford was later to make the basis of his first novel, *Mr. Isaacs* (1882). Jacob, who claimed to be a Turk but who was generally thought to be either a Polish or Armenian Jew, was probably born near Constantinople about 1850. He is said to have been sold as a slave at the age of ten to a wealthy pasha who had him educated in the languages, art, literature, philosophy, and occultism of the East. Manumitted at the death of his owner, Jacob, disguised as a Mohammedan, made the pilgrimage to Mecca and from there went to Bombay. His accurate knowledge of Arabic enabled him to obtain a clerkship at the Nizam's Court in Hyderabad where he laid the foundation of a large fortune in jewels. From Hyderabad, Jacob went to Delhi as a dealer in precious stones and then to Simla where he became an influential merchant and probably took an active part in the British secret service.[5]

When Crawford encountered him, Jacob was at the height of his fame. His fabulous wealth, the mystery of his background, his powerful personality, and his phenomenal knowledge of the wisdom of the East made him a man who was sought out by both the foreign and the native dignitaries in India. Crawford, meeting him in the dining room of the hotel at Simla, at first thought Jacob was an Italian; later he believed him to be a Persian. After dinner, Jacob and Crawford spent the evening in Jacob's apartment, and there Crawford probably heard as much of the life-story of "Mr. Isaacs" as Jacob chose to tell. Crawford, of course, had no idea that his chance conversation with this cele-brated man would one day change the course of his life and prompt him to remark: "If it had not been for him [Jacob] I might... be a professor of Sanskrit in some American college."[6] In 1879 Crawford may have still entertained the idea that he would have enjoyed the vocation of a professor of Sanskrit.

Equally as significant for Crawford as the encounter with Jacob was his conversion to Catholicism during 1879 or 1880. The circumstances of his conversion are not known, but very probably it was a gradual process begun in Italy and completed in India. Although Crawford had been reared in the Episcopalian faith of his mother, he had lived much of his life among surroundings pervaded by a Catholic atmosphere; but, had he avowed any sentiments toward Catholicism while in Rome, his mother would certainly have strenuously opposed them. In India, however, he was at liberty to follow his own inclinations without parental interference; and, under the guidance of a priest in Allahabad, he was converted. Later Crawford described himself as "a staunch adherent to the faith and a conscientious observer of prescribed duties."[7] Crawford's conversion had important consequences for his subsequent career. By giving him a more sympathetic understanding of the religious customs of the Italian people, it enabled him to use religious material effectively in his novels. As a contemporary Catholic reviewer noted, Crawford, when he became a Catholic, removed the one barrier which had prevented most foreign observers from "getting near to the Italians" and grasping "the meaning of Italian history and social life."[8] Although the Catholic influence becomes apparent in many of his novels and is especially evident in such volumes as *Saracinesca* (1887), *Sant' Ilario* (1889), *Don Orsino* (1892), *Marzio's Crucifix* (1887), *Casa Braccio* (1894), and *The White Sister* (1909), it is manifested primarily as subject matter and almost never as Catholic apology. He never attempted to convert his readers to Catholicism, nor did he address himself specifically to a Catholic audience; yet, had he remained a Protestant, or had he become a zealous Catholic apologist, the qualities of his fiction would have been different and perhaps less attractive to many of his readers.

In 1880, however, the question of writing fiction with or without a Catholic bias held no interest for Crawford, who was intensely preoccupied with the daily struggle for the continued success of an Anglo-Indian opposition paper and was severely handicapped by journalistic conditions peculiar to India. "The press in India," wrote Crawford, "is the result of the presence of Englishmen, who have always been used to a daily paper at home, and cannot do without it abroad—but there is a wide difference in the manner of their reading. The press in England has a great power over the reading public. In India the reading public consists almost entirely of the officials of a despotic government, who perfectly understand that nothing the papers can say will have the smallest influence on the affairs of the Empire." His conclusion was that newspapers in India "at best can only aspire to be favorably viewed in the light of agreeable literature" and "must be more or less servile to the despotism represented by the general reader."[9] These comments reflect considerable credit upon the insight of a young editor with very little if any experience, for even the most cursory glance at a file of the *Indian Herald* while Crawford was in charge shows that he was trying to make it something more than "agreeable literature" and at the same time survive himself.

Crawford's efforts to maintain the paper on such a level failed. Looking back upon the experience several years afterwards, he realized that he had been caught between two segments of the native and English population which were united in opposition to the English government but divided in respect to ultimate objectives. The English contributors were not willing to support a paper which continually hinted at the possibility of native rule, yet the natives were not satisfied with an organ which stopped short of the grossest invective against the English government. Each group withdrew its support, and, as Crawford remarked, the owner "found himself a poor man, and the editor a much wiser one."[10] Despite its bitter ending, the experience had been a good one for Crawford; he had learned from it that the man who wishes to succeed with the public must not offend too bluntly its tastes and prejudices.

The conflict of interest which Crawford rightly viewed as the fundamental cause of the failure of the *Indian Herald* was the most important but not the only reason for Crawford's departure from India. The breakdown of his health under the strain of work in an unfavorable climate doubtless contributed heavily to his decision to leave; but an even more pressing reason than health may have been an open quarrel with the proprietor of the paper. That Crawford's tenure as editor should end in a quarrel would not have been in the least surprising to anyone who knew him well; for, when Crawford went to India, he had never willingly submitted to authority—much less worked under a "boss." So long as Ajoodhya Noth allowed Crawford to be master of the paper, he worked with enthusiasm; but, when Noth began to assert his prerogatives and curb his editor's powers, Crawford rebelled and "retired in disgust."[11] He always found criticism difficult to accept; he never again worked directly for an employer.

Although Crawford left India in July, 1880, and never returned, what he had gained was of permanent value to him. He had gone there to perfect his knowledge of the Indian languages and had succeeded, but of far greater importance was the fact that he had learned to discipline himself, to work according to plan, and to meet precise deadlines. He had also settled the matter of his religion and unknowingly settled it in a fashion that would assist him materially when he later began to write fiction dealing with Italy. He had become accustomed to writing for publication, and unknowingly he had already acquired the material for his first novel. Finally, and perhaps most important of all, Crawford had acquired an ambition to utilize his talents and to make something of his life. The logical place for him to go was home—Italy, now, as it always had been, was his frame of reference.

III

Late in August, 1880, Crawford reached his mother's apartment at the "Palazzo Altemps" in Rome. From Bar Harbor, Maine, where she was trying to dispose of her art objects, his mother had written ahead to arrange an allowance to be paid him; and, upon his arrival, he found a hundred pounds enclosed in a letter expressing her heartfelt sympathy for him. Rather strangely she had nothing to say about his future plans and no suggestion to make about his present activities. She may have known that at this time Crawford needed no prompting from her and she wisely decided to remain silent. Certainly she had long ago realized what Crawford was to learn in the next four months: there was no acceptable opportunity for him in Italy. Once he assented to this premise, there was little choice for him but to seek his opportunity in the United States. Accordingly, after a rough voyage as the only cabin passenger on a tramp steamer, he arrived in New York on February 14, 1881. To the New Yorkers who met him, 'Crawford must have appeared as a foreigner who spoke English well but with an Italian accent. To Crawford, who was thoroughly familiar with almost every capital and large city of Europe, New York must have seemed a strange place that he only dimly remembered from his childhood.

In New York, Louisa Terry and Sam Ward welcomed Crawford as a man who had finally made a sound decision. A few days later, as they assembled in Julia Ward Howe's Boston home for a family council, Crawford had his first opportunity for private observation of the acknowledged head of the famous Ward family. At sixty-six, Sam Ward had lost none of the personal charm that prompted both men and women everywhere to seek his company. He had been a child prodigy in mathematics and had studied abroad for what appeared certain to be a brilliant career; but he had suddenly lost interest in the subject, had returned to New York, and had taken a job in his father's bank. In 1849 he went to California to prospect for gold, but he made instead a fortune in real estate. After his return to the East in 1854, he became one of the first lobbyists in Washington; and he has since been described as "the most engaging scoundrel ever to afflict Washington."[12] Meanwhile, he had been married twice; his first wife was the granddaughter of John Jacob Astor; the second, a celebrated beauty of New York society. By 1880, however, he was living by himself, was nationally known as "Uncle Sam," and was as good an example of a universal genius as nineteenth-century America had produced. While his left hand was lobbying for the magnates of big business, his right was busy in literary criticism, authorship, art collecting, and an endless round of dinner parties. Because of his personal charm and his vast number of influential friends in every profession, Uncle Sam was as good a person as Crawford could have found in America to help him find a career.

Crawford and Ward should have immediately attracted each other. Crawford's life, particularly in its lack of direction and apparent irresponsibility, had somewhat paralleled that of his uncle. Both men had received the same general type of broad, liberal education in America and in Europe; and Crawford had developed a charm of manner and conversation which promised to equal that of the older man. In the weeks that followed Crawford's arrival, however, the two men did not become friends very rapidly. Crawford tended to view the older man with great reserve if not open distrust, while Sam Ward felt that his nephew was being boorish and unfair. By May, however, the apparent coolness between them had vanished, and from this time forward Crawford and his uncle were such close friends that the occasionally sharp exchanges which passed between them did not in the least alter their affection for each other.

The chief problem that preoccupied Crawford and engaged the energies of the other members of the family was the finding of a suitable occupation for him. After the failure of the Indian venture, Crawford felt that he had to begin again, yet he hardly knew where. "I am as puzzled about Frank's prospects as you are," wrote Julia Ward Howe to Sam Ward. "He is full of talent, facility and pluck," she continued, "but does not know which way to turn in order to earn a dollar. This is not his fault. It is very difficult for a foreign-bred American to take hold and find employment here, even if he has what Frank has not, exactly—a definite profession for which he is fully qualified."[13] She could scarcely have stated the difficulty more succinctly.

Admittedly Crawford had not been trained for any profession, but such qualifications as he did have were carefully analyzed by Crawford and the Wards. Because his knowledge of Sanskrit might lead him to a professorship, Uncle Sam offered to send him to Vienna for an additional year's study of the language. Even before the offer was made, Crawford had enrolled at Harvard in a course in Sanskrit taught by Professor Charles R. Lanman. With Julia Ward Howe's encouragement and management, Crawford considered trying to turn his Indian experiences into public lectures and actually delivered one lecture entitled "The Origin of Sacrifice among the Aryan People" at the New England Woman's Club on May 10, 1881.[14] At the same time Crawford was also considering a singing career. That he had all of these projects in mind is evident from his letter to his uncle in May, 1881:

> It is now time that I should give a definite answer to your generous proposal to send me to Vienna. . . . I consider that my position with regard to my family requires me to maintain the ground I assumed in going to India [that is, his independence]. The small sum I lately inherited [presumably from his aunt, Jane Campbell] is

sufficient to discharge to my mother what she advanced to me for my journey to the East . . . so that I feel I am starting in this country without being indebted to her. In the meanwhile, until I can find a market for my philological attainments I shall try and support myself by my voice and my pen. As I have had the training of a professional singer I have no fear about the result, and indeed I have already earned money by singing in this city.

Next month I shall pass an examination in Sanskirt at Harvard for which I shall obtain a certificate that may be of some value in the future.

In accepting your most liberal offer, I should feel I was doing wrong for two reasons. First, because I should be standing in the way of those who have real claims on your generosity, whereas I have none, and secondly, because I should be giving fresh satisfaction to those who have known so well how to put the worst construction on every action of my life.[15]

Crawford's comments reveal the maturity he had achieved since the weeks preceding his departure for India when his mother felt that he would never amount to anything. From the confidence in himself which he had won in India, he could refuse both his mother's support and his uncle's offer.

Throughout the spring and summer months of 1881, Sam Ward successfully obtained for Crawford a number of opportunities to write short pieces for newspapers and periodicals. Most of these projects represented a continuation of the journalistic and linguistic work he had performed in India. One of the articles was a pamphlet "on the question of Silver and the Standards," which Crawford worked up from published sources and sent to Sam Ward. Through his uncle's influence with George S. Coe, president of the American Bankers' Association, Crawford presented it under the title "Our Silver" as an address at the bankers' annual convention at Niagara Falls in August. Although he was pleased at the New York newspapers' comments about his arguments, Crawford wrote his Uncle Sam: "I think I should be very careful how I make my next appearance before the public."[16]

Ward had also introduced Crawford to William Henry Hurlbert, editor of the New York *World*, to whom Crawford sent three articles on the Civil Service and waited vainly to hear that they had been accepted. Meanwhile, he had also written an essay about the "land question" in Europe, intending it for the *Atlantic Monthly*, and another about the Abruzzi region of central Italy which Ward had forwarded to Robert Bonner, editor of the New York *Ledger*. He had also prepared a second lecture on India. These articles represented a good deal of solid activity but not very much success in terms of money.

Crawford continued to feel the pressure upon him to make some definite commitment to a vocation. He was still dependent upon his mother, and privately Louisa Terry continued to think that his responsibility in money matters was his greatest weakness. Sam Ward shared her apprehensions about his character and at times spoke very frankly. In reply to one of his uncle's letters, Crawford wrote: "In your letter received to-day you further characterize me as 'unsystematic,' 'lazy' and 'loungy.' I regret that my conduct should have led you to form so unfavourable an opinion of my mind, my temperament and my character. I have nothing to say, however, except that, in future, I shall endeavour not to expose myself to your criticism."[17]

Sam Ward's remarks, however, had stung his nephew into a remarkable analysis of his own character. Crawford wrote:

Since you have raised the question of my character, I will say what I think of myself. I believe that, with merely an average intellect, I possess certain peculiarities in a unique degree. I am, I think, perfectly incapable of anything like enthusiasm and I have not the slightest trace of what is called imagination. I am conscious also of the power to work my mind with an absolute certainty of what it can do, at every moment of my existence. . . . I am your man and I have told you what I can, that you may know how to use me. I will endeavour to acquire some cis-Atlantic style of action, but it is useless to hope that I can acquire anything quickly, though I believe I can use what I do know with sufficient readiness.[18]

In the light of subsequent events it is obvious that Crawford underrated his imagination and that he possessed a better-than-average intellect though he was never to be an original thinker. Crawford probably knew, however, that Uncle Sam would discount these remarks. What really troubled him was a growing dislike for the rapid pace of American life, a dislike grounded in his European attitudes and in his fondness for European customs. At the same time he was certain of his own ability to surmount all obstacles; hence his plea for time to "acquire some cis-Atlantic style of action."

Crawford, moreover, was proud, defensively aggressive, and inclined to be stubborn; but, despite all the comments about his indolence and his irresponsibility, there can be little doubt that once he resolved "to strike out and be independent"—a decision he had made before he left Italy for India—he worked steadily to achieve his purpose. It is fair to comment that neither his mother nor his uncle made sufficient allowance for the fact that Crawford's educational background had not prepared him for any specific profession or vocation. Instead, it had fitted him for the life of a gentleman of leisure (with perhaps literary or artistic preferences) and given him an aversion to business as a vocation. When he came to the United States, he was prepared only for linguistic study and for writing, and these were the lines of endeavor which he followed; but, as Crawford himself realized, he had a great deal to learn about America before he could write on many American subjects.

IV

Early in the fall of 1881 Louisa Terry felt she had to return to Rome. Crawford knew that some decision had to be made about his future. He was discouraged because he had no prospects for permanent employment. "The future looks black," he wrote Uncle Sam; "I will work as a proofreader, or a farm hand, or I will go west...rather than be dependent on anybody. If I cannot touch bottom by the 1st of November, I will go, it does not much matter where."[19] Still depressed, he wrote again, a few days later: "If you know of an opening in a business house I would like to try it." He wanted to write, but as he said, "The important thing is... that I should be during this winter in a position, insignificant if it must be, but fixed and offering the possibility of advancement."[20] Crawford's remarks indicate for the first time a subtle change in his attitude. He said no more about a professorship, and in his mind employment was now only a means of subsistence while he continued to write.

Sam Ward sensed the change in his nephew's attitude. He saw clearly that Crawford was not fitted for a business career—a point of view strongly seconded in the family councils by Julia Ward Howe. When, therefore, Louisa Terry sailed for Italy in November, 1881, Crawford remained behind in Boston, established in the reception room on the ground floor of Julia Ward Howe's residence at 241 Beacon Street. His mother had been convinced that he should remain, and Sam Ward had seriously determined to make a writer of his nephew. In this undertaking, Uncle Sam was soon aided by "Uncle Adolph" Mailliard who had recently come to New York from California.

Although Crawford's progress during the next few months was not spectacular, both of his uncles were doing their utmost to promote his interests. "Uncle Do," as Mailliard was called, obtained for Crawford a sympathetic hearing from Richard Watson Gilder, editor of the newly founded *Century Magazine*. Gilder, who had known Mailliard since they had played together as boys in Bordentown, asked to see Crawford's "Origin of Sacrifice," but failed to publish it. The dinner party which Sam Ward arranged with Thorndike Rice, editor and owner of the *North American Review,* proved to be the beginning of a very profitable relationship for Crawford; and other dinner parties directed by Uncle Sam undoubtedly strengthened Crawford's position with Hurlbert of the New York *World,* with George Jones and Charles de Kay of the New York *Times,* and with Jeannette Gilder of the *Critic.* These last connections were particularly important, for between the end of November, 1881, and the middle of March, 1882, Crawford wrote more than twenty book reviews for these periodicals. The books he was assigned dealt primarily with religious matters (especially Eastern religions) and with Italian subjects—topics with which he was familiar because of his background. Reviewing was congenial work for Crawford; but, since it required an enormous amount of time and the rewards were slight in terms both of money and of reputation, Crawford saw that this work was merely a temporary expedient until he could do something else.

Crawford, in fact, already had in mind a much more ambitious project than reviewing. During the fall of 1881 he had translated a number of hymns of the *Rig Veda,* and shortly after Christmas he disclosed his intentions to his mother: "I have also made a number of imitations of the hymns of the Veda, into the original metres, and have today sent one to the Critic for approval. I am extremely anxious they should be published, as the novelty of the imagery and ideas must necessarily attract many persons here. . . ."[21] He believed that a small volume of two or three hundred hymns would be a profitable venture for a publisher, but the editors of the *Critic* were slow to publish the sample. Under the title "Hymn to Ushas," it finally appeared in the *Critic* (February 25, 1882) and in the New York *World* (February 26, 1882). Thorndike Rice of the *North American Review* admired the translation so warmly that he gave Crawford an introduction to George P. Putnam. Although nothing came of this project, it strengthened Crawford's connection with Rice who accepted from Crawford an article on "False Taste in Art" and ordered another on "Boston from a European Point of View."[22]

V

While Crawford was slowly establishing connections with the important literary periodicals, he was also beginning to participate in the social life of Boston. His singing lessons with Georg Henschel, who was well known as a voice teacher and who had recently been named the first conductor of the Boston Symphony Orchestra, represented an obvious pleasure—especially after Crawford had agreed with Henschel that he was not fitted for the career of a professional singer. Crawford's repertoire of gay, Italian songs, however, made him a valued guest at many a social evening. His satisfaction is evident from his comment to his uncle: "I have been a social success this year—constant dinner parties and the like, and I think I am learning to develop a little general conversation, in which I know you think I am lacking."[23]

Throughout the fall of 1881, Crawford considered himself engaged to Mary Perkins, the daughter of Thomas H. Perkins of Boston, whom Crawford, in European fashion, formally asked for the hand of his daughter. During the summer months Mary toured Europe; and, when she returned in the fall, Crawford went to New York to meet her ship. Before the vessel arrived, Crawford spent several evenings with the family of General Hiram Berdan in whose home he met "Bessie" Berdan, the general's daughter. Crawford wrote his mother, who had known the Berdans in Rome, that Bessie was "charming and her mother sympathetic."[24] Although Crawford was later to marry "Bessie," he thought only of the anticipated arrival of Mary Perkins; yet the two women were curiously associated in one of his letters to his mother:

> Last night there was a great ball to which I went through the kindness of the Berdans. Mary thought of going but was too tired at the last minute, but I had an amusing time though I did not dance. The Berdans have been kind and even empressées to a degree and beg me to give up Boston in favor of New York; they have had people to meet me at their house three times in these nine days—which have passed quickly enough considering the suspense I was in while M. was at sea in this dreadful weather. . . .[25]

Although Crawford thought that Mary Perkins would give him a definite answer when she arrived, it appears that she neither accepted nor rejected his suit forthwith. Instead she temporized, probably mentioned his financial insecurity, and sent him back to Boston. Yet Crawford continued to believe in the eventual realization of his hopes. What he did not know but what Uncle Sam fully suspected was that Mary Perkins was not in love with Crawford. When he finally learned the truth, as he did on Christmas Eve, he wrote a long letter to Lily Conrad, and another to his mother:

> With me, things have not gone well. I fear my dream of marriage is at an end—at least it is so for the present. First she lingered in New York. Then she avoided being alone with me and at last the scene came, on Christmas Eve. Interest, friendship, anything but

love. And so I told her I would not see her any more, and she said she was sorry—and there was an end of it. I do not believe I loved her after all. It was a bitter pill to swallow because it hurt my vanity and pride to be so slighted, but there is another [presumably Lily Conrad] who is dearer to me than pride or vanity, for to her I humbled myself to the very dust. The old allegiance is still the strongest, as it is now also the purest and highest.

I was cut up at first of course, and physically ill after my fashion. It is one more illusion gone, and what is worse it takes with it the immediate incentive to pecuniary success. I wanted money for her, and now I am indifferent again. Henceforth I am free to earn as little as will keep me alive.[26]

This letter reflects a transient mood; however bitter Crawford may have been at the time, he soon recovered.

Boston society afforded abundant consolation to a rejected suitor. Early in February, 1882, he wrote that he was engaged in "a whirl of dinners and parties and concerts"; and, if he considered society "all very unsatisfactory," he obviously found it very pleasant.[27] Of all those who helped to mend Crawford's broken heart, none assisted more satisfactorily than Mrs. John L. Gardner, who lived but two blocks away from "Aunt Julia's" house on Beacon Street. "Mrs. Jack," as she was familiarly called, was the daughter of David Stewart, a wealthy New York importer of linens and the owner of a Pennsylvania iron mine. In 1860, when Crawford was six years old, Isabella Stewart had married John Lowell Gardner, Jr. This marriage was a union of wealth with wealth and of beauty with position. Two years later "Mr. and Mrs. Jack" moved into the house which her father had given them at 152 Beacon Street, and it was there that Crawford first knew her in 1881.

Crawford was probably first attracted to Mrs. Gardner because she seemed the American equivalent of the women he had known in Roman society. The luxury of her surroundings—her town and country houses, her growing collection of *objets d'art*, her expensive clothes, and her servants—compared favorably with those of the Italian nobility. She lived as he wished to live, and he longed for the comforts of life which she so abundantly possessed. Mrs. Gardner, moreover, seemed to him a mature, intelligent, glamorous, cosmopolitan woman. Educated in Paris, she had also after her marriage traveled extensively in Europe, acquiring at least a conversational knowledge of art and literature—the subjects about which Crawford wished to talk. There can be no doubt that Mrs. Gardner gave him ample opportunity to explain his favorite ideas and to express his opinions. She listened sympathetically, appeared to understand his problems, and gently encouraged him to write. Crawford eagerly sought her advice. On her part, Mrs. Gardner found the tall, handsome young man with chivalrous manners and European tastes a distinctive personality unlike most Americans of his age. She was flattered by his respect for her judgment and charmed by his conversation.

Although Crawford may have been introduced to Mrs. Gardner shortly after he came to America in 1881, he probably saw very little of the fascinating "Mrs. Jack" until after his hopes of marrying Mary Perkins were dashed on Christmas Eve. In February and March, 1882, his letters indicate a rapidly growing friendship. By the middle of February Crawford was proposing to his uncle that they "join forces and make a square party" with the Gardners on a journey to Japan, China, and India the following summer.[28] A few days later he wrote again that "a married lady to whom I am both indebted and attached has begged me to escort her to town on Thursday week.... The lady admires you from a distance, and you will be charmed with her grace, conversation and consummate knowledge of the world."[29] Mrs. Gardner was going to New York to examine the widely discussed art collection of William Henry Hurlbert, and Crawford of course was making the trip in search of additional opportunities to write articles.

To Crawford there seemed nothing improper about their journeying together; but, after several such trips, Sam Ward, who began to have reservations about Crawford's eagerness to be with "Mrs. Jack," wrote Julia Ward Howe: "I don't know what will be the outcome of his present *affaire du coeur*. It seems to stimulate him to great efforts—But is the stimulus a healthy one?"[30] Crawford was soon aware—from Sam Ward, if not from Boston gossip— that accounts of his friendship with "Mrs. Jack" were beginning to circulate; and, lest Louisa Terry receive an erroneous impression, he wrote to her: "If you hear rumors of my attachment to a certain married lady, do not be distressed. She has been a good friend to me in trouble and is one of the purest and best women living—in spite of the slandering tongues of petty Boston."[31] Crawford concluded his letter on a note of confidence: "Do not be anxious about *me*. I am on the road to enduring success."

As events proved, Crawford wrote more truly than he probably realized; he was at last "on the road to enduring success." In the gloom which followed the break with Mary Perkins, he had declared that, since he no longer possessed any "incentive to pecuniary success," he was "indifferent" and free to earn as little as would keep him alive. But, under the spell of "Mrs. Jack," all his former eagerness to get ahead had revived with doubled intensity.

Next to Uncle Sam, and in a different way, she had become the most important factor in his life. As a result, his literary efforts increased until he could write his mother truthfully: "My pen flys [sic] most of the day and part of the night."[32] Indeed, he was on the point of beginning his first novel. For the importance of Mrs. Gardner's inspiration, there is Crawford's own testimony. In a letter written to her after *Mr. Isaacs* was published, he said: "I think of it [*Mr. Isaacs*] as someone else's work, as indeed it is, love, for without you I should never have written it."[33]

VI

Crawford had almost reached his twenty-eighth birthday. He did not know it, but he had lived half of his life and he was on the verge of writing the first of a long succession of novels that would bring him wealth and recognition during his lifetime as one of America's foremost writers. The writing of *Mr. Isaacs* happened by chance, yet it was one that seemed prepared for and made possible by a long chain of events leading back through India to his boyhood in Rome. Crawford could have looked back later and seen how the pieces of his life fitted together. An American with a Roman boyhood, a facility for languages and a particular interest in Sanskrit, the desire to study in India, the trip to Simla while editing the *Indian Herald,* the loss of his job, the difficulties of getting started in New York and Boston, and the efforts to make the Indian experience count for something—these were the elements in the Crawford story which was as romantic as his novel and which indeed became the basis for his novel. Could Crawford have looked ahead as he began to write it, he would have understood how the fact that he wrote and sold in America a story that had little to do with America was also appropriate. Even without this foreknowledge, Crawford knew the truth of what he confided to his mother, "Think, if I could get a publisher to take my imitations of the Veda I could come and live with you."[34] But the publishers resided in America, and there Crawford knew he must find them. Business was in the United States; the romantic life he longed for was in Italy.

CHAPTER 3

Success in America

I

LIKE HERMAN MELVILLE, Crawford lived most of his novels before writing them; and, also like Melville, Crawford began to write fiction at the insistence of friends and relatives who believed that a good novel could be made of his experiences that he had recounted to them. Hitherto Crawford had made no effort to write fiction, and, aside from the imitation of the Veda hymns, he had given no indication that he felt any inner compulsion or even desire for imaginative work. In the spring of 1882, Crawford, who still faced the imperative need for deciding upon a vocation, was exploring a variety of possibilities. Early in April he went to New York to discuss some of them with Sam Ward, and one evening, as Crawford later recalled,

> Uncle Sam asked me to dine with him at the New York Club, which was then in the building on Madison Square now called the Madison Square Bank building. . . . We had dined rather early, and were sitting in the smoking-room, overlooking Madison Square. . . . We began to exchange stories while smoking, and I told him, with a great deal of detail, my recollections of an interesting man whom I had met in Simla. When I finished he said to me, "That is a good two-part magazine story, and you must write it out immediately." He took me around to his apartments, and that night I began to write the story of "Mr. Isaacs."[1]

From Crawford's statement one infers that the idea of writing a story did not originate with him, a conclusion that is established beyond doubt by his remark to Sam Ward in a letter written on August 22, 1882: "I hope you will never forget that but for your suggestion Isaacs would never have been written and that I owe it therefore to you, as I do so many other things."[2]

In the context of Crawford's other activities, Sam Ward's suggestion that his nephew write a story about an incident which had happened to him in India is not the least surprising. Sam Ward knew that Crawford had the ability to write editorials, news-stories, essays, reviews, and even poetry; and, if Crawford could succeed in these areas, there was no reason why he should not write fiction. Sam Ward, however, was probably wise in advising him to write a "two-part magazine story" before attempting anything on a large scale.

Crawford made the transition to writing stories in what was the easiest manner for him by narrating the story in the first person, using the fictional name of Paul Griggs. About this fact there is certainty, for a year after he published the novel he wrote to A. Bence Jones: "I am the real Paul Griggs of the story . . . and the occasional allusions to my own history are for the most part true."[3] By making himself a character in his novel, Crawford was establishing a precedent that he would follow with but few exceptions throughout his career. The name of Paul Griggs would become familiar to hundreds of thousands of readers. In *Mr. Isaacs,* moreover, certain other characters and incidents were taken from actual persons and events. The disappearance of Shere Ali and the murder of Sir Louis Cavagnari, for example, Crawford had learned about during his work in India, while the character of Ram Lal was suggested by the Theosophist leader, Koot Hoomi.

At what point the "two-part magazine story" became a novel cannot be precisely determined. Talking to an interviewer in 1895, Crawford recalled that "part of the first chapter was written afterwards [that is, after he began to write in Sam Ward's apartment], but the rest of the chapter and several succeeding chapters are the story I told to Uncle Sam. I kept at it from day to day, getting more interested in the work as I proceeded. . . ."[4] Since the chapters mentioned by Crawford deal principally with Paul Griggs's first meeting with Mr. Isaacs, the fabulously wealthy jewel merchant, and with the incidents of Mr. Isaacs' life prior to the opening of the events which take place subsequent to this meeting, one concludes that they represent the original story related to Sam Ward.

After beginning the novel in New York, Crawford returned to Boston; and, by April 27, 1882, he had made considerable progress, for on that date he wrote Sam Ward: "I am at work on the story—the character and personality of Jacob [Isaacs] are a romance in themselves, *s'il en fut.* It is easy to make him fall in love with some fair English girl and to lead them through numberless adventures—weaving in stories of Nicoletts which I believe I told you—not to mention personal experiences in India."[5] The inference is clear that Crawford began with the intention of featuring his first encounter with Mr. Isaacs—including an account of Mr. Isaacs' career up to that point—but, as Crawford said, the possibilities of exploiting Mr. Isaacs' adventures became so evident that he continued to write. At some time he must have realized that he had already reached a point beyond the limits of a "two-part magazine story." For this reason, he was forced to make additions to what he had already written. In all probability, he knew by April 27 that he was actually writing a novel.

Further light upon the composition of *Mr. Isaacs* is afforded by Crawford's correspondence with Mrs. Gardner. In an undated letter to her but apparently written from New York, Crawford talked about his method of writing. After discussing a chapter which had caused him "trouble and vexation of spirit," Crawford continued:

> I shall not look at it again for a week—not until I read it to you— and then I may improve it. The people all say what I think they would, but they are *repeating parts*—there is not enough life in them. They ought to have more individuality. . . . I have made Isaacs tell his story, of course without my repeating any of it, and I have created a slight embarrassment for Miss Westonhaugh, and a little argumentative tiff, and I wound up putting Ghyrkins in a rage with Kildare's ideas about tigers. The latter, who is as brave as [a] terrier, has never seen a tiger, and talks wildly about them for the sake of egging Ghyrkins on. G[hyrkins]. at last vows that K[ildare]. shall see a live man eater before the week is out. Isaacs steals out to Miss W[estonhaugh]. while we are smoking, and I keep the men over their cigars as long as I can. So we break up. To-morrow we have the polo, in the eighth chapter.[6]

This letter provides further evidence, if any were needed, of the autobiographical nature of Crawford's writing, for here Crawford uses the pronoun *I* interchangeably with the character Paul Griggs.

Crawford's use of Paul Griggs as narrator proved advantageous because the device enabled him to write in the first person what was essentially his own experience. Griggs, speaking for Crawford, begins the story with a statement of fact: "In September, 1879, I was at Simla in the lower Himalayas . . . being called there in the interests of an Anglo-Indian newspaper, of which I was then editor." There follows an account of Griggs's meeting with Abdul Hafizben-Isak, a wealthy jewel merchant, who generally uses the name of "Mr. Isaacs." The remainder of the novel deals with Griggs's participation in Mr. Isaacs' efforts to win the love of Katharine Westonhaugh, an English girl, and to liberate Shere Ali, an Indian leader in revolt against British rule. The plot is sustained through a number of incidents, including a polo match, a tiger hunt, and a desperate fight in a mountain pass. Near the end of the novel, Miss Westonhaugh dies of jungle fever; and Ram Lal, the Buddhist priest, persuades Mr. Isaacs to accept the life of a religious. The love he has felt for this English girl, declares Ram Lal, will lead him to a transcendent love that will endure for all ages.

Crawford's correspondence during April, May, and June, 1882, reveals how heavily indebted he was to Sam Ward and to Mrs. Gardner for their advice in the writing of *Mr. Isaacs*. It is clear that Mrs. Gardner provided not only practical advice about plot and character interpretation but also encouragement and stimulus for writing that Crawford very much needed during the time he was composing the novel. The value of Sam Ward's contribution cannot be overestimated. Years afterwards, when Crawford was discussing the composition of the novel with Robert Bridges, he mentioned reading chapters "from time to time . . . to Uncle Sam."[7] Not only had Sam Ward suggested the possibility of making a story out of Crawford's experiences, but also he worked directly with Crawford in realizing them in fiction. The extent of his hand in the novel can perhaps be best indicated by Crawford's remark in a letter to him written on June 15, 1882, the date on which the novel was finished: "Isaacs is entirely finished and ready, if you will let me know what to do with it—whether to send it by express or to keep it until I come."[8] Crawford brought the manuscript to New York so that he could discuss its chances of publication with his uncle and with George Brett, an employee of the Macmillan Publishing Company.

From the very beginning, Sam Ward had favored serialization; and, after the two-part magazine story had become a novel, he continued to believe it should first appear as a serial. From a financial point of view the wisdom of this course of action could not be doubted. Yet Crawford rejected the idea because he felt very strongly that since the novel was "the exposition of an idea— namely that the love of woman, to a man of fine sensibilities and true purpose, is a step on the road to the attainment of the ideal life, whatever the religion of the individual," he questioned "whether this thought sufficiently pervades the book to be apparent in a serial form of its publication."[9] In the end, Crawford had his way; on June 26 Sam Ward sent the manuscript to the London office of the Macmillan Company. It was Sam Ward who on August 21 telegraphed the good news from New York to Crawford who was visiting the Gardners in Beverly, Massachusetts: "MacMillan [*sic*] accepts isaacs [*sic*] and I have authorized him to put it immediately in hand. Terms ten percent of retail sales."[10]

II

The writing of *Mr. Isaacs* by no means committed Crawford to
a novelist's career. Even while working on it, he was considering
other enterprises. James Robert Keene, a wealthy Englishman who
had for many years been a close friend of Sam Ward, offered
Crawford a position as traveling companion and tutor for his son,
but Crawford declined on the grounds of the responsibility involved
and the fact that it would break up the literary connections he
had already formed. He did accept an offer from M. T. Rothschild
to translate Baron Ferdinand Rothschild's *Vroni*, and he had
already completed about a third of a volume before the middle of
June, 1882. He also continued to write book reviews, and he
read widely in nineteenth-century philosophy. Moreover, he wrote
his uncle that he had "engaged to lecture at the Concord School
of Philosophy this summer."[11] Toward the end of June—shortly
after he had completed *Mr. Isaacs*—he was nearing the end of
Vroni and the "matter" for the lecture was almost formed in his
mind. Taken together, these activities represented a solid achievement: in the space of a little more than two months Crawford
had written *Mr. Isaacs*, read and reviewed a number of books,
prepared a lecture, and translated a novel. If he was not yet
willing to call himself a novelist, he was at least rapidly becoming
a man of letters, and he was beginning to make money.

Encouraged by his friends' approval of his literary efforts, Crawford began to consider subjects for a second book. He declined
Sam Ward's suggestion that he write "the history of the A. T.
Stewart conquest of East Broadway" on the ground that he
knew nothing about it and would be wholly dependent upon his
uncle for material.[12] Instead, he began *Doctor Claudius* which
was to be another semi-autobiographical novel presenting himself,
his travel experiences, and his circle of friends in fictional disguise.
The story which Crawford narrated deals with the adventures of
Doctor Claudius, a "Phil. D." at Heidelberg, who is suddenly
informed that he has inherited a fortune from an American uncle.
On the voyage to New York, he falls in love with a Russian
countess; and, after a series of extraordinary adventures, Doctor
Claudius obtains his fortune, recovers the countess' lost jointure,
and marries her.

By the end of July two chapters had been written; and, although
he admitted that "the ground work is less attractive," Crawford
was predicting that it would be a better performance than
Mr. Isaacs.[13] Early in August, he accepted the Gardners' invitation
to spend three weeks with them in their home at "Beverly Farms"

a few miles north of Boston. His letters to Sam Ward show how thoroughly he enjoyed the work and relaxation on the Gardner estate. Ten days after his arrival, he wrote:

> The life here is everything that a man could desire to nurture body and soul. I bathe often twice a day, generally row several miles on the bay, and in the afternoon I ride with Mrs. Gardner. I need very little sleep here, and so in the morning hours I have done a good deal of writing. Dr. Claudius progresses, and Mrs. G. thinks the work better and more highly finished than Isaacs, though not so striking as yet. As I have not told her yet of the subsequent plot, she of course cannot judge of the dramatic points which I shall make later.[14]

Once more he was under the spell of the fascinating "Mrs. Jack," but this time he was writing slowly and deliberately. During his stay at "Beverly Farms" he probably composed about six chapters, a little more than a hundred pages; but he was convinced that the result was worth the trouble and that "if Isaacs succeeds, Claudius . . . will succeed still better."[15]

Once Crawford left "Beverly Farms," the writing of *Doctor Claudius* suddenly became troublesome. Anxiety over delays in the arrival of the proofs of *Mr. Isaacs* was a factor, but the real difficulty seems to have been that, after he had composed the voyage episode in *Doctor Claudius*, he could not devise a satisfactory dénouement for the love story and, for that matter, a resolution of the other situations which he had already presented. For *Mr. Isaacs* and for almost all of his later novels, he prepared a blueprint of the entire work, chapter by chapter, before he began to write; but with *Doctor Claudius* he seems to have completed half of the novel before he knew what the conclusion would be. In a note to Mrs. Gardner, Crawford tried to justify his method by explaining: "I can only invent incidents and situations, my characters have got the bit in their teeth and will do whatever they choose, and I cannot for the life of me prevent them now that they are off, any more than I could influence real people that I know." After emphasizing his awareness of his characters as real people, he noted that "they have the most headstrong way of doing things without consulting me in the least."[16] To a degree, Crawford may have felt his characters to be real persons; but, so long as he invented incidents and situations, he could hardly say he did not control them. It required more than a month of concentrated work and several suggestions from Sam Ward before Crawford could write him: "I want to see you about Claudius, for my plan is now matured and it is too long an affair to write of."[17]

The plan was not, however, too long to be included in a

letter to Mrs. Gardner; in fact, during the composition of these vexing chapters, Crawford wrote for her a lengthy summary of each section as he composed it. These letters, of which only fragments have been preserved, afford a remarkable commentary upon Crawford's novel. He wrote:

Claudius develops. I have written a scene [Chapter XII] between him and Screw the lawyer which pleases me, and which defines the character better than I have hitherto done. When last you heard of Barker he was in the presence of Screw at the New York Club [Chapter XI]. He cleverly started Screw on the scent, keeping himself in the background, and so they parted. That was the same evening that the rest of the party were all dining together at the Brevort. The next day Screw finds Claudius and begins cautiously to ask for further evidence of the doctor's identity. He lets fall a chance word which makes Claudius think he takes him for an imposter, and Claudius accordingly loses his temper and Screw goes. So far I have written. A few minutes afterwards Barker walks in, and Claudius who is not inclined for company gets rid of him. Barker of course goes and calls on the Countess. Now I have an idea. Claudius is the son of a grand seigneur, who was secretly married to Lindstrand's sister. This same nobleman died shortly after Claudius' birth, without leaving any evidence or document concerning his marriage, or any mention of it in his will. As the marriage, however, was a bona fide affair, the legal papers proving it were in the hands of Claudius' mother. She being a fine character was foolishly proud and refused to take any steps towards securing the succession of the title to her son. He was sufficiently provided for, and when she died—he being still a boy—she left the documents sealed, to be opened by him when he came of age. This he did but being his mother's son, was too proud to appear as a claimant to the title and estates, preferring to make his own way in the world. Hence, when called upon by Screw to give a certificate of his birth, he refuses to do so, offering other evidence instead, to be obtained from Heidelberg. He feels outraged, however, at the insinuation that he is an imposter, and in his first feeling of wounded pride, he calls the duke and taking his English honesty . . . in pledge, he opens his little iron box [Chapter XII] and shews the peer his mother's certificate of marriage, and other papers, and the duke, on examination, is thereby satisfied that Claudius is person d'une tres grande qualité. The Duke instantly offers, if Claudius is in need, to give his ducal word in evidence that the doctor is the man he represents himself to be, still, however keeping the secret of his parentage, which Claudius would be very loth to divulge. The merit of this bit of plot is in its perfect rationality and sequence, and that at the same time it accounts for Claudius' character and manner. The next point may be less satisfactory, though it is quite as natural. The countess's late husband had a brother, who succeeded him in Alexis' estates. This brother gets into trouble over the Nihilist question and is compelled to fly. His estates are seized, and with them Margaret loses her jointure. This has occurred while they were at sea, and on arriving, or a day or two afterwards, this brother in law whom we will call Nicholas, appears and declares to his sister in law that she must help him. He need not appear on the scene, save that he would be a good character to describe. I have known Russians of that stamp. Do you see the consequence I am working at? Claudius finds out Margaret's difficulty. He then decides to go himself to Germany for his identification papers, and not to take advantage of the duke's offer of evidence. In reality however he goes to Russia, armed with certain powerful letters which the duke gives him—as he certainly could—and though he can do nothing for Nicholas, he succeeds in getting Margaret's jointure. He does not tell her however. Of course the parting between Margaret and Claudius will be a great scene, and the one where they will find out certain things of interest to them both. Claudius' return, the frustration of Barker's schemes and the satisfaction of the duke at the vault, will bring the book to a close. I like my plot and I think there is lots of room in it for good work. It was last night that I pieced these vague floating things together.[18]

This letter shows very clearly that, before writing the last sections of the novel, Crawford carefully thought out every action that was to take place in it. He was of course using the same method of writing that he had described to Sam Ward a year earlier when he wrote: "I compose everything I write before putting it down, so that the time needed for the mere writing is very insignificant."[19] Despite the fact that the evidence indicates that he is still far from a skillful novelist, the technique proved to be very satisfactory, for he never departed from it.

Crawford kept Mrs. Gardner informed of his progress, and as his novel was nearing completion, he commented:

In the last chapter, which opens on the day when Claudius is expected, I have worked hard to produce a feeling that something dreadful has happened to him. The duke is restless. There is heavy weather. At last the ship is sighted. . . . Claudius is *not* on board. The duke scans the ship, the register and everything. He discovers that a passenger who might be Claudius, was put ashore at Queenstown, the first day, desperately ill, but he had not registered his name. The duke is now in despair, and his only idea is to get back to the hotel to consult his sister. All this is worked carefully out and occupies a good many pages. At his own rooms he finds his sister—who tells him—that Claudius arrived two hours before and is now with Margaret. He came by another steamer which arrived the same day. So far I have written. This afternoon I will describe his meeting with Margaret, and the last words I will write when I am with you. There is little to be said. The whole question is ended the moment Claudius sets forth in New York, and I could think of no better device for sustaining the interest to the end, than raising a doubt about his coming back. I think the description of the duke's anxiety and disappointment is the best thing in the book.[20]

Crawford was, of course, writing his letter after his plan had matured, but his observations emphasize the complexities of the plot in the final chapters of the novel.

The tangle of motives and incidents in *Doctor Claudius* which are starkly revealed in Crawford's letters to Mrs. Gardner was the consequence of his failure to blueprint his novel before he began to write. These abstracts, once put on paper, would have revealed to an experienced writer the fact that the last half of the work was plot-ridden, packed with too much intrigue, and overburdened with the explanations which were necessary to make the intrigue plausible. Crawford did sense that something was wrong, but he felt that the fault lay in the lack of local-color pictures or perhaps the American coloring. It is true, as he realized, that the local color in *Doctor Claudius* is not so well presented as that in *Mr. Isaacs,* but the basic difficulty with *Doctor Claudius* remains the lack of initial planning.

After Crawford decided upon the details of the plot, *Doctor Claudius* once more began to "write itself,"[21] but it was not to be finished until the first week in December. Meanwhile, in the late autumn he had moved from the Howe home at Oak Glen to his aunt's house on Beacon Street. Before leaving Oak Glen, he had begun to read the proof sheets of *Mr. Isaacs,* and he had taken them with him to Boston where, as he said, "the finishing touches can best be put under the delicate feminine advice [that is, Mrs. Gardner's] I shall get there."[22] About the middle of October the corrected pages were returned to Macmillan; but, before the novel was published, Crawford was greatly surprised to learn that Sam Ward had unexpectedly and somewhat secretly gone to England to avoid a lawsuit. His departure not only deprived Crawford of easy access to one of his principal sponsors but also removed one of the most important reasons for Crawford's staying in America.

III

Mr. Isaacs: A Tale of Modern India, printed in Edinburgh by R. and R. Clarke Company, was published simultaneously in England and America on December 5, 1882, by the London and New

York branches of the Macmillan Company. The New York company imported one thousand five hundred copies bearing a title page slightly different from the English counterpart. In the United States, the novel was soon reviewed by a number of literary journals; in England it was discussed by Edwin Arnold, George A. Sala, and critics of such London papers as the *Daily Telegraph,* the *World,* and the *Guardian.* Among the most thorough reviews of the work was Maud Howe's lengthy article which appeared in the Boston *Evening Transcript.* On the whole, the critics were enthusiastic, and steady sales indicated the public's approval.

Although there can be no doubt that *Mr. Isaacs* was a popular and profitable book, authentic figures for its sale are not available. Macmillan obviously expected the initial supply imported for the American market to suffice for at least several months, if not longer. That the sales rapidly exceeded this estimate is clear from George Brett's comments to Crawford on January 20, 1883: "As to 'Mr. Isaacs' of which our first importation ... is exhausted I may just explain that I cabled for more upwards of ten days ago and hoped thus to avoid running quite out but the demand became so rapid at last that our supply became exhausted about three days since."[23] Brett may have been unduly hopeful, for a month later Crawford wrote Sam Ward: "I lost the sale of a thousand copies here alone—as all the *retail booksellers* tell me, by his [Macmillan's] allowing Isaacs to be *out of print 6 weeks* in spite of my frequent protests to Brett."[24] Meanwhile in London, Sam Ward joyfully declared that the demand "continues steady," the sales averaging about a hundred copies each week; and, when the book had been published two months, Ward declared that five thousand copies had been sold.[25] Although this sale was not spectacular, it was certainly more than anyone had predicted. In view of the fact that Macmillan found nine reprints necessary during the first year after publication, one can reasonably infer that Crawford's first novel was a success far beyond all expectations.

The recognition awarded to Crawford after the publication of *Mr. Isaacs* brought him offers of additional literary work and placed him in a good position to negotiate for the sale of *Doctor Claudius.* Thomas Bailey Aldrich, editor of the *Atlantic Monthly,* wanted to confer with Crawford about a novel for serialization or a series of short stories. He had already been commissioned to write two articles for the *Century Magazine.* In February, 1883, he wrote Sam Ward: "The *Tribune* has offered me 25 dollars a *column* for Eastern sketches. The *Century* asks for several short stories at 15 dollars a page, and *Harper's Weekly* has applied to me for stories at a 'liberal' price, not yet determined, however." His concluding comment in his letter was almost an understatement: "I have therefore plenty of work to do at high rates."[26]

When Crawford went to call upon Aldrich, he had in his portfolio the recently completed *Doctor Claudius;* but he refused to sell it to the *Atlantic* for serialization because he felt, as he had about *Mr. Isaacs,* that the novel should appear in one piece. Almost at the same time, Houghton, Mifflin and Company offered him $2000 for the American copyright, a proposal which Crawford did not immediately reject but which he later regretted not having accepted. In London, through Sam Ward, Macmillan offered $1200 (£250) for the serial rights, including, as Crawford understood, a stipulation that, after the novel had been published in England and America in book form, he was to be paid royalties of fifteen per cent.[27] Such a contract would have been everything that a young author could have desired, and Crawford would have agreed to it at once; but Brett of the New York branch of Macmillan submitted a different proposal under which the company would have paid $2000 for the American copyright on condition that John Morley accept *Doctor Claudius* for *Macmillan's Magazine.* Crawford considered this proposal ambiguous; and, when Frederick Macmillan clarified it by saying he would give $2400 (£500) for the entire copyright, Crawford was vexed. He wrote Sam Ward:

> Mr. Macmillan has evidently led you to suppose he would say to me the same thing he said to you, relying on my necessity for ready money to bring me to his terms. He has made an egregious mistake, and may take the consequences. I owe him nothing whatever as he must have made a clear 2000 dollars for himself on Isaacs already. I have lost the interest on the money Houghton was willing to pay me nearly two months ago, and that is all I have got.
>
> I am not in want of ready money as he supposes. But I will not let him have another book for publication *here* at a percentage bargain. . . . And I will not take 2400 dollars for a whole copyright when I can get 2000 for one half.[28]

Crawford, nevertheless, eventually sold the entire copyright to Macmillan for $2400, and in the later part of May, 1884, *Doctor Claudius* appeared without prior serialization. Perhaps Crawford needed money more urgently than he would admit.

Even while Crawford was negotiating for the publication of his second novel, he was completing his third, *A Roman Singer.* During his interview with Aldrich, Crawford had agreed to write it and sell it for serialization in the *Atlantic Monthly.* The price was to be $1200, and, after the final chapter appeared in the magazine, Crawford was to own the copyright.[29] Thus Crawford had disposed of *A Roman Singer* before a line of it had been written and even before he had found a publisher for *Doctor Claudius*.

In writing *A Roman Singer*, Crawford returned to the practice he had followed in composing *Mr. Isaacs:* he meticulously predetermined the characters and incidents of the story before he began to write it. He explained these matters to Mrs. Gardner:

Let me see. I, Cornelio Grandi, professor of philosophy, tell the story. I had an estate once, and on it was born of one of my tenants the boy Nino Cardegna. Since I lost all I possessed and have been obliged to live by writing, and teaching philosophy, I have helped to educate this boy, and he has been brought up in my little household. In spite of everything I could do, he would be a singer and so I bargained with old Ercole de Pretis the singer in St. Peter's to bring him through his training and produce him on the stage. . . . At the same time old Graf von Lira, who was wounded at Königgratz in 1860 and could not follow his regiment in 1870 has been settled in Rome with his only daughter Hedwig von Lira, now a grown maiden of 20. And so the story opens. You may imagine the wrath of the old Count, when he discovers that the successful singer is no other than his daughter's Italian master, as I described yesterday. It is not likely that he will tolerate her foolish fancy for this young man, and with the old feudal instinct he carries her off to Trevi, a place in the Abruzzi and undertakes to keep her there for six months. In that wild and desolate country I can introduce any romance I please. I know the scene very thoroughly, certainly better than any living English writer for I have visited many places where no foreigner has ever set foot. Poor Nino's situation is desperate. He can get no clue to the Graf's whereabouts; he has made a brilliant success and is engaged for a season in London or Petersburg, before he knows that they have gone. I persuade him to go where he is called and I undertake to find out what has become of Hedwig. It is no easy matter, and perhaps I may introduce some odd mystic machinery to aid me. (Apart from fiction I once knew of a man, tired of boredom, going into the. . . .) Nino together and threatens destruction. (I have seen enough of German fathers of that class through my sister's relations in Prussia.) Then comes a bit of sensation. Nino, baffled by the father, resolves like a true Italian to carry off the daughter, if she will consent. Love scene on Christmas eve in the pantheon in Rome. Hedwig is supposed to have gone to the midnight mass in St. Peters [*sic*], but manages to go to the pantheon instead. A tremendous picture, that, with the full moon streaming down through the round opening in the top, and the two lovers alone there at midnight. They plan an escape and they effect it. Wrath of the Colonel who condescends to come and see me and talks and acts like a live volcano. But meanwhile the couple are quietly married in a little church by the Tiber and the irate father is obliged to make the best of it in as few words as possible. So ends the tale, so I have thought it out. A comedy rather than a drama, but in that exquisite Italian air capable of much grace and softness. I am in love with the story. . . .[30]

This carefully planned blueprint helped Crawford to write *A Roman Singer*, as he remarked to Sam Ward, "at the double quick, without turning a hair, so to say."[31] He began to write on January 1, 1883, the day on which he wrote the sketch for Mrs. Gardner; and he completed it on February 21, 1883. The next day he declared to Sam Ward: "It is the most harmonious piece of work I have yet turned out, for it came in one casting, like Isaacs."[32] In comparison with *Doctor Claudius,* Crawford considered *A Roman Singer* the "more artistic work," but he believed *Doctor Claudius* was "altogether deeper." Although *A Roman Singer* fell short of the ideal conception he desired, he thought it the best work he had yet accomplished.[33]

IV

"Had anyone told me a year ago that I should ever write a novel, I would have laughed the suggestion to scorn," wrote Crawford to his mother; "And in less than ten months I have written three."[34] He had good reason to be satisfied with his accomplishments and confident of his future. So far as his financial position was concerned, there was certainly no immediate cause for worry. The profits thus far from the sale of his three novels had amounted to almost $6,000, and by April, 1883, he had made commitments that he anticipated would produce five or six thousand dollars for the coming year. Even a casual observer would have agreed with his family that Crawford had at last settled upon a career as a novelist.

Louisa Terry, therefore, must have been amazed when she read in one of Crawford's letters that he felt his success was due largely to a stroke of luck and that he had "no wish to write novels for themselves—and no feeling of special capacity"[35] for the work. In the same letter he continued: "You will ask perhaps, dear mother, what I intend in the future. I confess that I can no more answer you now than I could a year ago. . . . I rejoice, of course, at the worldly independence it [novel writing] gives me but it is not—it is not the one thing I have to do before I die. I must lay my hand to a greater implement than the story teller's pen, and do more than make people pass a pleasant half hour with an idle tale. To have all humanity for a pen and the world for a scroll on which to write—that were something worth doing!"

Crawford's condescending reference to the "idle tale" of the novelist becomes understandable in the light of his sudden ambition for a career in politics. The roots of his desire may have gone back to his editorial writing for the *Indian Herald* and to his knowledge of the conditions of life in India and perhaps in Italy. Politics, with the unlimited rewards of power and fame, may for a time have appeared to be what he wanted; but any practical politician could have told him that he was not likely to succeed politically in America and that whatever slight chance he may have had had vanished with the departure of Sam Ward. That Crawford should persuade himself that Europe (which meant Italy) was the proper place for him was logical, but his analysis of America reveals a curiously naïve attitude. He argued the point in a letter to his mother:

> Europe must ever be my camping ground, even though America become my home. America is uninteresting after the first blush, because with all its glaring faults one nevertheless feels that the country is growing in the right direction. Europe is not. It is entirely wrong from beginning to end. . . . America is the place for clever boys—Europe seems to me divided between a mass of effete humanity and a handful of great men, sweating blood in the enormous effort of government. American life makes men to be of one mind on all important questions of life and property—Europe breeds faction and discord in every separate furrow of its rack rented soil. There is little glory in helping the strong, but there is much good in strengthening the weak.[36]

With these arguments Crawford convinced himself that he did not want to be one of the "clever boys" who led America, and he ignored the fact that he had come to the United States mainly as a European unwilling and perhaps unable to enter sympathetically into American ways. The pace not only was too rapid, but American life, manners, art, and literature were not pleasing to him. In a country where public office rested upon inherited position, Crawford might have become a statesman, but that he could ever have won a political election in America is inconceivable.

Talk of a possible career in politics which would mean the abandonment of his literary work may have been merely evidence of the fact that Crawford was not happy in America. Between December, 1882, and April, 1883, his letters to his mother referred constantly to a feeling of restlessness and despondency. Shortly before Christmas he spoke of his literary successes but added:

"Still it is no use denying that I am wretchedly melancholy with it all."[37] Weeks later he was still complaining that he suffered from "dreadful fits of depression" and described himself as "intensely unhappy."[38]

Certainly part of his unhappiness was due to the mental letdown and loss of self-confidence that accompanied the completion of his novels. As he explained to Louisa Terry, "I suffer them [his books], like a kind of illness. Then, when the last stroke is done, I hate them, and am so melancholy that I am positively ill, as before I was only mentally sick."[39] To Mrs. Gardner, he said, "you cannot imagine what I suffered when Isaacs was finished."[40] After completing *Doctor Claudius*, he remarked, "The fit is on me, strongly, and I am inclined to say many bitter things about my work."[41] As he began *A Roman Singer*, he declared that, although he liked the story he had outlined to Mrs. Gardner, he supposed that it would seem a failure when he had finished it, "as all my work does."[42] From these periods of depression, produced no doubt by the mental fatigue of composing, Crawford recovered quickly; but they always remained a factor which contributed to his unhappiness.

Just as important as mental fatigue, and the temporary loss of self-confidence, in accounting for Crawford's increasing restlessness in America was the dissolving of the personal ties which had bound him to the United States. Sam Ward's departure had already deprived him of a close friend and powerful adviser. There was no one to take Ward's place, because Crawford did not easily make friends among his own sex. Instead, he sought, as he had since childhood, the companionship of women; but, if Mrs. Gardner carried out her plans to make an extended tour of the Orient, the circle of admiring women would be broken and, with "Mrs. Jack" gone, even Beacon Street would be uninteresting. Her friendship had meant much to him. He had enjoyed the comforts and artistic atmosphere of her houses in Boston and Beverly. She had praised his work, sympathized with his ambitions, and listened to his problems. Her advice had often counted as the deciding element for him. The anticipated loss of her presence presented a dismal prospect for Crawford.

As he daily became less satisfied with his present circumstances, Crawford began to think more and more about returning to Europe. By contrast it seemed inviting. During the composition of *A Roman Singer,* he recalled vividly scenes from his life in Italy, and these memories doubtless helped to turn his attention from the disappointing present to what seemed a happier past. He also longed to be with his mother once more. Crawford knew that there had been tension between them, but now that he had achieved recognition and a comfortable income, he could see no reason for further disagreements. He wrote her that he was sick for his home and his "native air," promising, "Dear, dearest, mother—we shall be very happy together."[43] Shortly before the end of April, 1883, he declared:

> Indeed, dear mother, I have hopes that we may not again be separated, save by the occasional journeys which will be necessary to me. The stirring interests that are beginning to act in my life make it necessary that I should be with my own people. Marriage has not come to me, nor will for years, and so long as I continue a productive power, it is wiser that I should be with you. . . .
>
> How I long to be there with you at last! It seems too good to be possible. We could be so happy together, and I am so unhappy here.[44]

And in the same breath, Crawford continued: "Mother—mother dearest—will it be wrong for me to be near her, if my lips do not speak and if I try to be only a honest and honouring friend among many others? Thank God I did not marry here, for I could never have made poor Mary [Perkins] happy, so long as my whole heart is breaking for the old love." Thus Rome possessed a three-fold appeal: a happy past, an adored mother, and the "golden haired" Lily Conrad, now lost to him irrevocably as the Marchesa Theodoli. Taken together they meant simply that Crawford wanted to return to Italy to live.

Early in May, 1883, Crawford left for London on his way to Rome. His sudden departure has been linked with his friendship for Mrs. Gardner. He had planned to accompany the Gardners to Japan, but Crawford had written early in April to his mother that he had decided against the Eastern trip and that he would leave for Rome on April 11. When literary work intervened, he postponed his going and reconsidered the tour of Japan. Shortly afterwards, he left this country unexpectedly for reasons that Crawford, his cousin Maud Howe, his aunt Julia Ward Howe, or later his sister Margaret Terry Chanler did not wish to reveal. When all of the vague contemporary and later accounts are considered, the best explanation seems to be that Crawford suddenly found that his friendship with Mrs. Gardner was on the verge of deepening beyond the bounds of what he considered proper. He hastily departed, and, after reaching London, he held himself in readiness to "be on the march" instantly if Maud Howe cabled that an additional move was necessary.[45] Ten years were to pass before Crawford would see Mrs. Gardner again.

V

The year that elapsed between the composition of *Mr. Isaacs* and the completion of *A Roman Singer* represented a turning point in Crawford's life. During these months he proved to himself, to his family, and to a number of publishers that he could write novels that would appeal to the public; and, although he was not yet certain that he wanted to continue to write fiction for the remainder of his life, he had learned that he could support himself by his literary work. Financially, at least, he had achieved independence; with it he had also gained a certain knowledge of the ways of marketing the products of his pen. In the years to come, Crawford would learn that there were still other means of realizing profits on his work.

Of perhaps greater importance to him than his initiation into the business side of an author's life was the knowledge that Crawford gained about writing itself. Like many a beginning novelist, he found that, after the first novel had drained off what seemed easily the best of his material, the second proved very difficult to write. Privately he fully realized how dangerously close *Doctor Claudius* had been to a failure; and, even if he lacked the self-criticism to analyze its deficiencies correctly, he instinctively rejected his method of composing it and returned to the technique that had proved successful in casting *Mr. Isaacs*. The essential rightness of his judgment was immediately evident in *A Roman Singer*. Never again would he begin to write a novel without carefully planning and blueprinting the plot and the characters.

In his personal life the net gain of this eventful year is difficult to measure. Partly because of his inability to decide upon a definite career and the consequent uncertainty of his future, Crawford was maturing late. At twenty-nine he was still inclined to rely upon others for guidance. The widespread sale of *Mr. Isaacs* had made him something of a public celebrity; but how long he would continue to depend in private upon Sam Ward, Mrs. Gardner, Maud Howe, and Louisa Terry was a matter about which none of them, including Crawford, would have cared to speculate. One permanent commitment he had made: he would like to live abroad. This decision stemmed from the surroundings of his boyhood and the influence of his parents, but it also reflected Crawford's inability to make much of American life. Europe, he believed, must ever be his camping ground. He could have said he was going back to Italy to resume the life of a cosmopolitan American expatriate whose home to Italians would always be a semi-foreign island in what would always be to him a semi-foreign land.

CHAPTER 4

Indecision in Europe

I

ALTHOUGH CRAWFORD frequently paused to analyze his attitudes and ambitions, he was never able to evaluate very objectively the real basis for his actions. He would have been the last person to describe himself as an opportunist; yet as one reviews the progress of Crawford's career, one becomes increasingly aware that Crawford's acknowledged intentions were consistently overturned by circumstances. He did what at the moment seemed best to do and thereby often abandoned what earlier had been formulated as long-range plans. There was a consistency to his life, but it was one premised upon two matters that Crawford never fully understood or admitted. Possibly because of his self-confidence, he never faced squarely the fact that the one genuine talent which he possessed was the ability to write novels that exactly satisfied the literary demands or desires of millions of readers. If one adds to his literary talent Crawford's unacknowledged but controlling dream of the life proper to an aristocratic gentleman of wealth, social position, and culture, the disparate facets of his life begin to assume definite configuration.

At no time were these forces more apparent than during the two years which followed Crawford's departure from the United States in the spring of 1883. Before he left, he had vehemently declared that the great mission of his life was to be politics instead of literature; then he had written his mother that he was fully determined to live with her in Italy; and he had stated flatly that he would not marry for many years. Although Crawford made these pronouncements sincerely, what seemed chance and opportunity, but was actually his talent and his idea of the good life, would in the months to come defeat them all. For the moment, however, it seemed as if his intention to remain with his mother in Italy would assuredly hold firm.

Immediately after arriving in London on May 16, 1883, Crawford sent a telegram to his mother in Rome to let her know of his safe journey; and probably with a backward glance at the causes of his sudden departure from Boston, he wrote her the next day: "You may imagine my happiness at being once more on this side and so near to you all—or you may not imagine it, for you do not know the manifold reasons I have for congratulating myself."[1]

After a visit with Sam Ward, who introduced him to such London celebrities as Henry Irving, John L. Toole, and Henry James, Crawford arrived in Rome on May 25. His welcome there was everything he could have desired. Louisa Terry and her daughters, Annie von Rabé, Mary Fraser, and Margaret Terry, were waiting at the "Palazzo Altemps" to repeat personally the praise of his achievements which they had already expressed in their letters to him. They had doubtless seen an advance copy of *Doctor Claudius* which had been published on May 22 and had probably also read *A Roman Singer* from the proof sheets; Crawford had corrected one set of them the night before he left the United States. He responded gratefully, as he always did, to their flattering adoration, and to Maud Howe he described his welcome as an ovation. One wonders if he hastened to call upon the "golden Lily," now Marchesa Theodoli; the chances are that he did. After a week in Rome, Crawford went to Sorrento with his sister, Mrs. Hugh Fraser, and her family; and there, on June 3, he began his fourth novel, then entitled "Ex Nihilo Nihil" but later published as *To Leeward*.[2] Shortly afterwards, the Terrys joined Crawford at Sorrento; in August, Sam Ward arrived.

The summer passed pleasantly for the family group in the small village of Sant' Agnello di Sorrento, one of the most beautiful spots in all Italy. Crawford described it in *To Leeward*:

> It is a beautiful place. Perhaps in all the orange-scented south there is none more perfect, more sweet with gardens and soft sea-breath, more rich in ancient olive-groves, or more tenderly nestled in the breast of a bountiful nature. A little place it is, backed and flanked by the volcanic hills, but having before it the glory of the fairest water in the world. Straight down from the orange gardens the cliffs fall to the sea, and every villa and village has a descent, winding through caves and by stairways to its own small sandy cove, where the boats lie in the sun through the summer's noontide heat, to shoot out at morning and evening into the coolness of the breezy bay. . . . Far along through the groves echoes the ancient song of the southern peasant. . . . And even the sapphire sea kisses the feet of the cliffs as though wooing the rocks to come down, and plunge in, and taste how good a thing it is to be cool and wet all over.[3]

His residence was the Hotel Cocumella, which a century ago had been a Jesuit monastery, but which for several generations had been operated by the Garguillio family as an inn. An apartment with a vinecovered terrace of its own could be rented there for six francs a day. The hotel, a large three-storied edifice, was built near the edge of high cliffs almost two hundred feet above the Bay of Naples. The Cocumella *caláta* or descent was cut or hollowed out of the brown, volcanic rock in which, half-way down, there was a recess. Here in this rock-lined "study" Crawford worked upon "Ex Nihilo Nihil," writing almost every day from nine until twelve o'clock in the morning, and, after a brief swim in the sea below, continuing until a daily stint of five thousand words had been accomplished. The entire area around Sorrento satisfied a craving within him for the sharp contrasts of color and the rugged terrain to be found at the meeting place of rock and ocean. To the extent that a man could love a place, Crawford loved Sorrento; he returned to it again and again until he himself owned a part of the coastline.

Here he had found the kind of surroundings in which he worked best. In his study recess he could find seclusion, peace, and absolute quiet; yet he had only to climb the *caláta* to the hotel to be applauded by a small circle of adoring women. The excellent sales of *Mr. Isaacs* and *Doctor Claudius,* the first numbers of the *Atlantic Monthly* which featured *A Roman Singer*,[4] and the rapid progress he was making with "Ex Nihilo Nihil"—these provided conversational subjects of the most pleasant type; and, when Sam Ward arrived, the mutual admiration society received a powerful addition.

Spurred by his family's enthusiastic approval of his work, Crawford wrote so rapidly that in seven weeks the novel *To Leeward* had been completed. The key to its personal significance Crawford confided to Maud Howe. "It is a sad story with a purpose to it," he wrote, "and I think it will hit hard. It has a portrait of a man you will recognize easily enough. The scene is chiefly laid here in Sorrento where the book has been written. Indeed it is more of a drama than a novel, more of a tragedy than a drama."[5] If it was truly more of a tragedy than a drama, Crawford conceived of the tragedy as his own; for the "portrait" which he mentioned must have been easily identified by Maud Howe as a sketch of the writer himself. A few details were changed, but otherwise the chief figure, Julius Batiscombe, portrays Crawford's view of his own life and character.

He [Julius Batiscombe] had conquered many difficulties in his life, and by sheer determination had turned evil fortune into good, winning himself a name and a position, and such a proportion of wealth as he needed. Of good family, and brought up in luxury and refinement, he had been left at twenty years of age without parents, without much money, and without a profession. He knew some half dozen languages, ancient and modern, and he had a certain premature knowledge of the world. But that was his whole stock-in-trade excepting an indomitable will and perseverance, combined with exceedingly good health, and a great desire for the luxuries of life. He had lived in all sorts of ways and places, getting his pen under control by endless literary hack-work. By and by he tried his hand at journalism, and was successively addicted to three or four papers, published in three or four languages in three or four countries. Last of all he wrote a book which unexpectedly succeeded. Since then the aspect of life had changed for him, and though he still wandered, from force of habit, so to say, he no longer wandered in search of a fortune. A pen and a few sheets of paper can be got anywhere, and Julius Batiscombe set up his itinerary literary forge wherever it best pleased him to work. He had fought with ill luck, and had conquered it, and now he felt the confidence of a man who has swum through rough water and feels at last the smooth, clean sand beneath his feet. His success had not turned his head in the least; he was too much of an artist for that, striving always in his work to attain something that ever seemed to escape him. But he now felt that he might some day get nearer to what he aimed at, and there were moments, brief moments, of genuine happiness, when he believed that there was wrought by his pen some stroke of worth that should not perish. Ten minutes later he was dissatisfied with it all, and collected his strength for a new effort, still hoping, and striving, and labouring on, with his whole soul in his work.[6]

Crawford's readers may not have been aware of the fact, but in *To Leeward* they were actually meeting Paul Griggs once more under another name.

The two principal feminine characters in the novel, Diana de Charleroi and Leonora Carantoni, likewise exhibit features which are unmistakable translations of the feelings and actions of real life into the guise of fiction. Crawford's family must have identified the Marchesa Theodoli with Diana de Charleroi and Mrs. Gardner with Leonora Carantoni. In the novel, Julius Batiscombe, like his creator in real life, loved a woman who had married someone else. The good and beautiful Diana de Charleroi had known great unhappiness, particularly after she had given up the man she loved and married a French aristocrat; but for more than a decade Julius had continued to love her and to seek her advice about his affairs. At times he believed he loved other women; but, in each instance, he returned in his dreams "to the one woman whom he had loved, and whom, down in the depths of his turbulent heart, he loved still."[7] He often imagined "how fair his life might have been with her."[8]

The most interesting biographical aspect of *To Leeward,* however, is the fictional account offered by Crawford of what *might* have happened in the "tragic situation" he had recently avoided in America. Although there is every reason to believe that, before he left the United States, Crawford's relationship with Mrs. Gardner had not progressed beyond the borders of impropriety, it seems likely that he wrote *To Leeward* as a warning both to himself and to Mrs. Gardner of the unhappiness that was latent in transgressions of the social code. In the novel, Leonora Carantoni, the wife of an Italian aristocrat, falls passionately in love with Julius Batiscombe. Although marriage is impossible, Leonora elopes with her lover, who knows that this is for him merely a passing affair. The only woman he has ever truly loved is Madame de Charleroi. Almost immediately after the elopement, Leonora begins to realize the enormity of her act:

> Then [in the morning when she "had not silenced her soul"], at last, she was honest. There was no more self-deception then, no more possibility of believing that she had done well in leaving all for Julius; she could no longer say that for so much love's sake it was right and noble to spurn away the world,—for the world came to mean her husband, her father and her mother, and she saw and knew too clearly what each and all of them must suffer. The pale faces came to her in her dreams, and their sad voices spoke to her the reproach of all reproaches that can be uttered against a woman. Her husband she had never loved; but in spite of all her reasoning she knew that he had loved her, and she understood enough of his pride and single-hearted nobility to guess what he must suffer while she dragged his ancient name in the dust of dishonour.[9]

Her lover, however, endeavors to quiet her doubts by asking, " 'How can true love, like ours, not be right?' " He answers his own question: " 'God has put it into the world dear, and into our hearts.' "[10] The condemnation, which Crawford as omniscient author places upon this passage, emphatically expresses the novelist's own moral attitude: "O, the blasphemy and the hollowness and the cruelty of those words! Even as Leonora lay in his arms . . . loving her sinful love for him out to the last breath, she knew that it was not true, what he said so fervently,—and she knew that he did not believe it, that no man can believe a lie so great and wide and deep and awful."

So long as Crawford continued to maintain these moral principles, he was not likely to transgress any marriage bond. Having approached the threshold of such a relationship, he was warning others—perhaps also Mrs. Gardner—of its potential consequences and at the same time turning the experience of his own life into fiction. Because of the subject matter and the unhappy ending, this novel occupies a unique place in Crawford's fiction. He never wrote another novel like *To Leeward*, and he later regretted having published it, possibly because he felt he had needlessly hurt Mrs. Gardner.

After completing *To Leeward* late in July, 1883, Crawford spent most of the remainder of the summer enjoying the pleasant company of his family and sailing in his newly purchased felucca, the *Margherita*, to Capri, Casamiccola, Amalfi, and San Vito—places which appear again and again as settings for his Italian novels. After the earthquake at Porto d'Ischia, Crawford wrote a series of articles to show that in the contracts for rebuilding the city the government was "being cheated on a gigantic scale by its employees here—engineers, commissioners and such fry."[11] These articles furnish evidence of his continuing interest in political and economic problems.

At the end of the summer, Crawford and his family returned to the "Palazzo Altemps" in Rome. There he worked on his fifth novel, *Zoroaster*, until he went to London with Sam Ward. Crawford hoped to arrange for the publication of *To Leeward* and of *A Roman Singer* and perhaps to dispose of his forthcoming *Zoroaster*. Although *A Roman Singer* had been promised to Macmillan in England, Crawford was not certain whether he would give the company *To Leeward*. Consequently, when Thomas H. S. Escott, editor of the *Fortnightly Review* and an advisor to the publishing firm of Chapman and Hall, approached Crawford in London with what seemed very profitable offers, he was immediately receptive. As a result, Crawford agreed to write articles on "Rome as a Residence" and "Italians at Home" for the *Fortnightly* and to permit Chapman and Hall to publish *To Leeward*.[12]

Under terms of his contract with his new publishers, Crawford was to be paid £200 for the right to publish fifteen hundred copies of *To Leeward*. Thereafter, a cheaper edition was to be issued for which he was to receive a royalty of eight pence per copy "for ever." Chapman and Hall also undertook to send the proofs of the novel to Houghton, Mifflin Company which would use them to publish an edition in the United States in time for the Christmas trade. Although the arrangements were complicated, Crawford felt that they were greatly to his advantage.

Chapman and Hall began at once to send Crawford the proof sheets of the new novel. Preoccupied with his corrections, he temporarily abandoned the composition of *Zoroaster*. Much of his time was occupied with social engagements which proved to be both a pleasure and a financial advantage. He wrote his mother:

> I seem to be fulfilling some object in seeing so many people, who all become attached to me *from the first*. It is very strange. . . . Escott the editor of the Fortnightly took such a fancy to me from the first that he has virtually managed my business with Chapman and Hall, in the most satisfactory manner. Henry James has got me in to the Athenaeum Club and is everything that is kind and friendly. Many other people seem no less well disposed to me, and altogether it almost looks as though I were to be a popular individual, for the first time in my life. Not that I desire it, or care in the least for popularity—but it is a new sensation, and I feel as though it were to lead to something.[13]

Ill health prevented him from returning, as he had planned, to Italy early in November; but the delay afforded him an opportunity to meet the editors of *Blackwood's Magazine* in Edinburgh and thus paved the way for the subsequent appearance of *Saracinesca* in that publication.

The sojourn in London proved to be a significant episode in Crawford's career. In addition to the sale of *To Leeward*, he had engaged to write a book for the *Fortnightly Review*, made a favorable impression upon publishers and critics, and received from Aldrich a request for a serial to appear in the *Atlantic* in 1885. In other words, he had obligated himself to write two new novels; and, by making these agreements, he had in effect committed himself more deeply than ever to a literary career. Once more his future was being shaped by the opportunities of circumstances rather than by the requirements of his ambitions.

II

Crawford began the year 1884 with a midnight supper party in what he called his "turret," actually the central tower of the "Palazzo Altemps." The room had been decorated with Chinese lanterns and furnished with an immense bowl of cordial brewed by the convivial "Uncle Sam." At midnight, nine picked chanters from the Pope's private chapel began to sing one of Palestrina's cantatas. Surprised and delighted, the guests applauded, and Sam Ward exclaimed: "Fancy what a leaf out of my book of styles!"[14] This was the first of many lavish entertainments which Crawford planned for important occasions. His thoughtfulness especially delighted Louisa Terry, who noted that she was "supremely happy," proud of her son's achievements, and pleased at the respect with which he was everywhere greeted. It seemed to her that Crawford now had almost everything—a profession, a reputation, and a comfortable income; and during the last several years she had known the girl who, she thought, would make the best wife for him.

During January and February, 1884, mother and son considered seriously the possibility of his marriage, and with her help he decided in favor of the girl she had already selected. Crawford had known Elizabeth Berdan slightly in New York. Since she was now living in Constantinople, Crawford hastened to that city. While at sea aboard the *Principe Addone,* he wrote his brother: "Every turn of the screw seems to confirm me in the certainty that I have done well in coming.... It is a great thing if a man can make up his mind to want a good thing—it is a greater thing even then to take it after he has decided. I think it may be heroic to have the strength for taking, but the knowledge of what it is good to have is godlike."[15] Crawford had left Rome with but a single purpose—to marry Bessie Berdan.

In Constantinople—or Pera, as the European quarter of the city was called—Crawford was the guest of General Lew Wallace, the American minister to Turkey and the author of the celebrated historical novel, *Ben Hur.* Wallace and his wife were friends of Crawford's mother. Since the Berdans were members of the diplomatic coterie, Crawford desired to make as many friends among this group as he could. Sam Ward had given him a letter of introduction to Lord Dufferin, the British ambassador. Crawford was already acquainted with the Marquis de Noailles, the French ambassador, and probably with the German ambassador, M. de Radewitz, whose wife was related to one of Louisa Terry's friends in Rome. The Berdans probably introduced him to Rustem Pasha, who was to become one of Crawford's most intimate friends and the godfather of his first child. No sooner had he arrived in Constantinople than invitations of all kinds were urged upon him. Confidentially, he wrote his mother: "As for the 'impression' I meant to make, it has been a brilliant one indeed. Every embassy and every private house is open to me and I am flattered and sought after all the day long. Most of the ambassadors have been to see me in person and all have asked me to their houses."[16] Aided by his friends, Crawford soon became popular with the diplomats stationed in Pera. Much of what he learned from them and from his rambles through the city, he later incorporated into *Paul Patoff*.

In his efforts to win the hand of the attractive Bessie, Crawford made such rapid progress that within a fortnight after his arrival he could report to his mother:

> The situation is not changed save for the better. The general [Bessie's father], likes me more and I am always welcome, generally dining or lunching there everyday. . . . We are constantly left to ourselves for a long time, and everybody seems very pleased. In all my life, I never saw or spoke to a more perfect woman of her age—so gentle and so brave and so high minded. . . . If her father and mother are not blind they must see it all—and yet perhaps I ought to speak to them. I have indeed managed to tell Mrs. B. that I meant to marry, and, that I am able to live comfortably, and that I came here simply for the purpose of seeing *them*.[17]

The Berdans, who fully recognized the meaning of Crawford's attentions, continued to give him every encouragement. Nothing interfered with the courtship until late in March when his uncle's illness suddenly called Crawford back to Rome.

When Crawford reached Rome on March 25, Sam Ward's doctors believed that he would recover; but, as the days passed, his pulse became steadily weaker. Louisa Terry, Margaret Terry, and Crawford nursed him as best they could, writing at his dictation the voluminous correspondence that Ward continued until the end. On the advice of the doctors in Rome, Crawford and Margaret Terry took "Uncle Sam" to Pegli, near Genoa, at which place he died on May 19, 1884. Crawford arranged for a simple Protestant service in the church at Pegli and subsequently joined with Lord Roseberry and William Henry Hurlbert in erecting a monument to him. Shortly after his death, Crawford wrote that "my impression of him in his last days was that he was a better man than he ever made himself out to be."[18] Although the remark was not intended for publication, Crawford's comment falls short of a very profound understanding of Ward's character and indicates nothing of Crawford's immense personal debt to his uncle.

Early in June, Crawford was again en route to Constantinople. He did not return to Pera but went, instead, to Büyükdere, where the foreign ambassadors to the sultan's court resided during the summer. He shared a small kiosk with Pangeris Bey, a young Greek in the Turkish diplomatic service and a close friend of the Berdans. There on the shores of the Bosphorus, Crawford, who was encouraged by the Berdans' obvious approval of his courtship, visited Bessie as often as possible until at last, on July 5, he wrote somewhat formally to his mother: "I am engaged to be married to Miss Berdan."[19] In the same letter he revealed his plans: "I am going to live in America for the present. I have determined to enter political life at home. I think I am adapted for it and many openings have suddenly presented themselves. For years to come I shall be dependent on my pen for my livelihood, but in the meanwhile I mean to lay the foundation of a surer career." This astonishing decision may be explained in part by Crawford's rather consistent refusal to believe that he could continue indefinitely to write novels, but the fact or circumstances which prompted him to desire to turn his back not only on the literary profession but also upon Europe as well cannot be understood except with reference to the Berdans.

Although the Berdans had spent a great deal of time in Europe, they could not be described as expatriates. Their frame of reference was emphatically America. Hiram Berdan, who had been a general during the Civil War but was now head of the Berdan Firearms Company, was currently in Europe to sell munitions to foreign governments. Thoroughly American, he was essentially a businessman who enjoyed good political and business connections at home and was endeavoring to market his products in Constantinople. Elizabeth Christophers Berdan, his daughter, had received part of her education abroad, but she fully expected to live her life in America. In this resolve she was strongly supported by her mother and by her aunt for whom she was named, Mrs. Elizabeth Christophers Hobson. From their point of view, the only permanent place for an American was in America; they were eager, therefore, to assist Crawford to establish himself and his family in the United States. To this end, Mrs. Hobson gave Bessie a farm of sixty acres in New Hampshire and offered the couple the use of her New York house for so long as they needed it.

Unable to withstand the Berdans' pressure upon him to return to America, Crawford revived his long-standing ambition to enter politics. Although he had never precisely defined his notion of a political career, he probably envisaged some kind of elective office; on the other hand, the Berdans most likely had in mind a government appointment. The "openings" which Crawford mentioned to his mother could only have been appointive positions which the Berdans, General Lew Wallace, and other diplomats in Constantinople hoped to secure for Crawford. None of these opportunities was certain, and the fact remained, as he intimated, that the only means of support he actually possessed was his writing. But he seemed oblivious to the equally apparent inference that if "for years to come," as he said, he would continue to be dependent upon his pen for his livelihood, he would hardly have time to make much progress in politics. To blind Crawford so completely as he was to the facts of his position, the pressures and offerings of the Berdans and his friends must have been very great.

The expectation of returning to America figured prominently in the couple's plans. They expected to marry in October, spend the winter in Rome with Louisa Terry, and leave for the United States the following spring. Crawford, happy almost to the point of ecstasy, began to order alterations in his mother's apartment to insure Bessie's comfort. In September, the details of the wedding ceremony were agreed upon. There were the usual difficulties attendant upon the marriage of a Catholic to a non-Catholic.[20] There was also a problem over the "double ceremony" which both Crawford and the Berdans desired; but, with persuasion and the assistance of the German and Austrian ambassadors, Crawford tactfully resolved every problem.

On the morning of October 11, 1884, Elizabeth Christophers Berdan and Francis Marion Crawford were married in the French Catholic Church at Pera. Present were the bride's family and the German and Austrian ambassadors, who were the official witnesses. At noon the Protestant ceremony was performed by the German pastor in the salon of the Berdans' villa. The reporter for the New York *Times* (October 13, 1884) wrote that "the whole of the diplomatic body and the élite of society were present." It seems, indeed, fitting that Crawford, a man whose life had been lived in many countries and whose novels contained characters of almost every nationality, should have been married before a gathering composed of men from many nations. In this cosmopolitan group, Crawford was very much at ease; he spoke their languages and understood their customs.

About the first of November, the Crawfords, after a brief stay in Athens, arrived in Rome; and shortly afterwards, Bessie's letters to Mrs. Berdan contained numerous references to their participation in the "wildly gay" life of Roman society. In January, 1885, for example, Bessie wrote:

> Last night's ball at the Pallavicini was a delightful affair. . . . I felt I was in fairyland. If I were to write a book full of the kindness of Italians to us, you would have no idea even then of it all. There was not the smallest party black or white that we were not asked to, and Marion is so pleased that even he enjoys himself. . . .

> To-morrow evening we go to princess Bandini's. Monday, dine at Mrs. Bruce's, a very nice English woman. The dinner is given to Cardinal Howard and Mrs. Astor. Tuesday we dine out again.

Thursday, dinner at the Astors'. She is charming, beautiful and simple, and all like her very much. The nicest men here are Prince Bandini, Count L. and the Duke of Sermoneta who is almost as nice as his wife, which is saying a great deal.[21]

Until the arrival of Lent ended all formal entertainments, Crawford and his wife continued to receive more invitations than they could accept from adherents of both the "white" and the "black" political parties. Doubtless, a portion of their popularity was due to Crawford's position as a rising young author.

III

The discussions about politics which Crawford had had in Constantinople with the Berdans and with members of the diplomatic coterie very likely encouraged him to deal with the subject in a novel. While in Rome helping to care for Sam Ward during his last illness, Crawford began to write *An American Politician*. When he returned to Constantinople in June, 1884, he took with him the nearly completed manuscript; and, shortly before his engagement was announced, the work was finished. On December 15, 1884, Houghton, Mifflin Company published it in Boston; on the same day Chapman and Hall issued a two-volume edition in London.

An American Politician was the fifth novel by Crawford to appear in print. In it he continued to follow the pattern that he had found successful in writing *Mr. Isaacs, Doctor Claudius, A Roman Singer,* and *To Leeward:* he built his story upon the foundation of a personal experience,[22] employing a protagonist representing himself and characters modeled after living persons. To these basic elements he added certain fictional episodes and unified his work around a central theme. Except in the case of *Doctor Claudius,* he always prepared a careful blueprint of the novel before he began to compose. The more that he wrote, however, the more he became convinced that dialogue was the essence of a good novel. While he was working on *An American Politician,* Maud Howe asked him for advice about writing fiction. Crawford replied: "Nothing develops character in a book like conversation.... Nine tenths of life is conversation, and to be lifelike you must give a great deal of it." In a significant afterthought, he continued: "Write dialogue as though you were speaking yourself. Listen to what the characters say to you and answer them *aloud*—it gives immense reality to one's thoughts to find oneself engaged in actual speech with an imaginary person."[23] Crawford himself followed this method of composing, and the extent to which he had come to believe in the value of dialogue is indicated by the perceptible increase in the relative amount of it in *An American Politician.*

The novel is interesting biographically because it represents Crawford's approach to politics. Much of the conversation in it takes place in the Beacon Street drawing room of Mrs. Sam Wyndham whose character is obviously modeled upon that of Mrs. Gardner. The plot is concerned with the efforts of John Harrington (that is, Crawford) to win a senatorial election and also the hand of the beautiful Josephine Thorn, whose character may owe something to Bessie Berdan. Harrington loses the election when, for reasons of political expediency, a group of powerful men in London, who control political fortunes throughout the world in the interest of democratic principles, fails to support his campaign. Harrington, however, becomes allied with this mysterious "X, Y, Z" society which finally elects him to membership. At the conclusion of the novel, John wins Josephine and, in the final chapter, a seat in the United States Senate.

The underlying theme of the novel is a plea for individualism in the party system. John Harrington's political views are obviously those advocated by Crawford. Although Harrington has associated himself with the Democratic Party, he is, essentially, an independent. In his opinion, the party system and its attendant evils—bribery, lying, and enslavement of the individual's freedom of thought—constitute a pernicious threat to the continuance of the American republic.[24] Harrington desires to become a reformer. He believes in "an established Civil Service" and "in something which if not exactly Free Trade, was much nearer to it than the existing tariff."[25] More than anything else, however, Harrington—and Crawford—believes in individualism. In his final speech Harrington declares: "Man is free, his will is free, his choice, his judgments, his capacity for thought, and his power to profit by it are all as free as air, just so long as he remembers that they are his own—no longer. When he forgets that he is his own master, absolutely and entirely, he becomes another man's slave."[26]

In other words, to "vote with the party" consistently means to lose one's own individuality. As part of his creed of individualism, Crawford also maintained that each man succeeds or fails in proportion as he is energetic or indolent. This lesson Crawford had difficulty learning himself, but once learned he never abandoned it. His point of view was based upon the assumption that each man must be responsible for his own acts and that the individual, not society, is to blame for failure. The concept lies behind Crawford's hatred of socialism, which he called anarchy, and his contempt for the Populist Movement.[27]

Explicit in *An Amercian Politician,* however, is Crawford's dislike of the party system. One surmises that he never thoroughly understood it, and he certainly never grasped the necessity for it in America. The basis of his aversion, however, lay deeper than the surface evils connected with political chicanery. Crawford's dislike originated in his personal individualism and in his concomitant hatred of authority. The best way to avoid becoming a "party man," Crawford must have reasoned, was to enter politics with the backing of a small group of powerful men like those of the "X, Y, Z" society. If the idea sounds naïve, one must remember that Crawford possessed no first-hand knowledge of practical politics and, for the most part, viewed American institutions through European eyes.

Crawford's politics, like his morality, was an expression of his religious, individualistic, and aristocratic point of view. In this and his other novels, the morality was that of all good Christians; and, so far as most readers of *An American Politician* were aware, his politics required only honest politicians who voted first as individuals and second, if at all, as party members. American readers were not inclined to take fictional incidents like the "X, Y, Z" society very seriously so long as the novelist tacitly affirmed, as Crawford did, the standards accepted by conventional, responsible citizens. Although *An American Politician* seems to the modern reader one of the least attractive of Crawford's works, the literary historian finds it remarkable as a very early study of the possibilities for corruption in political life; and he remembers that Crawford's novel anticipated by more than a decade such successors in the fiction of politics as Paul Leicester Ford's *The Honorable Peter Stirling* (1894), Brand Whitlock's *The 13th District* (1902), and Alfred Henry Lewis' *The Boss* (1903).

An American Politician differed greatly from the other novel which Crawford finished during 1884. He had written the first chapter of *Zoroaster* in August, 1883, at Sorrento; but he had put it aside because he found that, regardless of his familiarity with the subject, the Oriental material was difficult to transform into fiction. On November 3, immediately after his return to Rome, he began to work at it again and in thirty-two days he had finished it.[28] After a brilliant first-chapter prologue, Crawford wrote a partly fictional and partly historical account of Zoroaster's life. The novel was published on May 22, 1885, simultaneously in England and the United States by the Macmillan Company; and, although for the next four years at least it remained a popular historical novel, it cannot be ranked today among Crawford's best work.

IV

Late in February, 1883, after completing three novels in the United States, Crawford had declared that "Europe must ever be my camping ground" and indicated that his primary interest in life was politics. At the end of 1884, after having lived in Europe for almost two years and having written three additional novels, Crawford resolved to return to the United States to lay the foundation for a career in politics. When considered together, the two statements, contradictory as they are in one respect, throw a great deal of light upon Crawford's character and literary career.

Had Crawford realized in 1883 how ill-fitted he was for United States politics, he would probably have offered more resistance than he did to the pressures which were urging him in 1884 to return to America to begin a political career; but Crawford's enormous faith in his own ability prevented him from making the kind of self-analysis that would have shown him the unreality of the project. This same faith in his own powers led him to believe that he could succeed in European political life, regardless of the fact that he had never had any real training or experience in politics. He seems to have had no comprehension whatever of the fact that it was one thing to write a novel dealing with the evils in party politics but quite another to win an actual election in America or in Europe. The result was that he proved a willing convert to the arguments and opportunities advanced by the Berdans and by others in Constantinople.

Despite the acclaim that reviewers and readers accorded his work, a sound critic could have told Crawford that his sixth novel was not markedly better than his first. Although skills were essential to a writer, mastery of them would produce a competent workman but not necessarily a great novelist. And the basic difficulty lay in Crawford's attitude toward his work. His literary activities played a subordinate—even if essential—role in his plans. Without them he could not have married Elizabeth Berdan, and after his marriage they provided a resource which could be counted upon for income until his political ambitions were realized. Nevertheless, so long as he continued to view his continued literary success as problematical and to rank his literary work second to his vaguely defined political aspirations, he would not concentrate his full powers on the serious problems of his art; and his novels would lack, therefore, the depth and perception which he was capable of achieving. Before he could make significant progress in either field, he would need to commit himself wholeheartedly either to politics or to literature.

CHAPTER 5

The Prince of Sorrento

I

IN TIME the tremendous excitement engendered in Crawford by the events leading to his marriage diminished somewhat, and he began to make a more realistic appraisal of his qualifications and desires for success in the political field. Over and against the appeal of politics and the urgings of the Berdans that he return to America, he weighed his love for Italy, his already demonstrated talent for writing, and his lack of enthusiasm for American ways of living. The overwhelming argument that comprehended all other arguments was of course the simple fact of Crawford's awareness that only in Italy and only as a writer could it be possible for him to actualize his image of the good life. But, in the face of opposition from the Berdans, the decision to remain in Italy represented a final commitment that he made with great reluctance. Crawford could vacillate only so long as he believed the choice remained open, that is, so long as he believed there was time ahead for him to be successful either in literature or in politics. Ultimately, the choice had to be made, and in 1885 Crawford probably knew that the moment of commitment was rapidly approaching.

Circumstances and the romantic influence of Italy upon Bessie became important factors in the final decision. According to their earlier plans, Crawford and Bessie expected to sail for America after the publication of *Zoroaster* by Macmillan in May, 1885; but, since Mrs. Hobson and Mrs. Berdan planned to remain in Europe for the summer, the young couple decided to spend the summer at the picturesque Cocumella Hotel in Sorrento. Its influence upon Bessie is apparent in the letter she wrote her mother immediately after arrival:

> Never have I seen anything which could in any way compare with this place in point of beauty. The sky turquoise blue without one cloud, and the sea such a dark blue it looks almost black. Mountains all around us and as far as one can see to the right or to the left forests . . . of orange trees covered with golden fruit.

. . . To see Marion's happy face when we are out in our very smart little boat, with our four sailors perfectly equipped, flying over the dark blue water, is a thing of joy. . . . You should see the touching delight of the sailors on our arrival. Every day they come and bring us presents of large baskets of fruit or some pretty little box made for us as a welcome, and then some old man will take me one side and tell me how much they all love the "signore" who is so kind to the poor and not a bit "superbo." What a charm there is about these people of the South. . . . Oh, do make haste to come to us! for I now really feel that away from this place life is not life at all. Such perfect days as we pass![1]

However strong Bessie's convictions of what they ought to do may have been, she was certainly beginning to know the appeal of the expatriate's life in Italy. Her husband, of course, had long since been persuaded to this point of view and would have agreed wholeheartedly with her statement that "I now really feel that away from this place life is not life at all." The arrival of the Berdans, the Terrys, and Mrs. Hobson for an extended holiday heightened the enthusiasm of both Bessie and Crawford.

So pleasant were their surroundings that the Crawfords decided to remain at Sorrento throughout the winter. Neither Mrs. Hobson nor Mrs. Berdan approved this decision. The latter's comments in her journal provide a remarkable estimate of the impression Crawford would have made upon a contemporary American observer. She wrote:

My sister thinks that Marion and Bessie are making a great mistake in not returning to America, that continuing the habit of living abroad is not a good thing, and that both, belonging to the greatest country in the world, should make part of it and not live like exiles, as it were, in Europe. Marion says he cannot work to advantage unless he has a place sympathetic to him, and being brought up entirely abroad, I doubt whether he will ever be in full sympathy with Americans and their ways of living, therefore, should they have a family it seems to be desirable that they should be brought up in their own country and not have another generation of aliens. . . . I have lived over twenty years in Europe and have seen everything at its best, still I am only an American living in Europe. Yes, if I were to live my life over again, especially these last ten years, I would go back to my own country. It would, I am sure, have been best for my husband and perhaps best for my children.[2]

The strength of the Berdan pressure upon Crawford to return may be inferred from Mrs. Berdan's warning about "another generation of aliens."

Mrs. Berdan would have been even more apprehensive had she known that Crawford was contemplating the purchase of a villa at Sorrento. The place he selected was the "Villa de Renzis," a large three-storied house built upon a high cliff overhanging the Bay of Naples. The Renzi family, owners of the property, agreed to rent it to Crawford for a year and to give him the option of purchasing it. Early in November the Crawfords established themselves in the villa.

The occupancy of "Villa de Renzis," however, represented only one evidence of Crawford's increasingly firm commitment. Month by month he was becoming more and more involved in both the artistic and the practical side of the production of literature. The care, for example, that he took with *Saracinesca,* which he began to write during the summer of 1885, suggests that he was paying greater attention to problems of technique and content than he had ever done in the past. He was unwilling to hasten the composition of the novel. On October 1, when he suddenly discovered that Macmillan was expecting him to deliver a manuscript before the end of the month, Crawford refused to hurry the composition of *Saracinesca* to meet the deadline.

Instead, he began *A Tale of a Lonely Parish* which he described to his mother as "a strong story made out of simple elements, with a good moral."[3] For her information, he added: "I think it will succeed well and be popular, not because it is sensational but because it is *true. Do not tell* people that it was written in 24 days, a chapter a day, without a break except on Sundays. They would not believe it; but Bessie and Mrs. Berdan saw it done." Crawford's comment on its truth supports what has already been said about the connection between *A Tale of a Lonely Parish* and Crawford's schooling at Hatfield Broad Oak in England. For the right to print twenty-five thousand copies of the book, Macmillan paid 31,250 lire, the price being higher than usual because Macmillan did not wish to publish it first as a serial.

Before returning to *Saracinesca,* Crawford very hastily wrote a ghost story, "The Upper Berth," to appear in *The Broken Shaft,* an anthology edited by Henry Norman and published in 1886 by Fisher Unwin. Crawford contributed only because he considered it good publicity for his work to be included in an annual containing the work of other prominent authors; nevertheless, he was pleased to receive £40 for a few days' work. Curiously enough, this short story, which he dictated to Mrs. Berdan after his usual day's work was finished, has become one of his best-known works and now appears frequently in anthologies of ghost stories.

Crawford was forced to delay even longer any serious work on *Saracinesca* because *A Tale of a Lonely Parish* and "The Upper Berth" had scarcely been mailed to the publishers when Escott of the *Fortnightly Review* once more began to clamor for the long-promised Italian articles. Crawford laboriously began to collect material for the essay on Italian agriculture and its land system. The immediate necessity for correcting the proof sheets of his novels forced him to put aside his research. At the same time Crawford was helping to arrange for foreign editions of his novels. *Mr. Isaacs* had already appeared in French, *A Roman Singer* in Swedish, and *Doctor Claudius* in Danish; and Crawford's friend Giovanni Borghese, was having each novel, as it appeared, put into Italian. A second set of proof sheets of *A Tale of a Lonely Parish* had to be corrected so that the French translator, Charles Bernard Derosne, could begin his work at once; and Crawford and Derosne were already thinking about a forthcoming French edition of *Doctor Claudius*. Meanwhile the increasing volume of Crawford's correspondence with readers, publishers, translators, and editors required him to devote much time to the practical business of promoting the sale of his work.

Despite interruptions, Crawford returned to the composition of *Saracinesca* during the autumn and wrote it with far more care than he had devoted to any preceding novel. The result fully repaid the additional effort, for not only did Crawford realize that it was the best work he had yet accomplished, but also the editor of *Blackwood's Magazine*, to whom he sent it, expressed a very high opinion of the work and paid a large price for it. Greatly elated over his accomplishment, Crawford wrote his mother: "I am to receive the large price of £1350, nearly 34,000 francs for the serial and only fifteen hundred, 1500 copies, all the rest belonging to me, in England, America and abroad. At a low figure I shall get £2500 in 18 months from this one book."[4] A few weeks later he was still highly enthusiastic when he wrote her again, "I received a brilliant offer from Macmillan for the American edition of *Saracinesca*—750 pounds in advance. I shall have received altogether for this book £2100 by May 1st 1887, all contracted for, and independently of the English one volume edition which will bring several hundred pounds more."[5] Crawford had reason to congratulate himself upon his achievement. Not only had he written a good book and obtained a splendid initial price for it, but also he had safeguarded his subsequent royalties. By retaining his rights, he could demand a high royalty if the novel sold well; and, if not, he had already been well compensated.

II

"We are supremely happy in our house over the sea," wrote Crawford to his mother late in 1885. "Never were months so soon past nor more fully enjoyed."[6] As he looked back on his life since coming to Sorrento, he reflected that he had written two novels; and, though he did not know it at the time, one of these novels was to prove a high-water mark in his career. The prices paid by publishers for his work were rapidly increasing, and his reputation was steadily advancing. There was still another reason for the cheerful atmosphere which pervaded the Crawford household. Bessie was enjoying good health while waiting for the arrival of a "Marionette." As the time approached for her confinement, expected in February, 1886, Crawford wrote his mother: "I have some big things in contemplation, but I must make the personal acquaintance of my son—or daughter—before I can do anything."[7] On February 24, 1886, a daughter was born, and a few days later christened Eleanor Louisa Elizabeth Christophers Marion-Crawford. "Henceforth," announced Crawford, "the family name will be Marion-Crawford."[8]

Early in May, 1886, Crawford began to work upon *With the Immortals*. His idea, probably suggested by his wife, was to write a commentary upon various aspects of modern life, using famous men as vehicles for his remarks. The book began as a family project. Bessie Crawford and her mother planned to supply him with the necessary information about the characters; the former chose Chopin; the latter, Francis I, Heine, and Pascal. Crawford was to contribute the framework and interpret the characters of Julius Caesar and Samuel Johnson. A week after the work was begun, Mrs. Berdan noted in her journal:

> Yesterday all assembled in my room for afternoon tea and Marion read aloud to us what he has written. The description of the place he had chosen is most poetically imagined and beautifully written. He described us all as we are or would like to be and once we are settled in this new home he, Augustus Charde, is, for amusement to make all manner of experiments in electricity, and in this way he will evoke the spirits or ghosts of the great departed. But how these themes are to be treated and what they are to say to us or we to them will be seen. The opening chapter is delightful and I believe the book will be most original and interesting.[9]

As the writing of the novel proceeded, Bessie and Mrs. Berdan contributed less and less to it.

With the Immortals represented an experiment for Crawford. Hitherto he had utilized his own experience for the essential parts of his novels; the remainder had come from his imagination. In writing this book, however, he depended upon source material from books. For weeks he alternately read and wrote in the belief that the work would be either a great step forward or a great failure. It proved to be neither; for, although it sold well, Crawford realized that he was not adapted for such writing.

During the summer (1886), Crawford completed *With the Immortals* and made substantial progress with a new novel, *Paul Patoff*, which he asserted in the prologue was based in part upon his own experience.[10] The use of characters of widely different nationalities and settings in several different countries recalls *Doctor Claudius*, while the appearance of Paul Griggs as both narrator and participant in the plot reminds the reader of *Mr. Isaacs*. In *Paul Patoff*, Griggs emerges as a professional storyteller—as he says in the prologue, a "twister of words"—and he offers this story to his hearer, a young lady, as "emphatically a tale, and nothing else." Indeed, he would "almost call it a yarn, though the word would look strangely on a printed title-page." Crawford's apology was appropriate, for the plot of the novel consists of an improbable series of incidents.

The main action of the plot concerns the disappearance of Alexander Patoff from the gallery of the mosque of Agia Sophia. Alexander was watching the services ending the feast of Ramazán— Crawford himself had witnessed them in this same mosque. Since Alexander had been visiting his younger brother Paul in Constantinople and since there had been ill feeling between them, Paul fears that he will be suspected of having murdered his brother. Although the search for Alexander becomes the mainspring of the plot, Crawford leads Paul through a variety of highly improbable but exciting adventures in Germany, England, and Turkey. The final discovery that Alexander had been spirited away to a Turkish harem as a joke and then kept there because of the widespread alarm over his disappearance does nothing to lift the novel from the classification of "yarn."

Paul Patoff provides a good illustration of Crawford's tendency to emphasize incident over character and his unwillingness to penetrate very deeply into the psychological implications of the tension he creates between character and character. Early in the story, Crawford tells his reader that the animosity between the Patoff brothers is somehow related to the apparent partiality of their English mother for Alexander, and later the two brothers compete for the love of the same woman. Crawford solves the former complication by insanity and the latter by an instance of cowardice in the older brother. The result is a story that moves rapidly upon the wheels of incident and ignores the subtleties of character analysis.

By the fall of 1886, Crawford had made his decision to remain in Italy. Very likely the fact that he had written four novels—including two of very high quality—since coming to Sorrento weighed heavily in his decision; but certainly the enthusiasm which Bessie had shown for Sorrento must also have counted with him. The absence of the Berdans and the nearness of Louisa Terry, moreover, may have contributed. In any event Crawford's commitment to Italy was established beyond doubt by his efforts to purchase "Villa de Renzis." The price was fixed at 95,000 lire. Largely by borrowing from Frederick Macmillan against future novels and royalties, Crawford purchased the villa and obtained formal title on July 2, 1887. Louisa Terry's description of his pride in accomplishment as he became the owner contained also a suggestion of Crawford's final commitment to Italy:

> Our dear boy's unutterable joy, pride, happiness, are not to be described in the actual possession. To think that it was all his very own; won by his own hard work, was, is continually a source of delight: a permanent home for Bessie and his beautiful little Eleanor. He even rejoiced in the sense that the very noise of the waves dashing against the foot of the cliffs was his very own, for the contract gave title to seven metres of the Mediterranean along his shore.[11]

"Villa Crawford," as it was re-named, was built upon the edge of a line of cliffs, which rose steeply from the southern shore of the Bay of Naples. From the terrace which extended the length of the villa in front, the view was north, directly toward Mount Vesuvius. As one entered the house from the rear, after passing under a porte-cochere and through a large entrance hall, the library, tinted a Pompeian red, was on the left. To the right was a large dining room, while opposite the hall door and facing the terrace was an immense drawing room. Below the ground floor was a series of rooms which were used for servants' quarters and storage.

On the second floor of the villa was Mrs. Crawford's spacious bedroom, and adjacent to it her sitting room, elegantly furnished in the style of Louis XV. On the same level there were four other rooms. Directly above Mrs. Crawford's bedroom, and approximately the same size, was Crawford's apartment. These were connected by a winding staircase. Five additional rooms, somewhat smaller than Crawford's bedroom, completed the arrangements on the third floor.

Shortly after Crawford purchased the villa, he made extensive alterations both to the building and to the grounds. When he took possession, for example, the upper levels of the villa were reached by an exterior staircase on the east side. Crawford enclosed it in an octagonal tower, building a balcony at the top extending from the tower around the front of the house. Because of the seclusion and of the view it afforded him, the tower became his writing place. By certain devices he rendered it sound-proof so that he might work undisturbed by noise from the outside. Crawford redesigned the gardens, constructed a Moorish fountain, and built a tennis court around which he planted an orange grove.

In this magnificent palace, the Crawfords lived luxuriously. The master spared no expense. A staff of thirteen servants—"cooks, gardeners, footmen, groom, butler, maids, etc."[12]—were available to perform the wishes of their mistress. Clothes must be made of the finest materials; food must be of the choicest variety; wines must be of the finest vintage. Formal dress was required. Soon "Villa Crawford" was noted for the lavish entertainments which were the rule and not the exception. One of the many birthday fetes held in the villa has been described by Louisa Terry; from her account, one can form an estimate of the kind of celebration which Crawford thought appropriate:

> On the 15th of June [1887] beautiful golden haired Bessie awoke to be lovingly congratulated on the ending of her twenty-fourth and beginning of her twenty-fifth year. . . . As she came forth from her room on Marion's arm, she found flowers scattered before her, through the upper hall, down the long staircase through the lower hall to the very doors of the drawing and dining rooms. The servants and sailors were all assembled in this hall, with offerings of fruit and flowers, as also several of the charity protégées who came bringing eggs, cheese, such things as they had to show their gratitude and good will. In the dining room were collected the beautiful gifts, most of them Marion's loving kindness. I was there to receive my two with little Eleanor baby as they entered. . . . And finally as they entered Bessie caught sight of a most beautiful piece of carved furniture standing between the windows. A piece of gothic twisting and carving, inlaid with arabesques in brass, and in the centre, part and parcel of the furniture, a delightful old fashioned clock with a long pendulum, the large round disk of which looks like a sun by daylight and in the evening with the reflection of a high swing lamp looks like the moon. . . . Glass doors and crimson lining complete the "Meuble" which Bessie had been coveting, for many months. . . . But

The Prince of Sorrento

I must make speed and move on, not however without telling you
how touched and overwhelmed Bessie was. Now she was "faced
about right" and lo in the South East corner of the room six
charming bits of Cairo furniture, a tall corner piece with the peculiar
lattice work of the East, and a settee with four stools covered with
Bokarah carpeting in the same style. . . . Third rapture, when
standing on a table surrounded with flowers Bessie saw the desire
of her silver-loving heart. A beautiful mirror in a solid Louis XV
silver frame, matching or rather going admirably with her splendid
toilet table of silver articles, that M. had picked up in Constantinople,
increased by a gift of dressing case ornaments from her father and
mother, as also by some friendly wedding presents. . . . Bessie's
Cypher had been beautifully introduced in the frame so as to look
like the original design. I do not name the lesser gifts for they
sank into insignificance beside this splendid generosity. But I must
tell you of our pleasantest dinner and how the evening ended with
our favorite Tarantella danced most gracefully by Liacchino, the
Barber and Antonio the carpenter, with other costumed men and
women, four couples in all, costumes new for the great occasion. The
dance was on the broad terrace overhanging the sea. Hundreds
of coloured lamps illuminated the scene, with every now and then,
a Bengal to add fresh effect to the illumination. Between the dances
the little band, some of the performers half blind, waltzes were
played, or Neapolitan songs sung by our barber and carpenter,
who have such sympathetic voices and sing by nature as do all
these maccaroni eating people. We and our two or three guests
sat luxuriously under a carpeted tent at one end of the terrace,
upon divans, and I almost wondered in the midst of the fairy scene,
if we were not really orientals, so very much at home did we all
seem to feel.[13]

Although this was a family party, the entertainments to which
outsiders were invited were no less spectacular. The luxury for
which Crawford had longed since his boyhood days was now a
reality, and Bessie must have thought her adoring husband a
modern Alladin with a magic touch.

From this time forward, Crawford struggled to fill the dual
role of gentleman and scholar which he had formulated, perhaps
unconsciously, before Louisa Terry lost her fortune in the depres-
sions of the 1870's. "Villa Crawford" and its princely entertainments
were essential parts of the ideal of a novelist who liked to be
called the "Prince of Sorrento."[14] The standard of luxury which
Crawford now set for his wife and, to a lesser degree, for himself,
was so high that to sustain it he was compelled to write novel
after novel in quick succession. Thus there is some reason to
suppose that, if Crawford and his wife had been content to live

less extravagantly and in a less pretentious dwelling, he would have written fewer and probably better novels. From this point of view, the purchase of "Villa Crawford" was a mistake; yet to Crawford it represented in 1887 a magnificent personal triumph and the visible symbol of success.

III

Neither Crawford nor his family would have admitted that he was writing too rapidly. Stimulated by the demand for his work, delighted with his surroundings, and eager for the luxuries of wealth, Crawford wrote with what seemed an apparent lack of discrimination between good and bad work. Temperamentally unwilling to accept criticism from anyone, he could produce *Saracinesca* and immediately afterwards *With the Immortals* and *Paul Patoff;* and in the next few years he would intersperse such novels as *The Three Fates* and *The Witch of Prague* with the really outstanding volumes of *Marzio's Crucifix* and *Sant' Ilario.* Nor was Crawford able to foresee the effects of the physical strain of writing upon his health; yet, in the years which followed, it became evident that the pace which he had established for himself would, if sustained, prove ruinous. In 1887, however, he was too preoccupied with the activities of the present and with the prospects of the future to be concerned about his health and his ultimate literary reputation.

During the early part of his career, Crawford was often proud of his ability to write quickly; but, in declaring—for example— that he wrote *Marzio's Crucifix* in ten days,[15] he failed to mention that he had spent months learning about the silversmith's trade and carefully thinking through the events of the novel before he began to write. His fourth novel with an Italian setting, Crawford presented in *Marzio's Crucifix* the slightly sentimental story of a silversmith whose evil intentions are transformed into good motives as he makes a beautiful crucifix. Although not all critics would agree with him, Arthur Hobson Quinn has praised "the unity of the novel, the perfect preservation of tone, the art with which Crawford united the greatest symbol of Christianity and the love of beauty to bring peace to an unhappy heart" and has called it "one of the finest novels in the language."[16]

Although Crawford had been writing two full-sized novels each summer, in 1887 he wrote only *Marzio's Crucifix* and a long poem entitled "A National Hymn," which required more effort than the result warranted.[17] Aside from these, Crawford showed little interest in literary activity. Anxiety over the purchase of the villa and, subsequently, the demands of the constant parties and elaborate dinners at Sorrento prompted Crawford to seek relaxation. He spent most of the summer in the *Margherita,* cruising up and down the coast of Italy and in visiting unfrequented places along the shore.

On one of these excursions during August, 1887, Crawford anchored the *Margherita* outside of a shallow bay off the coast of Calabria, and with his wife and faithful servant, Luigi, went ashore in a small boat. Nearby was Torre San Nicola, an ancient fortress built by Charles V. After a picnic lunch, Crawford, accompanied by Luigi, explored the ruined tower, walked several miles to the wretched village of San Nicola, and returned carrying a large iron key. Mrs. Crawford was shocked to learn that this key fitted the castle and that her husband had leased it for thirty years. Bessie Crawford considered the place an impossible habitation. A round tower, with walls eighteen feet thick, wide at the base, and tapering slightly toward the summit, Torre San Nicola stood on the rocks of Calabria, miles from human habitation and without a single modern convenience. Inside were two apartments: one below, an immense square without windows, was presumably for animals; and above, a second large room dimly lighted by several windows. To Bessie it was a dismal sight; to Crawford it was a wild, romantic, solitary refuge from society. He soon whitewashed the brick tiles on the interior and furnished the two rooms with books and provisions.[18] Time after time, whenever Crawford wished to be alone, he returned to Torre San Nicola, especially in subsequent years after the happiness and optimism of the 1880's had faded away. At the moment, the tower was merely an episode in a pleasant summer.

In September, Crawford began to write *Sant' Ilario.* Two months later, when he interrupted his work to sing with the Pope's choir in Rome, Crawford had not made notable progress though he was warmly enthusiastic about his material. Because the story required careful plotting and accurate details for its setting, Crawford wrote slowly, yet by March, 1888, he had completed it.[19]

On February 1, 1888, Crawford's second child, Harold Marion-Crawford, was born. Crawford's family responsibilities, which he took seriously, were increasing. The family remained at the villa in Sorrento until the first sign of approaching hot weather when Crawford decided to move to a cooler place for the summer. On the last day of April, Louisa Terry disclosed the plans to Maud Howe, who was now married to John Elliott: "My Marions ... are stopping in Rome for two days only, on their way to Florence, where they stay a fortnight or so before going up for the summer to Vallombrosa. The summer is to be passed up there, Uncle Terry [Luther Terry] and I joining them in June or July. It is such a lovely place! Marion has hired what is known as the 'Paradiso,' a tiny hotel on the summit of the hill."[20]

So far as literary work was concerned, Crawford divided his time during the summer between writing *Greifenstein* and reading the proofs of *Sant' Ilario.* For the setting of *Greifenstein,* he recalled scenes from his student days in Karlsruhe. The symmetrical, though melodramatic, plot chronicles the fortunes of two generations of Prussian aristocrats. Years before the opening of the story, Kuno von Rieseneck married Clara Kurtz, and they had a son named Horst but called "Rex." During the revolution of 1848, Clara forced Kuno to become a traitor to his country. After he was sentenced to imprisonment for life, Clara married Kuno's half-brother, Hugo von Greifenstein, and they have a son named' Hugo but called "Greif." The two young men, unaware of their relationship, become friends at school. Greif plans to marry Hilda von Sigmundskron whom he has known since childhood. After forty years of imprisonment, Kuno von Rieseneck, now pardoned, returns home and tells his brother Hugo about Clara's perfidy. The two brothers strangle her; and, after leaving a note explaining everything to their sons, they commit suicide. By chance, Greif fails to receive his father's message and marries Hilda. Rex keeps his secret, but falls in love with Hilda, thereby re-creating in the second generation the tangle of the first. Hilda, however, proves her superiority to Clara by persuading Rex and Greif to pursue the path of honor instead of shame. The complications of the plot are thus happily resolved.

Despite Louisa Terry's assertion that *Greifenstein* was entirely different from any of his preceding novels,[21] it displayed a distinct resemblance to both *Saracinesca* and *Sant' Ilario.* In each of these novels Crawford dealt with the fortunes of a family throughout two or more generations. These books, moreover, prefigured a type of fiction which Crawford was to write again and again: the family novel. One has only to mention the titles of the others in this group—they include *Don Orsino, Pietro Ghisleri, Katharine Lauderdale, The Ralstons, Casa Braccio,* and *Corleone*—to realize that it represented the core of his best work. Although *Greifenstein* seems much less artistically attractive than the other family novels, it did serve to emphasize this new element in his work; nevertheless, the development actually began with *Saracinesca.* Unless Crawford's literary practices had changed greatly during the preceding three years, and there is no reason to suppose they had, it was not a fortuitous circumstance that his interest in the family as a social unit coincided with the growth of his own family circle. To be sure, he had always been, as Maud Howe Elliott remarked, "the most domestic man imaginable,"[22] yet Crawford's treatment of family life had to wait until the hero of his novels became a family man himself. By the time he began to write *Saracinesca* and *Greifenstein,* he possessed a family of his own, and the subject became sufficiently real and congenial to prompt him to employ it for fictional purposes. Thus the birth of his children, the "permanent home for Bessie," and the "mutual admiration society" began to leave an imprint upon his novels.

At Vallombrosa, the Crawfords, Berdans, and Terrys extravagantly praised *Sant' Ilario* and *Greifenstein,* reading the chapters as rapidly as the author finished them. In the fall, the Terrys returned to Rome, and the Berdans went to Sorrento with the Crawfords. Reflecting upon her son's apparent contentment in finding his intellectual stimulus almost exclusively among a family of women, Louisa Terry doubted, as she had long ago, whether living in a woman's world was good for him. When Crawford came to Rome in January, 1889, she wrote her daughter, Margaret Chanler: "His visit is doing him all possible good,... giving him such opportunity of seeing and talking with men, just what is most difficult for him to have at Sorrento. Clever as are his dear Bessie and paragon Mother-in-law he lives too exclusively among women."[23] A few weeks later the arrival of Margaret and Winthrop Chanler provided additional opportunities for Crawford to see and talk with men. Their circle of friends included Giovanni Borghese, Waldo Story, Lord and Lady Dufferin, the Marchese and Marchesa Theodoli, and Dr. Axel Munthe.

Throughout most of 1889 and 1890, Crawford suffered from fainting spells and stomach pains. During this time he continued to write novels, but he produced nothing that added greatly to his permanent literary reputation. In the summer of 1889 he completed *The Three Fates,*[24] a somewhat autobiographical novel dealing with the difficulties of a young writer in establishing himself in the literary world of New York. During the winter of 1889-90, which the Crawford family spent in Munich, he began *The Witch of Prague* and *A Cigarette-Maker's Romance,* but he made only slight progress with these volumes until after the birth of twins, Clare and Bertram, to the Crawfords on April 16, 1890.

Recently Crawford had used a German background for *Greifenstein*[25] and for portions of *Paul Patoff;* neither of these books could be included among his best novels. *The Witch of Prague* must be considered an even less attractive work. Like its German predecessors, it suffers from a multiplicity of improbable incidents and from characters who act solely in accordance with the exigencies of the melodramatic plot. Crawford's description of it on the title page as "a fantastic tale" may have been prompted by the knowledge that it could scarcely be defended as a credible imitation of life. The fact that he intended it for serialization probably accounts for the forced crises that occur every chapter or two and for the bewildering series of incidents which feature hypnotism, attempted murder, mistaken identity, and scientific experiments in the embalming of living persons.[26] Contemporary critics were as quick to denounce *The Witch of Prague* as they were to praise the totally different *A Cigarette-Maker's Romance* which Crawford completed about the same time.

A Cigarette-Maker's Romance, which Macmillan published in the fall of 1890, proved to be one of the most popular works ever written by Crawford. Within several years after its appearance, more than one hundred and fifty-three thousand copies had been printed for sale in England, and the demand in America probably far exceeded this number. Everywhere it was received with public enthusiasm and critical acclaim. After calling it "a beautiful story," the reviewer for the *Westminster Review* (May, 1891) continued, "we say it advisedly: no other word than 'beautiful' in any degree fits it." The critic for the *Athenaeum* (October 26, 1890) described it as "a story of exquisitely pathetic interest," and in the *Atlantic Monthly* (January, 1891) Crawford was highly praised for his masterly English and the "sureness of his movement." Reviewers for the *Spectator* (December 13, 1890) and the *Critic* (December 27, 1890) left little else to be said in the way of extravagant endorsement.

A number of factors could have contributed to the success of *A Cigarette-Maker's Romance*. The story, which relates the love of a young Polish girl for a Russian count who has been reduced to earning a meager living by making two thousand cigarettes each day, was well calculated to appeal to the romantic taste of the readers of the 1890's. Departing from his usual practice in the writing of his novels, Crawford reduced the number of his characters to a bare minimum, compressed the action of the plot into two days and an intervening night, and eliminated anything which did not directly contribute to the total impression he wished to achieve. By these measures he gave his romance an organic unity which reminds one of the Italian and German *novella*. Finally, he chose as his theme the unselfishness of woman's devotion and embodied it in a story with a happy ending, full of sentiment but, by the standards of the time, not markedly sentimental. The work continued for a long time to be a favorite with Crawford's readers.

In the fall of 1890, Crawford returned to Sorrento, but a renewal of the fainting spells and the severe stomach trouble from which he had been suffering forced him to abandon his plans to spend the winter at "Villa Crawford." Leaving their children in the care of Mrs. Berdan, Crawford and his wife made an extended journey to the East. On board the steamer, *Meno Minghetti,* they went to Izmir (Smyrna) and then directly to Pera. After sailing to Sevastopol at the extreme southern end of the Crimean Peninsula, they traveled leisurely to Tiflis, their ultimate destination, probably stopping along the route at Rostov, just north of the Sea of Azov, and at various ports along the northern shore of the Black Sea. Tiflis, with its picturesque scenery, cathedrals, palaces, and strange mélange of races, challenged Crawford's imagination. Sometime during the winter (1890-91), he traveled southward from Tiflis to Bagdad and thence to the northern edge of the Red Desert in Arabia. This is the locale of *Khaled,* a short novel, which he probably wrote during the spring of 1891 while still recuperating in the East.

Khaled, perhaps the most richly romantic of Crawford's novels, is the story of a genie to whom Allah gave a man's body and promised a soul if he could win a woman's love. Through faith and devotion, Khaled, "the believing genius," gains the love of Zehowah, daughter of the Sultan of Nejed. Crawford described her in prose that suggests the tone and atmosphere of the remainder of the work:

> One daughter only had been born to him [the Sultan of Nejed] in his old age, of such marvellous beauty that even the Black Eyed Virgins enclosed in the fruit of the tree Sedrat, who wait for the coming of the faithful, would seem but mortal women beside her. Her eyes are as the deep water in the wells of Zobeideh when it is night and the stars are reflected therein. Her hair is finer than silk, red with henna, and abundant as the foliage of the young cypress tree. Her face is as fair as the kernels of young almonds, and her mouth is sweeter than the mellow date and more fragrant than 'Ood mingled with ambergris.[27]

Although Luther Terry thought that *Khaled* was "totally unlike anything Marion has written before,"[28] the setting, fantasy, and semi-religious atmosphere which pervaded *Khaled* reminded Crawford's readers of the recent *Zoroaster* and, more remotely, of *Mr. Isaacs.* By the end of May, 1891, the novel had been published by Macmillan in London and New York, and the Crawfords had returned to Sorrento.

IV

Refreshed by the long voyage to the East and by the warm springs of Tiflis, Crawford believed that he was once more in condition to write. Since he had promised to send Macmillan in June, 1891, a third and final part of the *Saracinesca* trilogy, Crawford at once began to compose *Don Orsino*.[29] Although he knew that he could not meet the deadline, he worked steadily throughout the summer and fall; and, to avoid a recurrence of his illness, he made long voyages in the *Margherita* to Amalfi, Torre San Nicola, and so far south as Messina, often being away from "Villa Crawford" for a month at a time.

No one could say, however, that *Don Orsino* exhibited the marks of Crawford's illness, for he admirably sustained in it the high level of writing that he had displayed in the earlier *Saracinesca* and *Sant' Ilario*. Considered together, these three novels reveal perhaps better than any of his work the qualities which made Crawford a major American writer in the eyes of the reading public wherever novels were read during the 1880's, 1890's, and the first decade of the twentieth century. Since then a changing literary taste may have diminished Crawford's fame; but, for its kind or type, the *Saracinesca* trilogy has probably never been surpassed.

In these novels Crawford was chronicling, as he said, the history of a Roman family from 1865 "down to the present day,"[30] 1885. In other words, he was writing about a period of time within his own memory. He considered the work as a three-act drama; each volume, though a complete story in itself, comprised one act. On one level of interpretation, the three volumes represent an analysis of the effect of changing political and social conditions in Italy upon the members of a noble Italian family; yet this was neither the sole, nor to Crawford, even the most important element of the work. On a second plane, the trilogy is an account, full of suspense and action, of the activities of a group of people bound together by social and, or, consanguine ties. From yet another viewpoint, the novels constitute an analysis of the relations and emotional development of two, and perhaps three, generations of the house of Saracinesca. Any one of these three interpretations would be valid, but incomplete by itself and thus partially false. Even the briefest examination of the work makes this inference evident.

In *Saracinesca*, the action of the plot covers less than two years. Don Giovanni Saracinesca, thirty years old in 1865 and the heir of the ancient house of Saracinesca, has not married because he loves Corona, the Duchesa d'Astrardente, wife of the Duca d'Astrardente, a "broken-down and worn-out dandy of sixty." In Crawford's words, Corona had "accepted Astrardente with his dukedom, his great wealth, and his evil past, on the day when she left the convent where she had been educated; she did it to save her father from ruin, almost from starvation; she was seventeen years of age; she was told that the world was bad, and she resolved to begin her life by a heroic sacrifice. . . ."[31] Five years later her father is dead, and Giovanni and Corona are aware of their mutual love; but each possesses too much honor to reveal it openly to the other. This is the situation at the opening of the "first act."

Skillfully exploiting the possibilities of the triangular situation, Crawford narrates how Giovanni's resolution never to avow his love is broken while Corona sits beside her husband in their box at the opera. When she makes no reply, Saracinesca leaves the opera house, bitterly disgusted with himself and angry at his own impetuousness. A few days later, they meet again at a magnificent ball given by the Frangipani family, and on the terrace of the palazzo Giovanni again pledges his love to her. Loyalty to her husband and her sense of honor prevent Corona from revealing her feelings to Giovanni. Upon discovering that Ugo del Ferice, an unscrupulous political schemer, has witnessed this rendezvous, Giovanni challenges him to a duel. After the encounter which follows, Del Ferice, though severely wounded, escapes, recovers, and plots to ruin Giovanni.

The narrative continues to unfold rapidly. The sudden death of the old Duca d'Astrardente removes the only apparent obstacle to the union of the lovers, and after a period of mourning—and courtship—the day of the wedding is fixed. Meanwhile, Donna Tullia Mayer has promised to become Del Ferice's wife if he will destroy the happiness of Corona and Giovanni. Donna Tullia's hatred of Saracinesca arises from the fact that, after Giovanni's father had opened negotiations for a marriage between Donna Tulia and his son, Giovanni had refused to marry her. Del Ferice furnishes Donna Tullia with marriage certificates which purport to prove that Giovanni is married to a peasant girl. When Corona's engagement is announced, Donna Tullia confronts the duchess with these papers. Investigation, however, discloses that the certificates belong to Giovanni's distant cousin of the same name, an innkeeper at Aquila. The lovers are married with great splendor. In the final scene, Giovanni, at the request of his wife, permits Del Ferice— now revealed as a spy for the liberal party and one of the "scum which remained after the revolution of 1848 had subsided"[32]—to escape from Gouache, the painter, who has enlisted in the Papal Zouaves.

As may be seen from the foregoing summary of *Saracinesca*, the political background of the novel is slight and is rigidly subordinated to the action. On the other hand, the plot moves rapidly, from scene to scene, through a series of climaxes to a happy conclusion; and, within the framework of events, the characters are made to act from rational motives. There are no psychologically enigmatic characters, no descent to the commonplace, and no obvious "purpose" or thesis. The great subject is love—love opposed first by social custom and second by hate. In a larger sense, the theme becomes the attainment of happiness by individuals through their own emotional and intellectual development. Crawford had once written:

> There is something beyond mere greatness, beyond the pursuit of even the highest worldly aims; there is something which is not a means to the attainment of happiness, which is happiness itself. It is an inner sympathy of hearts and souls and minds, a perfect union of all that is most worthy in the natures of man and woman; it is a plant so sensitive that a breath of unkindness will hurt it and blight its beauty, and yet it is a tree so strong that neither time nor tempest can overthrow it when it has taken root; and if you would tear it out and destroy it, the place where it grew is as deep and as wide as a grave. It is a bond that is as soft as silk and as strong as death, binding hearts, not hands; so long as it is not strained a man will hardly know that he is bound, but if he would break it he will spend his strength in vain and suffer the pains of hell, for it is the very essence and nature of true love that it cannot be broken.[33]

In *Saracinesca*, Giovanni and Corona achieved such a union as Crawford described. In *Sant' Ilario*, the novelist was to demonstrate the validity of his assertion that "true love ... cannot be broken."

Although the principal theme of *Sant' Ilario*, the "second act" of the trilogy, is the jealousy which threatened to break the bond of "true love" between Corona and Giovanni, Crawford gives the plot three or four separate facets. One develops Gouache's courtship of Faustina Montevarchi; another traces the rise of the second Giovanni Saracinesca, the former innkeeper, now known as San Giacinto; a third presents an account of the Montevarchi forgery; and a fourth, of course, deals with the central plot. The task of the storyteller is to unite the different episodes into a harmonious whole. Crawford adroitly provided connecting links between them, but the focus of the novel shifts so frequently that Sant' Ilario (the Giovanni of Saracinesca) never quite emerges as a memorable character.

The political and social background of Roman society, moreover, occupies a less important position in *Sant' Ilario* than it does in the first novel. There is, to be sure, a brief reference to the Revolution of 1867, but no special emphasis is placed upon contemporary events. With *Don Orsino*, however, Crawford introduced a considerable amount of social and political material; but again, and for the same reason, he used only what was essential for his purposes. Twenty years have elapsed since Corona and Giovanni were married. Their son, Don Orsino, is growing up in a united Italy. Unification has been attended by a building and speculating boom which is at its height in 1885. The law of primogeniture has been abolished, and the leadership of the old Roman nobility has been superseded by a new order of businessmen and bankers. Representative of the best of this group is San Giacinto who has, by this time, claimed his titles of nobility, married a daughter of the house of Montevarchi, and become a financial magnate. The worst element of the new order is exemplified by Ugo del Ferice whose services as a spy have been rewarded by political patronage and opportunities for graft.

Into this environment Crawford projected Don Orsino, a youth whose family's ideas and prejudices are those of the older generation of the Italian nobility. To a considerable degree, Crawford himself had, as a young man, shared the views of Don Orsino's parents. Orsino, however, has become surfeited with the idle and aimless life of his class and earnestly seeks purposeful activity. He is, as Crawford wrote, a "young man of the Transition Period."[34] Orsino finds, temporarily, a vocation; but he becomes so entangled in the meshes of Del Ferice that only the sacrifice of the woman who loves him deeply (and whose love he does not return) can set him free. At this point, Crawford concluded the novel. The implications are that Orsino has tried business, found it not agreeable to his taste, and assumed a position somewhat analogous to that of his parents and, one may add, to that of Crawford. In Crawford's opinion, however, these implications do not represent the essential issue.

Crawford summarizes the essential meaning of Orsino's experience near the end of the novel. This passage may be also taken as Crawford's account of his own development.

> But these things which I have described have made a man of him at an age when many men are but boys, and he has learnt what many never learn at all—that there is more true devotion to be found in the world than most people will acknowledge. He

may some day be heard of. . . . Or he may never love at all and may never distinguish himself any more than his father has done. . . . And Orsino Saracinesca is not extraordinary in any way. His character has been formed by the unusual circumstances in which he was placed when very young, rather than by anything like the self-development which we hear of in the lives of great men. From a somewhat foolish and affectedly cynical youth he has grown into a decidedly hard and cool-headed man.[35]

The emphasis in the novel supports Crawford's remarks. Finance, business, construction, industry—these things do not interest Crawford. For Orsino to have become an industrial czar or a financial leader would have been counter to Crawford's own experience. On the other hand, to Crawford—as well as to the millions who in the nineteenth century committed themselves to the values of Victorianism and its American counterpart now called the Genteel Tradition—love, faith, and devotion represented the highest ideals of human life. That in novel after novel Crawford's heroes and heroines affirmed these beliefs accounts for a large measure of his popularity.

By no means the least of Crawford's achievements in the *Saracinesca* trilogy was the creation of an imaginary web of figures who seem to have actually lived; and their experiences, moreover, are inter-related, usually plausible, and exciting. What he accomplished, in effect, was the transformation of the reality of his own past into the romance of fiction. No incident, however trivial, was too insignificant for Crawford to use in his novels. Once as a child, Crawford received a blessing from a Catholic prelate in the same fashion as he described in *Saracinesca:* "Many a time, too, Pius IX. would descend from his coach and walk upon the Pincio, all clothed in white, stopping sometimes to talk with those who accompanied him, or to lay his gentle hand on the fair curls of some little English child that paused from its play in awe and admiration as the Pope went by."[36]

It is not a coincidence that the three novels span the period from Crawford's boyhood until 1885 when *Saracinesca* was written. The place names, descriptions of Rome and the characters, and even the incidents Crawford "lifted bodily" out of his own life. With regard to the characters, Mother Marion-Crawford, the novelist's daughter, has said: "Giovanni Saracinesca was most certainly a portrait of Giovanni Borghese. He . . . was an intimate friend of the family and came to Sorrento very often and entertained my family frequently in Rome. Corona Astrardente was a portrait of Princess Vittoria Colonna as she appeared in her outward manner and looks, it was not a portrait of her character. . . . The melancholy Spicca was a portrait of Mayendorff, a Russian Diplomat . . . and a great friend of the family."[37] To this list others, including, of course, Cardinal Antonelli, might be added. Likewise, the hunting scenes, the description of the Frangipani ball,[38] and the duel were based upon actual experiences. In addition, the stopping of the runaway horse and the account of Montevarchi's library in *Sant' Ilario,* as well as the description of the Jubilee in *Don Orsino,* were facts before they became fiction. These examples could be multiplied, but even these few serve to demonstrate the solid foundation in reality of Crawford's romances. By the time he had completed *Don Orsino,* Crawford had fully developed, though not expressed, the theory and practice of his craft; and, in the opinion of a vast international audience, he was one of the greatest living American writers.

V

The six years between 1885 and 1891 were probably the happiest years of Crawford's life, for during them he came closer than he had in the past, or would ever reach in the future, to realizing his ideal of what the perfect life should be. Influenced partly by circumstances but perhaps even more by his own inclinations, he resisted the pressures which were driving him toward a political career in America. His final commitment to Italy was symbolized by the acquisition of "Villa Crawford." Meanwhile, his increasing family responsibilities and the continued success of his literary work, which notably increased the prices that publishers were willing to pay for his novels, became decisive factors in his commitment to literature. Although he paid a price in hard work, everything he wrote became a success; he had no failures. For the first time since his boyhood, Crawford had sufficient money to satisfy his luxurious tastes. He spent his income as rapidly as he made it; and he set for himself and his family an extremely high—probably too high—standard of living. He could, as he probably did, repeat what he had said earlier—he had astonished them all.

After a time, however, he appeared somewhat less self-assured to his friends. Sir James Rennell Rodd, who saw Crawford in the summer of 1891, remarked: "I found him much changed since his marriage with a daughter of the well-known military inventor, General Berdan. He [Crawford] was less cynical and self-assertive. Success had made him a kindlier critic, and he was extremely modest about his own accomplishment."[39] Crawford's outward modesty did not mean that his self-confidence had in any way diminished, but it was less evident than formerly. His obstinacy, moodiness, and proud spirit, however, were always apparent. Sir James recalled an incident which took place during the same summer:

> One night we had returned very late . . . from a picnic in an undecked felucca . . . when a sudden impulse prompted Crawford to propose sailing to Capri. His experienced boatmen who knew their own seas protested; they had families dependent on them and the passage could not be attempted in an open boat. This roused his demon of opposition, and he denounced their lack of courage. Seeing that argument was useless, I said I would go with him, and we put out again about midnight. Beyond the shelter of the bay every bit of canvas had to come down at once. . . . I foresaw catastrophe and reflected on the obituary notices. Crawford managed the boat well enough, but he had been up at dawn, and I was not sorry to see sleep overpowering him, whereupon he relinquished the rudder to one of his boatmen and resigned himself. We steered for a little creek half-way to the end of the peninsula and found shelter.[40]

Neither in personal affairs nor in his literary work did Crawford willingly accept criticism.

There was, indeed, almost no one at "Villa Crawford" during these years who seemed to want to criticize him. On the contrary, Crawford appeared to be always surrounded by an adoring circle of females who praised his every word and submitted without question to his commands. As the "Prince of Sorrento," he dispensed a lavish hospitality to those who admired him; and, when he became weary of society, he could find solitude at sea in his felucca and at San Nicola in his isolated tower. The apparent domestic and literary harmony at "Villa Crawford" forecast only a happy future which would continue the present. If there were any signs of a rift between Bessie and Crawford, they were well concealed by the multiplicity of Crawford's literary activities and by the incessant social events at the villa.

CHAPTER 6

The Man of Letters

*

I

BY JUNE, 1892, Francis Marion Crawford had been a practicing novelist for ten years. By that date he had already written more novels than either of his contemporaries, William Dean Howells or Henry James, both of whom had been producing fiction twice as long as Crawford. Every one of his eighteen novels had been an astonishing success with both the critics and the reading public. Hundreds of thousands of Americans and Englishmen who could not have recalled even the title of a single novel by either Howells or James had willingly succumbed to the charm and power of Crawford's romances. Henry James, who had watched Crawford's brilliant success with a bitterness he did not wish to reveal, wrote Howells from Paris shortly after *A Roman Singer* appeared in 1884:

> What you tell me of the success of [Crawford]'s last novel sickens and almost paralyses me. It seems to me (the book) so contemptibly bad and ignoble that the idea of people reading it in such numbers makes one return upon one's self and ask what is the use of trying to write anything decent or serious for a public so absolutely idiotic. It must be totally wasted. I would rather have produced the basest experiment in the "naturalism" that is being practised here than such a piece of sixpenny humbug. Work so shamelessly bad seems to me to dishonour the novelist's art to a degree that is absolutely not to be forgiven; just as its success dishonours the people for whom one supposes one's self to write. Excuse my ferocities, which (more discreetly and philosophically) I think you must share; and don't mention it, please, to any one, as it will be set down to green-eyed jealousy.[1]

"Ferocities" and "green-eyed jealousy" aside, James was applying his own theory of fiction to Crawford's novels which were written according to a totally different concept. Crawford could have retorted—and there were many who would have agreed with him—

that, judged by his notion of what a novel should be, the fiction of both James and Howells left something to be desired.

In the last ten years Crawford had learned much about the practical methods of selling novels to the public. He knew that most established novelists endeavored to sustain their popularity by broadening the scope of their literary efforts, and in 1892 he abruptly took the first step in that direction by accepting an offer from Major James Burton Pond, the leading lyceum manager in the United States, to give a series of readings from his novels. To the public Crawford remained of course primarily a novelist, but in the next few years he became successively a public reader, lecturer, critic, and dramatist. To fulfill this new role of the professional man of letters, Crawford, perhaps willingly, spent much of his life away from "Villa Crawford" and worked harder than he ever had in the past.

His sudden readiness to leave his home in Sorrento and to give a series of public readings in the United States was very likely prompted by personal as well as by professional reasons. In recent years the atmosphere at "Villa Crawford" may not have been so harmonious as it had been in the days immediately following Crawford's marriage. The mutual admiration society, which in the past had gathered frequently in Sorrento, had been dissolved and its members scattered. Louisa Terry, in Rome and suffering from ill health, no longer participated actively in Crawford's career. Bessie Crawford, who during the first years of their marriage had manifested an eager delight in his novels, no longer cooperated in his work; she now gave her attention to society. Crawford, who had begun to care less and less for social activities, gradually perceived a change in the domestic life at Sorrento. Beginning about 1891 there were persistent rumors that Crawford and his wife had separated—rumors that were not dissipated by Bessie Crawford's fondness for society and by Crawford's preference for the solitude of Torre San Nicola and by his visits to the still beautiful Marchesa Theodoli, who with his help was writing a novel that she dedicated to him.[2] Despite his assertions of indifference, this gossip must have hurt Crawford personally and perhaps even professionally. Just how serious it could become, Crawford made clear in *Pietro Ghisleri* in which the sufferings of the hero and heroine are caused for the most part by the spread of malicious rumors. Written about the time he decided to leave Sorrento for the United States, Crawford said it was the novel which "possessed most reality for him."[3]

Whatever the cause—whether from a sense of spiritual isolation at "Villa Crawford," from marital difficulties with Bessie, or from the gossip about his domestic troubles—Crawford saw his wife at very infrequent intervals during the next few years; and his outlook on life was that of a man for whom life held very few satisfactions and even fewer pleasures. Mrs. Elliott, commenting upon *The Three Fates*, written late in 1889 and published in 1891, remarked that Crawford was "a sadder man than the author of *Isaacs and Claudius*."[4] Significantly, she added: "The zest of life is diminished. Sadness, even bitterness, is creeping upon him." The tenor of Crawford's letters and novels during the 1890's confirms her observation. Not long after his return to the United States he wrote:

> There is no more room for phrases, and the deeds that speak are always few in life, and far between, and often hard to understand. The deeds that have no story to tell wear out the strength there is, and there is little between me and nothing, but the impossible bridge of little nothings, which must nevertheless be passed to reach the end of all and be at peace. When I was younger I used to think it might not be so far for me, but I have given up even that hope, and am resigned to the idea of another thirty years of this existence. I am deplorably strong, still. It is only illusions that shorten life.[5]

At thirty-eight Crawford believed that he had already enjoyed his allotted share of happiness and that his energies must henceforth be directed toward attaining a permanent literary reputation and providing financial security for his children. Ultimately, these were the reasons for his return to America.

Early in November, 1892, before Crawford sailed from Genoa, he wrote Maud Elliott and Mrs. Gardner to tell them of his expected date of arrival. When he left the ship in New York, he found a note from Maud awaiting him but nothing from Mrs. Gardner. He hastened to write Maud: "There is one question, dear Maud, which I can ask only of you and which you must *please* answer me by return. Before leaving Sorrento, I wrote to a certain person of very dear memory—for the first time in ten years, and asked an answer, giving my address at 33 Wall Street. None has come. Is she in Boston? Or possibly abroad? I am convinced that if any letter had been received it would have been answered."[6]

A few days later he declared: "I shall certainly not write again [to Mrs. Gardner] ... as a meeting is so near. If I did so in the first instance and could have done so again, it was out of a feeling that in common courtesy I could not appear and meet, without myself announcing my coming. For of course meeting is inevitable. Whatever there is to tell—as you write—you can safely write me here, and I should be forewarned, if it is a warning."[7]

Finally, Crawford in still another letter to Maud Elliott remarked: "For the rest—about what you wrote me—I understand it better than anyone. . . . Nevertheless, I did well to write, that once—and once at least we must meet."[8] They did meet, and whatever coolness or resentment Mrs. Gardner may have felt during the ten years since they parted completely vanished. Their friendship, founded upon tender memories surrounding the composition of Crawford's first novels and nurtured by Mrs. Gardner's sympathetic understanding of Crawford and his work, matured into a lasting bond of mutual affection which endured so long as Crawford lived. From her, he had no secrets. She discussed his future with him, read his novels from the proof sheets, and comforted him in his moments of depression and unhappiness. With her he was happy, and away from her he refused to admit they had parted. Once, when leaving her, he wrote: "Goodbye, dearest, till we meet again—and soon I hope. This is not a goodbye at all, you know. There is only to be one more goodbye between us, and I do not think it will be spoken aloud, nor written, for it will come when one of us two reaches the end, and it will be very long before that. Goodnight then, and sweet dreams. You have been long asleep for the day is almost breaking—while I say goodnight, dear."[9] Of the vast number of letters which they exchanged, none of hers has been preserved because Crawford burned them; and of Crawford's letters to Mrs. Gardner, only a few remain, the majority of which she cut into fragments, destroying the portions which she apparently did not wish anyone else to read.

Upon reaching New York, Crawford talked with reporters in Everett House before discussing the details of his readings with Major James Burton Pond, his manager. According to the New York *Times* (November 8, 1892), the reporters saw a hard-working, successful man of letters who towered over "ordinary men like an oak among underbrush." The reporter added: "He has a strong, bronzed face, lit up by a pair of clear blue eyes, and his accent and manners are such that, barring the little fact that his clothes fit him perfectly—an item hardly to be found in connection with most selfrespecting Britons—he might well be taken for an Englishman." Crawford's brown hair, closely cut and already thin about the temples, was beginning to turn gray. His beard, familiar to Americans from his pictures, had recently been shaved, but he retained the straight mustache common to many men in his circle during the 1890's. All in all, he appeared to be, what he was: an intellectual, cultured, and serious personage.

When reporters asked about his plans, novels, and experiences, Crawford replied at length, for he was fully aware of the importance of publicity to his career. With regard to his work, he was quoted as saying:

> I have completed two more novels, which will soon be published. One of them is what would be known in Europe as a "one-volume" work and the other "three volumes," although each of them will be published as a single book. The single-volume novel has about 60,000 words, and its title is "The Children of the King." It deals with the sailors on the coast of Southern Italy and the scene is laid in Calabria and Sorrento. The three volume work contains about 150,000 words, and is entitled "Pietro Ghisleri." It is a tale of modern Roman society, and the scene of it is laid entirely in Rome. . . . These works will probably be published as serials in a periodical magazine.[10]

Crawford's admirers soon found in *The Children of the King* a slight novel about a young Italian sailor who sacrifices his own life to free a beautiful Italian noblewoman from an unscrupulous count who has almost trapped her into marriage. The theme of unselfish love and devotion on the part of a lower-class character for a member of the aristocracy suggests a comparison with *A Cigarette-Maker's Romance;* and, had Crawford been able to sustain the high degree of unity of plot and character that he had displayed in the earlier work, *The Children of the King* might have been one of his most artistic productions.

Crawford's readers and contemporary critics were pleased to see the re-appearance in *Pietro Ghisleri* of such characters as the melancholy Count Spicca, the artistic Anatase Gouache, and the Marchese di San Giacinto who had been previously introduced in the *Saracinesca* trilogy. The new novel featured the exciting story of the machinations of a selfish, ruthless, society woman who circulates slanderous rumors about her step-sister, murders her step-sister's husband by innoculating him with scarlet fever, and falls herself a victim to the morphine habit. Contemporary reviewers asserted that, because of excellent motivation, there was really nothing sensational in the plot and found in the work an exposition of the "thinness of the veneer with which modern civilization has glossed over the primitive instincts of the Italian race."[11] Those who had followed the progress of Crawford's work over the past few years must have recognized that addiction to morphine was a far more credible device than the insanity of *Paul Patoff* and that the "evil eye" represented an improvement over the hypnotism of *The Witch of Prague.* Few objected strongly to the noticeable increase in Crawford's obtrusions upon the story to present his own opinions as omniscient author. Although Crawford had indulged himself in this practice from the very beginning, in *Pietro Ghisleri* he allowed it to become a marked defect. What gave the novel its appeal was its, for the most part, easy, rapid flow of narrative and Crawford's obvious mastery of the Italian setting.

After his interview with the reporters, Crawford reached an agreement with Major Pond about public readings from his novels. Pond had engaged him to alternate with Sir Edwin Arnold in a series of Lenten matinee performances at Daly's Theatre. At Pond's suggestion, however, Crawford first practiced reading selections from his works before an elocutionist and made professional appearances in Brooklyn, Boston, Concord (New Hampshire), Philadelphia, Washington, Providence, and Newark before appearing in New York. During these engagements, Crawford generally read scenes from the initial chapters of *Zoroaster* (probably Belshazzar's feast in Chapter I), Keyork Arabian's mock-courtship of Unora from *The Witch of Prague* (Chapter IV), and the song of the sirens from *With the Immortals* (Chapter XIV).[12] His program was not rigid; and, in response to particular requests, he willingly read passages from his other novels.

The critics uniformly complained of his lack of dramatic sense and his disregard of the rhythm of his prose. The reviewer for the Boston Evening *Transcript* (December 13, 1892) found that Crawford had "precisely the abilities and claims, and no other, of any wellbred and intelligent gentleman who may pick up a book from a drawingroom table and read a chapter or two to his friends." He concluded that "it is amusing to note that he has not . . . outgrown the exceedingly primitive idea that intense feeling is invariably to be indicated by raising the voice."

Audiences and critics alike, however, were pleased when Crawford began to depart from his set programs and either related anecdotes he had heard in his travels or commented upon his literary practices and theories. These extemporaneous remarks were responsible for the success of his second and third performances in Boston. The series there was adequately characterized by the reviewer for the *Daily Advertiser* (December 19, 1892):

> It is not amiss to say that Mr. Crawford's initial appearance was his least satisfactory. Unaccustomed to public reading, he probably felt a constraint that affected his manner and deprived it in a measure of the frankness and spontaneity that were the charms of his later readings. From all tricks and manners of the elocutionist, he is delightfully free, reading with the trained intelligence of the thinker, the intuition of the artist, the keen sympathies of the poet.

There is absolutely no affectation in his easy, graceful, sympathetic rendering of the dramatic scenes conceived by his mind and perpetuated by his pen. His voice is low, sustained, resonant, vibrating and unusual in a rare degree and expresses every tone in the gamut of human emotion without effort.

But perhaps the most enjoyable portion of the entertainment was that in which he laid his books aside and chatted as if to a party of friends about the strange unwritten legends of Italian villages unknown to travellers, in which he has passed many months in the years of his life in Italy. Mr. Crawford has a great deal of quiet humor and evidently felt the friendly and appreciative atmosphere to a degree that rendered his chat unconventional and free as if in a drawing-room, so that when he made his final bow there was a murmur of regret in the audience that spoke sincerest flattery.

During his engagements in other cities, Crawford continued to supplement his programs with the brief extemporary talks. The public found them charming, instructive, and at times compelling; and they demonstrated that, even though Crawford was not a very successful reader, he could be a well-paying boxoffice attraction as a writer and a personality.

During the Lenten season of 1893, Major Pond presented four series of morning "courses" at Daly's Theatre. Because each course consisted of four presentations offered in successive weeks, by performing four times in one week an artist could appear in each course. Thus Crawford, who began the series, read to the four different audiences during the week of February 19-26. In successive weeks, he was followed by Henri Marteau (a violinist), Francis Hopkinson Smith and Thomas Nelson Page, and Maud Howe Elliott. Sir Edwin Arnold, who had been originally scheduled to alternate with Crawford, did not participate in the performances.

Crawford used the selections he had practiced before other audiences and varied his readings with the informal talks which earlier had proved successful. He told an anecdote about Judas Iscariot, described the Italian seacoast, and discoursed "on the art of making love."[13] The critics likewise repeated substantially what had been said earlier during the tour. The reviewer for the New York *Tribune* (February 21, 1893) spoke for the general reaction when he declared: "The most interesting portion of Mr. Crawford's programme, however, was not a reading at all, but a little description of Calabria, where he has spent much time."

Despite the remarks of the critics, Crawford characteristically persisted in the task. He had come to America to read and he would continue to read until the tour was either completed or pronounced a losing venture. As a matter of fact, both Crawford and Pond made money. By keeping his name before the public and by giving thousands of his readers the opportunity to see and hear him in person, Crawford also stimulated the sale of his books and aroused interest in those yet to appear. His successful extemporaneous talks, moreover, seemed to imply that, if he wished, he might become a skillful lecturer for the lyceum circuit. Finally, by means of these informal comments Crawford began to take the case for his own critical theory of the novel to his readers; and, by so doing, he actively entered the most important literary controversy of the 1890's.

II

In May, 1891, at the urging of his agent and advisor who thought it would be a good business venture, William Dean Howells had selected from his essays in the "Editor's Study" a number of his comments about the theory of realism and had arranged them to form a book published as *Criticism and Fiction*. Although it was hastily compiled and in places badly pieced together, the volume represented the culmination of the critical ideas which Howells had already expressed in many of his book reviews and had illustrated by his own practice in writing fiction. By collecting and publishing his ideas, Howells had in effect issued a critical manifesto that invited opposition.

Before his return to the United States in November, 1892, Francis Marion Crawford had not publicly advanced any critical theory about the novel; yet, even to the most unobservant contemporary reader, a work by Crawford must have seemed vastly different from the majority of Howells' novels. An observant reader could probably have guessed accurately the nature of Crawford's ideas from comments about literary theory that appeared in such novels as *A Tale of a Lonely Parish* (1886), *Paul Patoff* (1887), *With the Immortals* (1888), and *The Three Fates* (1892). Like Howells, Crawford developed his theory of fiction at the time that he was writing his novels; and it may be that each man derived his theory from his own practice. But in both cases practice and theory were the products of widely divergent views about human life. Probably it is more accurate to say that the practice and theory of both men were facets of their views of human life before they were expressed as artistic theories.

Crawford's actions imply that he considered that the appearance of *Criticism and Fiction* forced him either to accept tacitly Howells' rebuke of Romantic fiction or to enter the critical debate with a statement of his own position. Crawford's reputation was to a large extent at stake in the matter. Accordingly, when he arrived to begin his readings under Pond's managership, Crawford was prepared to assert his own theory and to attack the concepts of realism through every medium open to him. By departing from his announced program of readings to lecture informally on his concept of the novel, he obtained a hearing from his immediate audience and from the readers of the daily newspapers which printed his remarks in full. He reached an even wider audience through two lengthy articles entitled "What Is a Novel?" and "Emotional Tension and the Modern Novel," published by the *Forum* in successive issues (January and February, 1893); and in April, 1893, he published his own volume of criticism, *The Novel: What It Is*. These sources, when combined with the pronouncements which he made in his novels, furnish a complete exposition of his critical position.

Crawford began his volume of criticism with a frank recognition of the financial rewards of literature. He remarked that the "army of fiction-makers" would continue to write novels because "most of us do not know how to do anything else, and . . . are dependent upon it for bread as well as butter; and lastly and chiefly, because we are heavily backed, as a body, by the capital of the publisher, of which we desire to obtain for ourselves as much as possible."[14] Since there is a demand for novels and a profit in producing them, "who shall prevent us, authors and publishers," he asked, "from continuing the production and supplying the demand?"

The economics of literature thus provided Crawford with his first answer to the question, "What is a novel?" A novel, he replied, "is a marketable commodity, of the class collectively termed 'luxuries,' as not contributing directly to the support of life or the maintenance of health. It is of the class 'artistic luxuries' because it does not appeal to any of the three material senses—touch, taste, smell; and it is of the class 'intellectual artistic luxuries,' because it is not judged by the superior senses— sight and hearing. The novel, therefore, is an intellectual artistic luxury."[15] Although neither Crawford nor Howells would have been content to rest the matter here, both men fully recognized the importance of the market place in modern literature.

One of the major points of disagreement between them, however, was Crawford's next assumption that "the first object of the novel is to amuse and interest the reader."[16] This position he had taken implicitly ever since he wrote *Mr. Isaacs*, and he had explicitly stated it as early as 1886 when in *Paul Patoff*, speaking through his fictional representative, Paul Griggs, he had declared that he wrote "for the sole purpose of amusing you [the reader]."[17] In *The Three Fates* (1892), a novel pervaded by autobiographical references, he had reaffirmed his stand:

> It is certain that since those who live by the pen have made it their business to amuse rather than to admonish and instruct their substance has been singularly increased and their path has been made enviably smooth. Their shadows not only wax and follow the outlines of a pleasant rotundity, but they are cast upon marble pavements, inlaid floors and Eastern carpets, instead of upon the dingy walls and greasy mud of Grub Street. The star of the public amuser is in the ascendant, and his "Part of Fortune" is high in the mid-heaven.[18]

To say, however, that Crawford's theory of the novel dealt merely with the means of entertaining the public greatly over-simplifies his critical position. "The novel must amuse, indeed," wrote Crawford, "but should amuse reasonably, from an intellectual point of view, rather than as a piece of good fun."[19]

While asserting that the principal objective of the novel is to amuse, Crawford declared as a corollary that the novel should not instruct the reader. When the novel was written to instruct, it became the "purpose-novel" and thus an " 'intellectual moral lesson' instead of an 'intellectual artistic luxury.' "[20] In other words, the purpose novel, in Crawford's opinion, is "a simple fraud"; for the reader "has simply paid money, on the ordinary tacit contract between furnisher and purchaser, and he has been swindled."[21] Classification, however, could not always be absolute; for Crawford recognized that a novel written to amuse might also improve the reader. As he wrote,

> What we call a novel may educate the taste and cultivate the intelligence; under the hand of genius it may purify the heart and fortify the mind; it should never under any circumstances be suffered to deprave the one nor to weaken the other; it may stand for scores of years—and a score of years is a long time in our day—as the exposition of all that is noble, heroic, honest, and true in the life of woman or man; but it has no right to tell us what its writer thinks about the relations of labour and capital nor to set up what the author conceives to be a nice, original, easy scheme of salvation, any more than it has a right to take for its theme the relative merits of the "broomstick-car" and the "storage system," temperance, vivisection, or the "Ideal Man" of Confucius. Lessons, lectures, discussions, sermons, and didactics generally belong to institutions set apart for especial purposes and carefully avoided, after a certain age, by the majority of those who wish to be amused.

The purpose-novel is an odious attempt to lecture people who hate lectures, to preach at people who prefer their own church, and to teach people who think they know enough already. It is an ambush, a lying-in-wait for the unsuspecting public, a violation of the social contract—and as such it ought to be either mercilessly crushed or forced by law to bind itself in black and label itself "Purpose" in very big letters.[22]

Crawford would have had no difficulty in assigning to the category of purpose novels such emphatically economic works as Edward Bellamy's *Looking Backward, 2000-1887* (1888) and Howells' *A Hazard of New Fortunes* (1890), *The World of Chance* (1893), and *A Traveler from Altruria* (1894). The confusion arose over the moral content of fiction. Crawford tried to clarify his position by saying:

In art of all kinds the moral lesson is a mistake. It is one thing to exhibit an ideal worthy to be imitated, though inimitable in all its perfection, but so clearly noble as to appeal directly to the sympathetic string that hangs untuned in the dullest human heart; to make man brave without arrogance, woman pure without prudishness, love enduring yet earthly, not angelic, friendship sincere but not ridiculous. It is quite another matter to write a "guide to morality" or a "hand-book for practical sinners" and call either one a novel, no matter how much fiction it may contain.[23]

On this basis Crawford might have considered Howells' *A Modern Instance* (1882) and even *Dr. Breen's Practice* (1881) as works written primarily to instruct; and, had he lived to read Lloyd C. Douglas' *Magnificent Obsession* (1932), *Green Light* (1935), and *The Robe* (1943), he would have undoubtedly rejected them also as purpose novels. But he would have found it very difficult to classify rigidly Howells' *The Landlord at Lion's Head* (1897) and *The Son of Royal Langbrith* (1904) as either amusement or instruction.

As he was writing *The Novel: What It Is*, Crawford could have illustrated his critical theories from his own novels. *Mr. Isaacs, Doctor Claudius,* and *To Leeward* had each been written to explicate a given thesis and to persuade the reader to adopt that idea as his own. These novels could be classified as purpose novels. On the other hand, Crawford had steadily moved away from the use of a single governing idea in the novel toward the depiction of an ideal character; and the recently published *Saracinesca* volumes had been products of this new direction in his work. Corona and Giovanni Saracinesca, for example, had been presented as characters whom readers "might like to resemble, acting in

scenes in which they themselves would like to take a part"[24] and
offering the reader an ideal of human conduct. Crawford, nevertheless, could rightly claim that these were not really purpose
novels, for the intention had been to show the ideal and not to
preach a moral lesson. This distinction between fiction which
presented the reader with an ideal to be emulated and that which
aimed to inculcate a moral lesson was basic to Crawford's theory
of the novel.

If Crawford possessed little admiration for Howells' purpose
novels, he showed even less respect for Howells' theory of Realism.
Up to a certain point the two men could agree. They could agree,
for instance, on the fact that Zola was a great writer and that in
his hands the novel had reached new heights of achievement.
Crawford qualified his approval by adding that Zola was "mistaken
perhaps, possibly bad, mightily coarse to no purpose, but great
nevertheless—a Nero of fiction."[25] Both men agreed also that, if
the novel in America were addressed only to adults, it could deal
with the subjects which Zola discussed. Howells, however, argued
that in America those subjects were not essential to the practice of
Realism—that the realistic novel could be written so that it would
not shock "the tenderest society bud at dinner"[26]—but Crawford
believed that they were the inevitable concern of Realism. "The
result," wrote Crawford, "of the desire for realism in men who
try to write realistic novels for the clean-minded American and
English girl is unsatisfactory."[27] And he added in words that
applied directly to Howells' novels, "It is generally a photograph,
not a picture—a catalogue, not a description." Crawford was convinced that "the realistic method is better suited to the exposition
of what is bad than of what is good."[28] As Realism broadened into
Naturalism in American fiction, the validity of Crawford's observation became evident.

From the first Crawford had associated Realism with coarseness
and coarseness with sexual frankness. He never abandoned the
reticent attitude—inculcated in him during boyhood by Louisa
Terry and almost universal at that time in genteel circles—toward
the frank expression of sexual matters or the use of impolite words
in literature, art, or conversation. Crawford had discussed the
matter in several of his novels. In *With the Immortals,* for example,
Crawford, speaking through Heine, declared:

> I think music has advanced [in the nineteenth century] better than
> literature. They were both little boys once, but the one has grown
> into a great, dominating, royal giant—the other into a greedy,
> snivelling, dirty-nosed, foul-mouthed, cowardly ruffian. There are

bad musicians and good writers, of course. The bad musicians do little harm, but the good writers occupy the position of Lot in the condemned cities—they are the mourners at the funeral of romance. The mass of fiction makers to-day are but rioters at the baptismal feast of Realism, the Impure.[29]

In *Saracinesca,* he had indicated his disgust at the "Dirty Boy" in painting.[30] In *Paul Patoff* he had reminded his readers that "the world is not yet turned into a farmyard" and that "it is not every one who cares for the beauty of nature in a horsepond."[31]

Realism, Crawford believed, led not only to coarseness but also to the narration of commonplace events which were boring to the reader and conducive to the production of formless fiction. In *The Three Fates,* he argued:

> There are people who, when they hear any unsual story of real life, exclaim, "What a novel that would make!" They are not the people who write good fiction. Most of them have never tried it, for, if they had, they would know that novels are not made by expanding into a volume or volumes the account of circumstances which have actually occurred. True stories very rarely have a conclusion at all, and the necessity for a conclusion is the first thing felt by the born novelist.[32]

A mere transcript of life or a photograph in words, however truthful to fact and faithful to nature, reasoned Crawford, would result in formless, colorless productions unworthy to be called artistic creations. In *The Novel: What It Is,* he expressed this idea in terms of the stage: "The most dramatic scene of real life, if it actually took place on the stage of a theatre, would seem a very dull and tame affair to any one who chanced to find himself in the body of the house."[33]

Crawford's distrust of Realism did not rest upon a disbelief in the relationship of "real life" to fiction. On the contrary, Crawford insisted that a good novel possesses elements of both Realism and Romance. "Why must a novel-writer be either a 'realist' or a 'romantist'?" asked Crawford in his volume of criticism. "And, if the latter, why 'romanticist' any more than 'realisticist'? Why should a good novel not combine romance and reality in just proportions? Is there any reason to suppose that the one element must necessarily shut out the other?"[34] Crawford demanded a basis of reality, but he insisted that that reality be shaped, heightened, and even transformed by the artist. And in words that recall Henry James's phrasing, Crawford declared that "art, if it is 'to create and foster agreeable illusions,' ... should represent the real, but in such a way as to make it seem more agreeable and interesting than it actually is."[35]

To achieve this quality, Crawford felt the novelist must write out of his own experience. In Crawford's words, "the writer must have seen and known many phases of existence."[36] He must "know and understand... men and women who have been placed in unusual circumstances."[37] He must "have loved, fought, suffered, and struggled in the human battle. I would almost say that to describe another's death he must himself have died."[38] The foundation for the novel, concluded Crawford, was reality; but it was not the kind of reality that Howells was contending for in fiction. Howells' notion of Realism led to authentic and accurate descriptions, to the natural grasshopper of the field and not to the ideal grasshopper of wire and cardboard.[39] Of this kind of Realism, Crawford could only remark: "Generally speaking, I venture to say that anything which fixes the date of the novel not intended to be historical is a mistake, from a literary point of view. It is not wise to describe the cut of the hero's coat, nor the draping of the heroine's gown, the shape of her hat, nor the colour of his tie. Ten years hence somebody may buy the book and turn up his nose at 'those times.'"[40] Crawford could have turned the same argument against Howells' "purpose-novels," for a social or political issue could be as dated as the shape of the heroine's hat.

The dialect writers of the local-color movement seemed to Crawford to be restricted almost to the same degree as the Realist who used excessive details or contemporary issues. Some novels consisting almost wholly of dialect were bad because they lacked dramatic interest and form, but there were, Crawford believed, some good novels "in which more than half the pages are filled with dialogues in a language not familiar to the English-speaking public as a whole." With reference to these works, Crawford asked:

Is not the writer wilfully limiting his audience, if not himself? Is he not sacrificing his privilege of addressing all men, for the sake of addressing a few in terms which they especially prefer? Is he not preferring local popularity to broader and more enduring reputation? Could he not, by the skilful use of description, by a clever handling of grammar and a careful selection of words, produce an impression which should be more widely felt, though less warmly received, perhaps, in that one small public to which he appeals? Is he not, although he be a first-rate man, often tempted to lapses of literary conscience by the peculiar facilities he finds in the literary by-way he has chosen? How much of what is screaming farce in the dialect of the few, would be funny if translated into plain English for the many? Wit and humour are intellectual, and when genuine are susceptible of being translated into almost all languages; but dialect seems to me to rank with puns, and with puns of a particular local character. A practical demonstration of this is found in the fact that stories in dialect, when told and not read, are duller than any other stories, unless the teller has the power of imitating accents. Almost all limitations which a man willingly assumes afford facilities for the sake of which he assumes them.[41]

Crawford knew that he was criticizing local color at the "risk [of] wounding the sensibilities of many writers and attacking the individual tastes of many readers of fiction."[42] In fact, as Crawford wrote, the local-color movement had just reached the peak of its popularity in both the literary periodicals and the book trade. One can imagine Crawford's reactions as he tried to read Joel Chandler Harris' *Uncle Remus and His Friends* (1892) which was popular throughout the country when Crawford was writing *The Novel: What It Is.* Crawford's judgment, nevertheless, was consistent with his theory of the novel. He saw very clearly that the local-color movement was intrinsically hostile to his position; and a later generation of writers, for somewhat different reasons, has confirmed the essential rightness of his attitude.

While making clear his objections to the purpose novel, to the literary technique of Realism, and to the methods of the local-color writers, Crawford was also trying to define his own position. In distinguishing between Realism and Romanticism, for example, he had observed that "the realist proposes to show men what they are; the romantist tries to show men what they should be." He then admitted that there was merit in both positions, but declared, "For my part, I believe that more good can be done by showing men what they may be, ought to be, or can be, than by describing their greatest weaknesses with the highest art. We all know how bad we are; but it needs much encouragement to persuade some of us to believe that we can really be any better. To create genuine interest, and afford rest and legitimate amusement, without losing sight of that fact, and to do so in a more or less traditional way, seems to be the profession of the novelist who belongs to the romantic persuasion."[43] The general aim of the novelist, Crawford argued, ought to be to present the ideal; but, in delineating that ideal, the novelist must build character and incident upon reality. One did not *transcribe* reality; instead, the novelist created the *illusion* of reality very much as the dramatist sought to represent life on the stage. The connection between the theatre and the novel was indeed so close in Crawford's mind that he referred to the novel as a "pocket theatre."[44]

By insisting upon the foundation of reality and the creation of
the illusion of reality, Crawford was also incidentally answering
the objections of Howells to the sentimentalities and absurdities
of romantic fiction.

Unquestionably the most important point in Crawford's theory
of the novel was his insistence that the novelist write of the
human heart. Stated more accurately, Crawford was saying that
the novelist should embody in his work the verities of human
experience. In *The Novel: What It Is,* Crawford wrote:

> The foundation of good fiction and good poetry seems to be ethic
> rather than aesthetic. Everything in either which appeals to the
> taste, that is, to the aesthetic side, may ultimately perish as a mere
> matter of fashion; but that which speaks to man as man, in-
> dependently of his fashions, his habits, and his tastes, must live
> and find a hearing with humanity so long as humanity is human.
> The right understanding of men and women leads to the right
> relations of men and women, and in this way, if in any, a novel may
> do good; when written to attain this end, it may live; when
> addressed to the constant element in human nature, it has as good
> a right and as good a chance of pleasing the men and women of the
> world in our day, as it had to appeal to the intellect of Pericles or
> to thrill the delicate sensibilities of Aspasia.[45]

The ethical bias of Crawford's theory is immediately evident. He
believed that, although each age saw the problems of human
conduct in a different light, the essential elements of humanism
remained the same and that works of fiction which sought to
dramatize them partook of their permanence in proportion as they
were artistically excellent. In advocating fiction that dealt with
the principles of ethical conduct over fiction that concerned
itself with political and economic problems, Crawford was much
closer to Henry James than to Howells.

By the publication of *The Novel: What It Is,* Francis Marion
Crawford became the recognized leader of the Romantic school of
fiction both in America and in England. In opposition to him
was the powerful and influential William Dean Howells, whose
Criticism and Fiction almost certainly occasioned Crawford's volume. Although Howells' cause would apparently prevail among
the most important American novelists of the succeeding decades,
many of Crawford's comments proved to be sound literary criticism.
His warning that the realistic method could result both in dated
and in uninteresting fiction had a bearing upon the novels created
by the followers of Realism. There was likewise merit in his
reminder to the Realists that, if they failed to create men and
women in their eagerness to discuss political and economic issues,

their novels would not possess lasting interest. The disappearance of the dialect novel and the demise of the local-color school have likewise demonstrated the soundness of Crawford's estimate of the literary fashions of his time.

On the other hand, Crawford endeavored to construct a theory of the novel that would contribute to the production of lasting literature. To this end he argued forcefully that the novel must deal with the permanent and perpetually challenging aspects of human life. It must demonstrate right relations among men and women in society, and it must have an ethical bias. The human personality or conduct exhibited by the novelist must be ideal; for, by setting forth the ideal standard, the novelist may best create in the reader a desire to emulate it. To achieve this goal, the novelist should use the material of real life to create an agreeable illusion of reality. The most important deficiency in Crawford's theory, of course, was his failure to see that "non-agreeable" illusions of reality could also be of lasting literary value; nevertheless, what he said had a measure of permanent value and made good sense to a vast segment of novel readers in America and Europe. Better than anyone else, he had provided the rationale of the novels which were popular during the 1880's and 1890's.

III

Crawford's activities at the beginning of the 1890's seem to have been prompted by a conviction that a successful literary man should engage in as many as possible of the profitable ventures open to his profession. He knew that each such project would gain support from his other activities and, in turn, further his overall career. Crawford, moreover, probably estimated that the new copyright law of 1891 would greatly strengthen the position of American authors with publishers and producers. The market for all forms of American literature, particularly novels and plays, should improve rapidly. Although he had never written a play, Crawford believed, as he said, that "a successful play is incomparably more lucrative than a successful novel."[46] He knew also that even more lucrative than a successful play was a successful novel that became a successful play, or vice versa. These were facts, of course, known to almost anyone who was aware of the facts of literary production. Henry James and William Dean Howells, for instance, were as well acquainted with them as Crawford.

When Crawford returned to his country to prepare for his readings at Augustin Daly's theatre during the Lenten season of

1893, he offered Daly a play entitled *Marion Darche*. The plot dealt with the fortunes of a woman whose life was ruined by her marriage to a swindler and thief. Although Daly accepted it, his request for changes in the script prompted Crawford to make extensive changes in the original draft. The manuscript was still unfinished when Crawford left for Europe in March, 1893. During the following summer, Crawford rewrote the play as a novel, and Macmillan published it in the fall of that year. Although the play was announced for the London season of 1893, it was never staged. Crawford's first effort as a dramatist could not exactly be termed successful.[47]

During 1893 Crawford had little reason for satisfaction over either his professional or his personal affairs. On the whole, he probably felt somewhat dissatisfied with his first ventures in the role of the professional man of letters. "These have been tiresóme, not to say harassing times," he wrote Mrs. Gardner, "and many things are crooked still which it seems hopeless to straighten. I have worked hard, too, and have not accomplished much, which is always disappointing, though I am used to it."[48] His readings had been only moderately successful and his play writing ambitions had produced nothing definite. The one bright spot in the otherwise dim picture was the re-establishment of his friendship with Mrs. Gardner, and, when in Europe, he greatly missed the encouragement and comfort she gave him. Early in June, he took his sister, Annie von Rabé, to Vienna; and from there he traveled southeastward on the Danube to Orsova. From a Danube steamer, near Belgrade, he wrote Mrs. Gardner:

> The rain is pouring down in thick sheets, which one might cut with a knife, and it looks as though it meant to go on pouring for a week. So I am sitting in my cabin and thinking of you. Not that the rain is associated with you—far from it. You make me think of summer days, and flowers, and wind blown water and the happy rustling of spring leaves—of much that was and of all that is not any more. But I often think of you when I am all alone, and know how much alone I am. . . . But I am not going to bore you with my sentiments—if I have any. This is principally to say that I am alive and distressingly strong and well as usual. . . .
>
> This thing—letter or not—shall be posted in Belgrad[e] this evening. I believe I am going to Constantinople. At least I was the other day when I spun off to Orsova. What difference does it make? I send you such thoughts as are still whole—gentle and very tender thoughts of you, dear.[49]

There was evidently not much happiness for him at Sorrento where his main interest seemed to be his children. He commented to Mrs. Gardner: "I think when I last wrote to you I was in one of my uncomfortable moods, and was thinking of doing something of the same kind. But I did not, you see. I never shall, because I have a sort of conscience which makes me hang on for the children's sake—and that will probably last me until nature is tired of me, or I break my neck."[50] This mood persisted, and his letters to Mrs. Gardner continued to reflect the gloomy tenor of his thoughts. Shortly after his return to the United States in the fall of 1893, he wrote: "I have much to tell, for much has happened to my unquiet existence—though little which really and truly touches my real me. It might be better if there was something left to touch. Perhaps you will find it for me again some day, as you did long ago."[51]

Sometime during this depressing summer Crawford had agreed to assume the general direction of the legal proceedings which had been initiated by the Berdan Firearms Company (now owned by Crawford's mother-in-law) against the United States government for use of the Berdan patents. The judgment of the United States Court of Claims had been appealed to the Supreme Court. Crawford's task was to obtain passage of a private bill in Congress waiving the statute of limitations until the appeal was decided.[52]

Crawford expected that the Berdan matter would require his presence in Washington throughout most of the winter of 1893-94; and, while he was living there, he planned to write two long novels which he had promised to deliver to Brett of Macmillan Company by the end of December, 1894. Despite the continual interruptions of the Berdan affair, he managed to complete *Katharine Lauderdale* and *The Ralstons* before Christmas[53] and to make short visits to Bar Harbor, Boston, and New York. During this period, his letters to Mrs. Gardner furnish a weekly account of his literary progress. As he worked, he divided his time between the Capitol and his writing table in Mrs. Hobson's home. He described his life for Mrs. Gardner: "I am living quite alone in a big house.... I never go out except to go to the Capitol, or to dinner when some one asks me, which is not often as I have made no effort to see people.... I am often at my writing table almost continuously from half past seven in the morning until ten o'clock at night. You will understand that I have not much to tell about myself under the circumstances."[54]

Before he finished *Katharine Lauderdale,* he wrote again about a visit he expected to make to her early in November:

If you could let me come for a day about the first of November, and if there is to be nobody else staying with you, I think I would manage it. . . . Will you forgive me the *proviso* about there being nobody else? It sounds arrogant—which I am, perhaps—and rude, which I am not, except under provocation. The fact is that by working very hard I may just have finished my third and last volume by that time, and shall not be fit for human food, so to say, though I shall certainly be an object of charity, and for your kindness if you can spare me a little. These big three volume novels are exhausting, and there is little left, intellectually, to exhaust in my composition. The small amount of flesh I have is as indestructible as sole leather, but the same cannot be said of my imagination, which alas, is all my fortune. As soon as I have done this thing, I have to begin another, which must also be finished forthwith, at a stretch, and if I could have twenty four hours of your gentle company between the two I should be a better man —on paper—as indeed I am in some other ways when I have been with you.[55]

Since he was receiving the proof sheets almost as rapidly as he composed the work, he promised to bring a complete set for her to read.

By November 25 he had completed half of *The Ralstons*, and, although he longed to see Mrs. Gardner again, the pressure exerted upon him by his publishers forced Crawford to continue working. As he said:

I am fiercely chased. . . . They want to "liberate the type" of "The Ralstons" by the 15th of December and I cannot, by working every day, finish the last volume till Saturday the 9th. . . . I have written a whole chapter every day since I saw you, except on Sunday and have got eighteen done out of thirty. I suppose I shall get to the end without stopping, for land is in sight, and things are terribly urgent. If, however, I should be obliged to stop—which would leave me a free conscience I will telegraph, take a night train and arrive early the next morning.[56]

Writing ten hours daily, Crawford finished the fifth "volume" of *The Ralstons* shortly before Thanksgiving (November 30); thereafter, the concluding section was dispatched to the printer, chapter by chapter, as fast as he wrote it. The necessity for haste, he explained, "is that just now I am bound by contract to deliver the MS at a certain time."[57] Finally, as Crawford had predicted, *The Ralstons* was finished on December 9, 1893. In less than four months he had produced two major novels, the second (and longest) of which he wrote in less than six weeks. In view of the superior quality of the work, his was a significant achievement.

As Crawford himself intimated, *Katharine Lauderdale* (1894) and *The Ralstons* (1895) were originally designed as the first two parts of a *Ralston* trilogy, corresponding to the *Saracinesca* trilogy.

The similarities between these groups of family-novels are striking. Crawford tended to view each novel as a single act in a dramatic sequence. In both sets, moreover, the characters belong to aristocratic families whose members are divided by conflicting interests and confused by a changing social order. Romantic love, jealousy, and misunderstanding constitute the principal theme; and—had the American novels been continued—Crawford would undoubtedly have presented a study of mature love comparable to that in *Sant' Ilario*. He would probably also have emphasized much more than he did the contrast between American and Italian marriage customs. Finally, the close resemblance between Orsino Saracinesca and Jack Ralston, both young men "of the Transition Period" in pursuit of a vocation, is immediately apparent to readers of both series.

On the other hand, there are important differences. Crawford may have intended to emphasize the difference between American and Italian customs by his discussion of the marriages of Katharine Ralston and Corona Saracinesca. There is also the fact that in the *Saracinesca* trilogy, Crawford began with the generation which matured during the 1860's, thus unfolding his chronicle historically; in the *Ralston* novels, he precluded such a development by beginning with the younger generation of the 1880's. Hence he could only treat incidentally the effect of the post Civil War decades upon the Lauderdales and the Ralstons. Nevertheless, if the *Saracinesca* volumes have a broader scope, the *Ralston* novels possess a greater unity. Although the time factor contributes to it, the superior unity of the American novels results mainly from a greater concentration upon the principal characters, fewer digressions, and less emphasis upon the actions of the minor characters.

Although each volume or act of the *Ralston* novels is more or less complete in itself, the two American novels form essentially one continuous story. In the first volume, Katharine, the youngest daughter of Alexander Lauderdale, secretly marries John Ralston, her distant cousin, for what seem good and sufficient reasons. Unfortunately, Jack Ralston has established a reputation for drinking, wildness, and irresponsibility. An extreme individualist, disliking the routine, subordination, and confinement of business, he has never been able to keep a steady job, and seems content to live upon his allowance from his widowed mother. After the marriage Katharine hopes to obtain for him a comfortable position from her wealthy uncle, Robert Lauderdale. Informed of the secret wedding, the multi-millionaire patronizingly offers Jack a check for a hundred thousand dollars—he at once raises the sum

The Man of Letters

[123]

to a million dollars—for Katharine's support. Jack angrily refuses the money because he believes that the offer is based upon the assumption of his inability to provide for his wife. Immediately afterwards, Jack temporarily loses his sense of direction as a result of an accident. After being waylaid by a professional boxer, he returns home bruised and beaten. This incident produces misunderstandings between Jack and his mother and between Jack and Katharine which are not resolved until the conclusion of *Katharine Lauderdale*.[58]

By failing to disclose (except to Uncle Robert) the marriage between Katharine and Jack in *Katharine Lauderdale*, Crawford created a suspenseful plot which he continued in *The Ralstons*. In the second novel, Jack reforms his drinking habits and attempts once more to begin a business career. Uncle Robert dies, after making a will in favor of the Ralstons. Subsequently, Katharine's father, Alexander Lauderdale, a selfish, miserly hypocrite, endeavors to break the will, quarrels with his daughter, and attempts to secure Jack's discharge from the bank. Alexander succeeds in nullifying his brother's will, but a second, unsigned will is found and with it is Katharine's marriage certificate. Thus the marriage is disclosed, although the disposal of Uncle Robert's enormous fortune is not completely settled. Presumably, Crawford intended to explain this matter in the never-written third novel of the series.

As has been previously remarked, the essential pattern of the *Saracinesca* novels is a central action supported by a number of episodes involving in greater or lesser degree subordinate members of an imagined social group. A minor character, introduced briefly in one novel, becomes a leading participant in a succeeding volume where his "history" is fully developed. Crawford employed a similar method in the *Ralston* novels. Although Walter Crowdie, for example, appears as an insignificant character in *Katharine Lauderdale*, he plays an important role in *The Ralstons*. Alexander Lauderdale's part in the series affords another illustration of the same technique. The device was a success in *The Ralstons* where it linked the two novels together, but it was almost a failure in *Sant' Ilario* since it tended to halt or blur the progression of the central plot.

Crawford probably expected to link the American and the Italian series by a similar method; in fact, he partially accomplished this intention through the story of Paul Griggs. During the past ten years Crawford had kept alive his readers' memories of his fictional representative, the narrator of *Mr. Isaacs*, by occasional references in novels to Paul Griggs's career. In *The Ralstons*, the novelist strongly emphasized the mysterious relationship between Crowdie and Griggs, pointedly wrote of "the strange story of Griggs' life,"[59] and remarked that Katharine knew him later;[60] but Crawford purposely neglected to satisfy the curiosity he was obviously seeking to arouse in his readers. When, in *Casa Braccio*, Crawford finally wrote the story of Griggs and revealed Walter Crowdie's true identity, he reintroduced several characters who had already appeared in the *Saracinesca* trilogy or in related novels.[61] Thus the two series were, in effect, connected by Crawford's device of carrying over characters from novel to novel. It is quite possible, however, that he intended in 1893 to make the relationship between the American and the Italian novels more forceful than he later did; and, if this surmise be valid, there seems no fully satisfactory explanation of his failure to do so. The fact that the American series was not so well received as the Italian group may have been an important factor in his decision not to emphasize the relationship between them. It may also help to account for his refusal to complete the American series, although there were probably other, more personal reasons.

Crawford had gone to New York to make the final arrangements for printing *The Ralstons;* and, after they were completed, he returned to Washington to endure the seemingly interminable delays and endless conferences over the Berdan case. He felt that he operated under constant pressure and that he was called upon to accomplish more than was possible in the time allowed. Before Christmas, however, he was forced to cease all work and return to New York for treatment of a severe back ailment. For three weeks he lay in the New York Hospital on Fifteenth Street. None of his family, not even his wife, knew that he was there; but he informed Mrs. Gardner who visited him several times. Although the enforced rest helped him physically, the gloom which for almost two years had characterized his private confidences to Mrs. Gardner continued. Scarcely a week had passed since he left the hospital when he wrote: "Dear—your letter ends with a few words which mean more than a commonplace. To 'be good' is a very wide term. In a sense I am—negatively—whatever the busybodies may say of me. My sins are spiritual ones, I think—the rather bitter and perhaps blasphemous reflexions of a man for whom life holds nothing, and who would readily part with it—the unbelief in any possible enduring happiness, or even satisfaction."[62] In view of the fact that Crawford was a writer whose unvarying practice had been to embody his own feelings and experiences in his fiction, it would have been almost beyond belief if this disillusionment and bitterness which he poured out to Mrs. Gardner had not found expression in his subsequent fiction.

IV

During the first five months of 1894, Crawford was occupied in Washington and in New York by a remarkable variety of projects. In Washington, his main task was to advance the Berdan bill in the Congressional committee which was considering it. The center of his literary work, however, became his New York apartment which was really the top floor of the Macmillan Company's offices at 66 Fifth Avenue. Since he had become the company's most important author, George Brett, the president of the firm, made it available to Crawford so long as he wished to use it. Here Crawford hastily wrote a short novel about a young man who fell in love while visiting three old maids in Bar Harbor. Originally, Crawford intended to call it *The Three Miss Miners*, but at the last moment he decided to give it the present title, *Love in Idleness*.[63] He was also planning to translate Nikolai Notovich's *La Vie inconnue de Jésus* and to write a book about the streets of New York, a children's story, and a life of Christ. For various reasons he abandoned all these projects and instead wrote a long review of Mrs. Humphry Ward's *Marcella*, a three-installment essay on mysticism for *Book Reviews*, two articles for the *Century*, and a travel sketch for *Scribner's Magazine*.[64] While completing these projects, he also wrote a major novel, *Casa Braccio*.

By references near the end of *The Ralstons* to "the strange story of Griggs' life, which no one had ever suspected,"[65] Crawford had led his readers to believe that there would be a third part of the *Ralston* series and that the novel would deal with Paul Griggs. Later he commented to Miss Katharine Lauderdale, whose name he had borrowed for the series: "There is to be a sequel to the Ralstons, but not for some time. I know what it is to be about, but I do not know what it is to be called. One reason for putting it off is that Katharine and Jack Ralston have not been married long enough to be horrid, so to say."[66] That he changed his mind is evident from his remarks to Mrs. Gardner late in April, 1894, when he wrote: "I have almost decided that it will be *necessary* to write the long book about Griggs at once and take my chances of being over here long enough to finish it. It is not for money, of which I have plenty just now, but on account of the sequence of stories—too many American ones coming together."[67] In terms of the practical considerations of a man of letters, Crawford's reasoning was logical; but there may have been another and perhaps more subtle reason for his sudden decision. Just as he had felt the need to express in *To Leeward* the emotional crisis

which in 1883 had resulted in his leaving America for Italy, he
may have again felt in 1894 the need to discuss in fiction the
circumstances and feelings which had prompted him to return to
America.

For the core of his novel Crawford selected an incident that
he had recently heard related by his wife's aunt, Mrs. Hobson.[68]
In Lima, Peru, Mrs. Hobson had met the granddaughter of a former
Catholic nun who "under unusual circumstances" had deserted the
convent of Nuestra Señora de los Dolores, married a Protestant
physician, and escaped to Scotland. Crawford transferred the setting to Italy, changed the names of the characters, and added
several fictitious episodes. The remainder of the novel, however,
which comprises the story of the novelist, Paul Griggs, was Crawford's own invention. In the second part, the former nun's
daughter, Gloria Dalrymple, returns to Italy, marries a young
artist named Angelo Reanda, but leaves him for Paul Griggs, who
loves her deeply. After the birth of their natural son, Walter
Crowdie, Gloria poisons herself. In the final part, Griggs, although
grief-stricken, finds consolation and even some happiness in the
memory of their perfect love until he learns that Gloria actually
loathed him.

The disclosure of Gloria's lies and deceptions has a profound
effect upon Griggs:

Outwardly he was very much the same man as ever. . . .

But within, the difference was great and deep. He felt that the
man who sat all day long at the writing-table doing his work was
not himself any longer, but another being, his double and shadow.
. . . Life was to him a vast blank, in which, without interest of
sensation, he moved in any direction he pleased, and he pleased
that it should be always in the same direction, from the remembrance
of a previous intention. . . . It was all precisely the same, and it was
perfectly inconceivable to him that he should ever care. . . . Nothing
could make any difference.[69]

Griggs is described in the novel as "beyond the possibility of
pain, even though beyond the hope of happiness."[70] He is "beyond
feeling anything,"[71] yet in the last sentence of the novel Crawford
tells his readers that with a woman who has also suffered Paul
Griggs found—as Crawford himself had found—"the truest [friend-
ship] that ever was between man and woman."

Although the exact relationship between the story of Paul
Griggs as told in *Casa Braccio* and Crawford's own experiences
may never be determined, certainly many of the sentiments attributed to Griggs—who had been Crawford's fictional representative

ever since his first novel, though perhaps heightened for effect—probably did represent Crawford's personal feelings. His comments in letters to Mrs. Gardner during this period make the parallels unmistakable. In passages from letters already quoted, Crawford had written that his sins were "the rather bitter and perhaps blasphemous reflexions of a man for whom life holds nothing, and who would readily part with it—the unbelief in any possibly enduring happiness, or even satisfaction." Again, he had said that his conscience forced him to "hang on for the children's sake" and that he was "resigned to the idea of another thirty years of this existence."

Even while writing *Casa Braccio* he told Mrs. Gardner that he was "past hurting,"[72] and, after the death of his sister's child, he declared: "Life is such an unmitigated evil to most of us that it is hard to regret, for the child's sake, that it has escaped the 'heartache and the thousand natural shocks'—the bruising and battering of fifty or sixty miserable years. What would not many of us give to have died at five years old!"[73] Four years later he was still writing to Mrs. Gardner in language that suggests that his attitude had not changed: "Sometimes I feel now as if I were writing after my own death, in a curious, posthumous way—disembodied as it were. I do not write any better, perhaps, but it is different from what it used to be. Do you understand? In some ways I like it better—but I seem to feel nothing any more, and I think I miss the pain more than the pleasure—I had got so used to it."[74]

The memoirs of Nellie Melba furnish another link between the fictional experiences of Paul Griggs and the real-life experiences of his literary creator. During the winter of 1893-94, Crawford formed a lasting friendship with the great soprano. He was often a guest in her hotel suite where they frequently sang together portions of *Faust* and of *Romeo and Juliet.* One day an incident occurred which Melba never forgot and which, after Crawford's death, she related in *Melodies and Memories.* Of Crawford she wrote:

> He was . . . acutely sensitive to beauty—so much so that when he was emotionally affected he would throw absolutely all restraint to the winds and bring out the deepest secrets from his heart. One afternoon when he had come to see me and I had sung to him, I noticed that when I had finished, the tears were streaming down his face. . . . I suggested lightly that perhaps he might care to write in my autograph book. He looked at me strangely for a moment and then said:
>
> "I wonder if you would understand what I should like to write."

"Let me see," I said. And as I bent over his shoulder I saw that he had written:

"*Credo in resurrectum mortuorum.*"

(I believe in the resurrection of the dead.)

He . . . told me the following story:

Years ago, when he was quite a young man he had fallen deeply in love with a girl who, at first, seemed to return his love. And then one day he discovered that she was untrue to him. The shock of this discovery was so great that instead of breaking his heart it seemed to kill it. "I became hard," he said, "and absolutely without feeling. In fact, I had lost faith in all women."[75]

In the winter of 1893-94 the incident would have been vivid in Crawford's mind. It remained vivid to him, for, years later, he wrote part of it into *The Primadonna* in which Paul Griggs bears the same relationship to a fictional operatic singer as the novelist did to Melba; but the story he told Melba in 1893-94 Crawford left out of the novel.[76]

Crawford finished *Casa Braccio* by the middle of June, 1894, and as soon as the printer returned the last proof sheets, he forwarded them, uncorrected to Mrs. Gardner. Meanwhile, he had spent a few days with her in Boston. The quiet of the Gardner home seemed all the more enjoyable by comparison to the noise and tension of Washington, and after he left, he wrote gratefully: "I shall always remember those dear, quiet days—as we have many good ones to remember in years gone by. May there be others to come!"[77] Several days later Mrs. Gardner sailed for Europe while Crawford fretted impatiently at the Congressional stalemate which was detaining him in Washington. While waiting for his bill to be presented in the House of Representatives, he corrected the proof sheets of *Casa Braccio.*[78]

Near the end of July, 1894, the bill for the relief of the Berdan Firearms Manufacturing Company was scheduled to be presented; but, just before it was to have been called, the House adjourned. Crawford knew that he would be forced to wait until the next session to try again to obtain passage of the bill. Consequently, on August 15, 1894, Crawford sailed for Genoa knowing he would return when Congress assembled again.

V

In the slightly more than two years between June, 1892, and August, 1894, Crawford initiated a number of projects which helped to shape his subsequent career. Very likely many of his actions were prompted by domestic troubles in Sorrento. The details of what happened there are much less important than the results. It is clear that the hopes and optimism of the 1880's faded quickly when Crawford realized that only in romance did a man always live happily ever after. For him there seemed no solution, only continued work in the career that had now become a demonstrated success but had been drained of much of its pleasure to him. Pride, obstinacy, ambition, concern for his children—a variety of motives operated in his decision to increase the range of his literary activities. There may even have been a connection between his need to defend his personal position and his public defense of his literary practices. Probably more than he realized, the re-establishment of his friendship with Mrs. Gardner provided a new frame of reference for his private life, while the writing of his volume of criticism was an unvoiced assertion of his determination to pursue his literary calling. What actually happened was that the "Prince of Sorrento" became the professional man of letters. His first efforts, it is true, were not entirely successful, but during these months he reached the decisions which made possible the transformation.

CHAPTER 7

Restless Wanderings

I

THE CONTINUAL MOVEMENT that characterizes the life of F. Marion Crawford during the last decade of the century threatens often to blur the essential unity of his activities. After "Villa Crawford" ceased to be a compelling attraction for him, Crawford roamed the Mediterranean in his boats, sailing for weeks at a time along the French and Italian riviera southward along the coast of Calabria to Sicily and back northward to the Islands of Sardinia and Corsica in what seems now like a perpetual odyssey. While he was ashore, the names of such cities as Palermo, Messina, Rome, Zurich, and Paris often provided the return addresses for his letters. About six months of every year he spent in America traveling back and forth on a line running from Boston to New York to Washington until he made his coast-to-coast lecture tour that took him as far south as New Orleans and the small towns of southern Texas, westward to the Pacific, and then back to New York on a northern route that included Oregon and Montana. Always a stranger but paradoxically one who was at home wherever he was, Crawford liked to wander, but he often seems like a man forever on his "passage out," a person with no fixed center or known destination to make his voyage complete. Beneath the seeming aimlessness of his movement, nevertheless, he had a consistent purpose, a firm resolve to practice his profession of letters and to succeed even in the areas that seemed most difficult and forbidding.

In the four months between September and the end of December, 1894, Crawford wrote two long novels, *Taquisara* and *Adam Johnstone's Son,* which Macmillan published in 1896. Featuring Italian castles in Sicily, duels, poison, embezzlement, and heroic self-sacrifice, the plot of *Taquisara* is so melodramatic that the novel cannot be considered among his best work. It is an interesting example of Crawford's practice of using, in minor roles, characters who have had major parts in his earlier novels.

Adam Johnstone's Son could be described as an "international novel" set in Amalfi and Salerno; the leading characters are Englishwomen who have no home in England and generally live "abroad, more or less, in one or another of the places of society's departed spirits, such as Florence."[1] In the plot Crawford uses a complicated situation in which a man's son by his second marriage falls in love with the man's first wife's daughter by her second marriage. In the final paragraphs of the novel Crawford restated some of the theories he had expressed in *The Novel: What It Is.*

Between December, 1894, and November, 1895, Crawford accomplished little. He was exhausted from the literary work (four novels completed) of the past year, and he probably realized that he could best restore his energy through travel. He made a quick journey to America and back in a futile effort to advance the Berdan case. The remainder of the spring and summer of 1895 he spent cruising alone in the Mediterranean,[2] sailing his felucca as far north as Elba, then south by way of Montecristo to the Lipari Islands, and then back along the Italian coastline to Sorrento. In Rome he gathered information for an article which eventually appeared in the *Century Magazine* as "A Kaleidoscope of Rome,"[3] and in Paestum and Sicily he collected material which he thought he might someday use in a novel. In July, he actually began *A Rose of Yesterday,* but he made very little progress with it.

The long vacation, however, helped to prepare Crawford for the coming winter's work in America. A few days after arriving in New York on November 14, he remarked that "everything is upside down and topsy turvey in my literary life, as the result of a long period of idleness which has given me strength, if not peace."[4] With only minor variations, the pattern of 1893-94 seemed about to repeat itself. In New York, he rapidly wrote several articles about Pope Leo XIII and the Vatican for the *Century,*[5] and during the winter he completed two novels of decidedly uneven quality, *A Rose of Yesterday*[6] and *Corleone.*[7] In Washington he planned to try to secure passage of the Berdan bill. As events proved, Crawford's presence was not often required in Washington this year, but the Berdan bill, although approved by a House committee, was "held over" a second time.

A Rose of Yesterday seems a definite retreat from the critical convictions which Crawford had expressed in *The Novel: What It Is.* Although he had vigorously objected in his criticism to novels that contained preaching or lengthy discussions of contemporary issues, in *A Rose of Yesterday* he illustrated the problem of divorce in the story of a woman who for twenty years refused to divorce her husband because of her loyalty "for the vow, for the meaning of the bond, for the holiness of marriage itself."[8] Not only did he dramatize the issue in his plot but in the role of omniscient author he also commented tiresomely upon the moral issues involved in relations between men and women. The result was the embodiment of a realistic issue in the lives of characters who are almost absurdly ideal. This curious combination brought Crawford dangerously close to failure and to a denial of his strongest artistic convictions. It almost seems as if Crawford had half-heartedly attempted for once to venture into the literary province of Howells.

Although Crawford featured members of the Saracinesca family in *Corleone*, the novel should not be regarded as constituting the fourth volume of the *Saracinesca* trilogy. He thought of his three earlier novels as a completed unit embodying his analysis of the political and social aspects of Italian life over a half century, and he considered such Italian novels as *Pietro Ghisleri*, *Taquisara*, *Corleone*, and *Casa Braccio*, which he wrote during the middle years of the 1890's, as stories of modern Italian society. In these novels the Saracinesca family appears as a kind of standard of measurement by which other members of the fictional Italian society created by Crawford may be measured, and in this sense perhaps the term "Saracinesca series" properly describes them.

In marked degree *Corleone: A Tale of Sicily* possesses the good and bad features that are often simultaneously present in Crawford's novels. The plot, which turns upon mistaken identity and the inviolateness of confidences given to a priest during confession, is as improbable as any Crawford ever devised; but the manner of telling the story is representative of the narrative skill of Crawford at his best. What gives *Corleone* its distinction and particular merit, however, is Crawford's use of his own extensive knowledge of Sicily and the Sicilian people. The Sicilians in the novel, who for the most part are the villains, are credibly motivated and realistically characterized. The three Sicilian brothers, Tebaldo, Francesco, and Ferdinando, and the two young girls, Aliandra and Concetta, are particularly acceptable persons. Furthermore, Crawford's analysis of the organization, purpose, and operation of the Sicilian Mafia seems consistent with modern studies of the famous criminal society. Contemporary reaction to *Corleone* may be summarized in the comment of the reviewer for the *Atlantic Monthly* who found it "difficult to overpraise."[9]

Throughout the winter of 1894-95, Crawford saw Mrs. Gardner as often as possible. His friendship with her had not in the least been lessened by what he considered an unfortunate incident in Italy during the preceding summer. Before he reached New York in November, he had written, "I think we shall read our Dante this year, though things may be different from what they were eighteen months ago. You see I feel very much that Madame's behaviour has put a stop to my stopping under your husband's roof, when I cannot even have you to dinner in my own house."[10] He added, "If I had been in Sorrento when you were here, it would not have been much worse. Perhaps I should have forced the situation and insisted upon at least inviting you both. As it happened, I was in Sicily and knew nothing of your coming." Crawford was much relieved when he found that she understood the situation. There was no alteration in their feelings for each other, and they continued to meet whenever they could arrange a place and a time.

In New York Crawford once more took over the "den" or "loft," an apartment twenty-five feet by sixty, above the Macmillan offices. The room was rather sparsely furnished with a long table, a desk, several chairs, bookcases, a bearskin rug, and pictures of "Villa Crawford," his children, and his boats. Here Crawford worked long hours, rarely venturing into society, except to dine occasionally with his brother, Arthur Terry, or his friend, Mrs. Mary Cadwalader Jones. At her house Crawford met John La Farge, Augustus Saint-Gaudens, John Sargent, and Elizabeth Marbury. As a rule Crawford avoided large social functions, and Mrs. Jones later recalled that he did not admire many of the people he knew in New York and that he often insisted that no other guest be present when he came for dinner. Observing that Crawford had very few friends among other men, Mrs. Jones called him "a woman's man."[11] Among men, George Brett, whom he met daily for lunch, was his closest friend; yet Crawford undoubtedly knew him better than Brett knew Crawford.

Few men could penetrate Crawford's reserve. As an acquaintance, Crawford was usually amiable, even friendly, and his conversation was often brilliant, enlivened with anecdotes and accounts of strange incidents he had seen or heard about during his travels. On the rare occasion when he dropped his formal manner, he was likely to exhibit an intense interest in astrology, in occult manifestations, and in superstition. Although these matters were the subject of widespread discussion during the last decades of the century, Crawford's persistent and intense interest in them dated back to his experience in India. During the 1880's Mrs. Berdan mentioned the matter several times in her journal. On October 3, 1885 (Berdan memoirs), she remarked: "Marion startles us constantly . . . by the odd beliefs he has, if they really are beliefs. Now he seems to have a certain faith in astrology or in the influence of the stars over us. For instance, he says: 'I am under the influence of

Venus, Mars and Mercury which accounts for my temperament, and Bessie is under the influence of Mars and Jupiter.' It is very amusing to hear him and Bessie talk of these things so seriously, although I laugh at it, for to me it is utter nonsense." Among other evidences of Crawford's interest which could be cited, perhaps the most indicative are to be found in his letters to Mrs. Gardner. On one occasion he wrote:

> Of late I feel an odd sort of uncertainty about the future. Do you remember that old astrologer who predicted so many things which have come true? He foretold that from September of this year till November of next year, was to be an unfortunate time, but that after that things were to go very much better than ever before in my life, in every way. I suppose it is foolish to pay any attention to such things, but I cannot get rid of the impression that there is a change coming before long.[12]

A few months later he declared, "You may remember that this year, until the 1st of next November is the last adverse one before the immortal glory my old astrologer predicted."[13] Although many of these comments cannot be interpreted as establishing beyond doubt Crawford's attitude, the fact remains that the character of his remarks and the frequency of their occurrence lend support to the assertions of Mrs. Jones and others who knew him that he was superstitious and believed in astrology.

Usually Crawford kept his opinions and feelings to himself. His cousin, Samuel Prescott Hall, remembered that Crawford "had something of the New England reserve...and had few real intimates."[14] Hall considered Norman Douglas' reference to Crawford's "lustrous Vatican-society veneer"[15] a very good characterization of one side of Crawford, but Hall added immediately that "at the same time, he did not always show this face, and he was ever a golden talker." There was a certain stiffness in Crawford's manner which precluded discussions of his personal affairs and kept men from seeking his friendship. On the other hand, there were times in the 1890's when Crawford longed to revive the circle of feminine admirers whose flattery he had enjoyed at Sorrento during the early days of his marriage. Embittered and melancholy, he sought and received companionship, appreciation, and sympathy from Mrs. Gardner and, to a much lesser degree, from the Marchesa Theodoli, Mrs. Jones, Nellie Melba, Sarah Bernhardt, and others. With them, he was relaxed and warmly sociable. For mixed society, especially that with which his wife was preoccupied, Crawford had only contempt. He frankly stated his attitude in a letter to Mrs. Gardner: "The sea is a nice place, because there are no people in it. It would be nicer if the whole world were all sea, and if there were no one, not even one-self, anywhere."[16]

II

The remarkable combination of the romantic and the practical in Crawford's nature often resulted in strangely juxtaposed, if not actually contradictory, actions. There was the Crawford who was intensely absorbed by all kinds of occult manifestations, and there was the Crawford who drove advantageous bargains with practical business experts in the dollar profits and losses of the literary market. There was also the Crawford who appeared as a disil-lusioned idealist seeking to assuage his melancholy with the adulation of a highly select circle of feminine admirers, and there was the Crawford who as the professional man of letters determined in cool and logical fashion the alternation of American and Italian novels with an eye to maintaining his popularity with thousands of readers. Nowhere may the two traits be seen more evenly balanced, however, than in Crawford's romantic attachment to the sea and in his practical skill in seamanship. Crawford was indeed as romantic a sailor as ever appeared in a pirate story; but, when his judgment was not upset by his temper or his pride, he was fully as competent as many professional sea-captains.

By 1896 Crawford was a veteran sailor. Shortly after purchasing "Villa Crawford," he had acquired several boats, and in one of them, the felucca *Margherita*, he had sailed extensively the coastal waters of the Mediterranean; but, after he began the yearly trips to America, Crawford felt he needed a larger boat. In April, 1896, he purchased the *Ezra Nye*, a pilot-boat seventy-five feet in length, with a nineteen-foot beam, built in 1859 for the New Jersey Pilots' Association. Crawford renamed the boat *Alda*, ordered extensive repairs, and, while the work was being completed, passed the examination for a first-class captain's license so that he might sail his ship across the Atlantic to Italy. Impressed by Crawford's enthusiasm, his sister remarked that "he seemed happier than I have thought him for years. The idea of sailing his own boat across the Atlantic was better than an elixir of life to him."[17]

Once the ship was considered sea-worthy, Crawford was eager to sail. He had not accomplished a great deal of literary work since his arrival in November, and the Berdan bill, which had been the ostensible reason for his return to America, was no nearer passage than it had been a year earlier. The prospect of sailing the *Alda*, however, blurred for a time his troubles in America and in Italy. By comparison with the gloom of his letters during the winter, the tone of his comment to Mrs. Gardner seems almost enthusiastic: "The schooner is all but ready, and the stores are on board. She is to have one trial sail in the bay tomorrow, to stretch things a little, before we get off for good. We may put into the Azores for fresh things, before making Gibraltar, but it is not sure. Most probably I shall sail the yacht back again in November, for I have not finished the fight in Washington, and I still mean to win it."[18]

On May 24, 1896, Crawford sailed from New York bound for Sorrento, expecting to stop only at the Azores and at Gibraltar. The *Alda,* flying his colors, a white Maltese cross on a blue field, carried a crew of six. After encountering several bad storms, the yacht reached Gibraltar on June 24, but seemingly endless calms in the Mediterranean kept her from arriving at Sorrento until July 13. For a brief period thereafter, several members of his family cruised with him, but later only Clare, his daughter, accompanied him on excursions in the *Alda.* He spent a great part of the remainder of the summer at sea.

The Atlantic voyage had provided almost seven weeks of relief from the problems he had left behind him in New York and in Washington and from the troubles he knew were ahead in Sorrento. By August, when he wrote Mrs. Gardner about his plans, the enthusiasm which he had shown in anticipation of the crossing had been dissipated:

What am I doing? Writing a novel of course! What am I always doing? But I am meditating other things in such spare time as I can find. The old fashioned novel is really dead, and nothing can revive it nor make anybody care for it again. What is to follow it? That is what we are all trying to find out and some are already making experiments. A clever German who is here suggested to me last night that the literature of the future might turn out to be the daily exchange of ideas of men of genius—over the everlasting telephone of course—published every morning for the whole world. The mere suggestion shows what we are drifting into.

For my part, I sometimes fancy that an age of meditation may follow this era of screaming. We shall come back to our next lives, if we must come back, tired of this one, and wishing a change. But then—perhaps some may not come back at all. Why should you, for instance? You have peace in your existence. . . . If you could see my life from within me for a week, you would understand what war means, and how blessed you are, compared with me. I shall have much more to fight through before I get at real hope. But I think that this next year is going to make the main difference, and I mean to win. Perhaps I may have won by next spring—or failed altogether. Sancta Isabella, ora pro me! . . . What should you care about my crossing the ocean in a forty ton schooner? Our bodies do not matter in the least any more, do they? But ourselves do matter—our Selves with a big S.

As for average news I have none to tell. I see something of my children and that gives me pleasure. My wife is in Switzerland at a cure. My mother is in Lucerne, very infirm, and that gives me anxiety. There is a handful of people here—less than usual—and we see something of each other and exchange banalities. That is the sum of the summer situation, outside me, and so far as surroundings are concerned. What difference does it make? They are the atoms that come into contact with my atoms—not the selves that come near my Self. A thought, a memory, has more reality than all society put together.[19]

Since 1892, when Crawford made his first return voyage to America after his marriage, the state of affairs in Sorrento had remained virtually unchanged. The "Prince of Sorrento" returned after nine months' absence to find some pleasure in seeing his children; otherwise "Villa Crawford," which he continued to maintain in comfort and even luxury, held nothing for him.

III

Crawford hoped that during the next year he would be established as a dramatist. He had always had certain misgivings about his ability to continue indefinitely as a novelist; and now, having written almost thirty novels, his estimate of the current literary situation greatly increased his confidence in the wisdom of his decision to enter new areas of literary activity. Until proved no longer a marketable product, Crawford would continue to write the "old fashioned novel" as he had written it in the past; but, at the same time, he would explore other avenues. In 1892 he had been convinced that the drama offered a new opportunity for him; and despite a not very promising beginning Crawford remained convinced in 1896 that he could "win" as a playwright. In the fall of 1896, therefore, Crawford returned to New York to attempt to achieve success in the theater. The play was to be a dramatization of *Doctor Claudius.*

Perhaps no previous literary effort proved as exhausting and frustrating as that expended on the dramatization of the novel. To help with it, he secured the assistance of Harry St. Maur, an actor and dramatist of considerable experience in adapting novels to the stage. After the script was completed, an excellent company was selected for the production. The arrangements, in fact, were all that Crawford desired. Confidently he wrote Mrs. Gardner:

> There is a great deal to do just now, and I think it is being well done—but the work is perpetual and the days seem to be only five minutes long—and four out of the five are spent at the theatre. Monday is the first night, and there is going to be a big crowd, for the house is almost sold out already—and I am *glad* you are not to be there. For I should like you to see the piece when it is at its best, and not in the unfinished fury of a first representation.[20]

On February 1, 1897, *Doctor Claudius* was presented to a capacity audience at the Fifth Avenue Theatre. The production was a dismal failure, and the next day the reviewers seemed to enjoy venting their sarcasm at Crawford. The man who had never written an unsuccessful novel had at last failed. A critic for the New York *World* (February 7, 1897) began his discussion of the play:

> Have you heard of the new charitable society that is being formed? It is called "The New York Charitable Society for the Distribution of Illuminated Mottoes Among Novelists." The motto selected is "Keep Off the Drama." This will hang in a prominent position over the author's desk, and we pray much from its constant admonitory appearance there.
>
> Marion Crawford's "Doctor Claudius" is the last sacrifice offered up on the altar of dramatic ambition. You might as well try to dramatize the city directory or one of Richard Harding Davis's Harper Magazine essays!

Although other reviewers were more temperate in their remarks, almost without exception the notices were unfavorable. The principal weaknesses of the dramatic version seem to have been an overemphasis upon dialogue and a corresponding lack of action, a failure to make dramatically satisfactory the intrigues which dominate the second half of the novel, and the weak performances of the feminine roles. Although the deficiencies in acting could have been remedied, the essential defects of the play were inherent in the novel. Several weeks after the play was withdrawn, Crawford wrote Mrs. Gardner: "The critics killed Claudius, as I dare say you heard. It was a disappointment, but I shall be more successful next time."[21]

The failure of *Doctor Claudius* and the stinging blasts from the critics, humiliating as they were, served only to intensify Crawford's determination to succeed. His chagrin had scarcely begun to subside when he began a new play "which," he declared, "is *not* to fail."[22] More than ever, Crawford was convinced that he could achieve the same degree of recognition as a playwright that he had already attained as a novelist. The new play, he determined, would have a historical setting.

Crawford's choice of a historical subject was partly influenced by his estimate of literary trends in the novel. From his own observation, which was confirmed by the lists of best-sellers published in the *Bookman* after 1895, Crawford fully realized that the historical novel was becoming an increasingly heavy favorite with the reading public. Crawford believed, therefore, that a play with a historical setting would have a good chance for success and that, if the script were so written that it could easily be turned into a historical novel, he might profit two ways. What was unusual here was Crawford's intention to write the play first and later to derive the novel from the play. For his setting he decided to use the palace of King Philip II of Spain, and the title of both play and novel became appropriately *In the Palace of the King*.

Although the venture in playwriting seemed very important to Crawford, he characteristically refused to stake everything on one project. Accordingly, when Major Pond approached him with an invitation to deliver a series of lectures on Italian subjects in the fall and winter of 1897-98, Crawford listened receptively. During the past two years he had become interested in Italian history and had already published several articles on the subject. The research which he had accomplished for these articles would provide part of the material for the lectures and subsequently for a non-fiction book on Italy. Doubtless Crawford estimated that the lecture tour would afford him a good return at a minimum output. In addition, the lectures would keep his name and person before the public across the country, thereby stimulating interest in his previous and future work.

As the negotiations with Major Pond were being concluded, Crawford was suddenly called to Sorrento because of an accident suffered by his mother. Early in March, 1897, Louisa Terry fell, cracking her breast bone. To be with her, Crawford sailed from New York on March 13. When he first saw her after his return to Italy, he believed she was dying, but gradually she seemed to improve. Crawford, nevertheless, restricted his voyages in the *Alda* to the Island of Corsica and to the waters near Sorrento, and he would have canceled his lecture tour except for the ruinous financial loss which would have been involved. As events proved, Crawford's anxiety over his mother's health was justified, for she died on September 21, 1897, a few days before he had expected to return to the United States.

During Crawford's boyhood and even in the early years of his maturity, Louisa Terry had exercised a profound influence over her son's personality. A large part of his longing for feminine companionship, his polished and urbane manner, his conservative moral and political bias, his love for Italy, and his enjoyment of luxurious, sensuous living he owed to his mother's teaching and example. After his marriage, her influence had been replaced by that of Bessie Crawford and later by that of Mrs. Gardner; but Crawford always considered his mother a strength and a center to which he could return should the need arise. Her death deepened Crawford's now habitual melancholy, for she was one of the few persons who meant a great deal to him. The loss of his mother also emphasized to him the value he attached to his relationship with Mrs. Gardner. Crawford concluded the letter in which he told her about the death of Louisa Terry with a comment about distance and separation, asserting,

> Not that distance makes much difference to us, now, if we cannot see each other. For my part the sense of distance—mere length of miles, has disappeared. Distance is forgetting, and nothing else— and that is very far from me—and from you, I hope. Surely you and I have earned friendship of each other—with pain—and that sort of friendship does not go out in a flash like a falling star. It is much to me, though I am sometimes silent for a long time—yet I do not think that a day passes in my life in which there is not a tender thought of you. Is it so with you sometimes? Please let it be, my dear.[23]

Despite his concern over his mother's health, Crawford had accomplished a good deal of work during the summer of 1897. He had begun *In the Palace of the King;* he had finished the lectures which he would deliver under Pond's management; and he had virtually finished the book on Italy entitled *Ave Roma Immortalis.* He had worked hard on this last book, and he considered it an important one. Of its composition, Crawford wrote Mrs. Gardner:

> It . . . has been a long and troublesome piece of work. A whole year will go by before it is published, as the American Macmillans think illustrations absolutely necessary. . . . The writing of it has taken me through many strange and interesting old volumes of Chronicles. The story of Rome is surely the grimmest and grizzliest of all possible stories, and I have tried to tell it so that a girl may read it and see the horror, but think no evil—which is not easy. No one can guess what things were done in those days, who has not studied the chronicles, and they are not within everyone's reach. Muratori's collection alone has sixty volumes, half of them folios and out of print for the last hundred and fifty years—you may

imagine from that what my workshop is like—I am using four
tables, a swinging bookcase and a fixed bookcase, just for the books
I read all the time. And when I read Gibbon and see the names
of the authors he quotes, remembering that he possessed most of
them, I am filled with envy and wonder.[24]

Ave Roma Immortalis, which Crawford finally completed during
his lecture tour, is not, as some critics said, a mere "guidebook."[25]
Rather, it is a novelist's reading of the chronicles of Rome, a
fusion of a sympathetic study and appreciation of the great artistic
monuments of the city with the characters of the men who were
prominent in Roman history. The organization of the two volumes—
an introductory chapter, thirteen essays describing the regions of
Rome, and three chapters dealing with Catholic centers—suggests,
it is true, a guide-book; but Crawford superimposed upon historical
fact his own impressionistic rendering of the atmosphere surrounding each famous landmark of Rome. What the public received
in two superbly bound and illustrated volumes was a kind of
romantic history of Rome by an American expatriate who had
known and loved the city from his earliest childhood. The two
volumes were not only important in themselves, but also important
as an indication of a change in Crawford's literary interests.

IV

When Crawford returned to the United States early in October,
1897, to begin his speaking engagements under the direction of
Major Pond, he found his itinerary already planned in detail. He
was to begin with performances before small groups in the East, to
make his first appearance in front of a large metropolitan audience
in Chicago, and then to return East for lectures to Boston and
New York audiences. In February and early March of 1898 his
tour would take him as far south as New Orleans and thence
to Kansas City and across the continent. He would reach California
during the last week in March. For the following six weeks he
would lecture on the West Coast and then turn east for engagements
along the northern route until the tour ended in Duluth, Minnesota.
Pond later remarked that this was "one of the most extensive and
successful tours I have ever made with a star."[26]

Crawford opened with a lecture before a literary club in
Bridgeport, Connecticut, on the night of October 28, 1897. Later
he went to Chicago where he was the guest of honor at a banquet
and a reception given by the Press Club and by the Quadrangle
Club. He delivered two lectures there at Central Music Hall, and

between these engagements he addressed the students of Notre Dame University. Since the performances in Chicago represented the first real test of his powers to attract large audiences in metro-politan centers, Crawford must have been greatly pleased by the excellent press notices which he received in the Chicago papers and by the fact that the New York *Herald* (November 14, 1897) reprinted virtually his entire speech at the Press Club banquet.

Early in December, Crawford was speaking in the Boston area. The press reviewed favorably his lecture before a large audience at Boston College Hall and at Sanders Theater at Harvard. Throughout December and January, he continued to lecture in the East, concluding his performances in this section of the country with talks in New York at the Astor Gallery of the Astoria on January 7, 1898; at Xavier College on January 31; and at the Staten Island Academy on February 1. In view of the fact that many of these places were schools, one infers that his lectures were considered educational as well as entertaining; indeed, throughout the tour Crawford spoke on many occasions to students and faculties of educational institutions.

After arranging to meet Major Pond in Kansas City on March 12, Crawford left for a tour of Southern cities. Very probably this Southern tour was planned around his participation in the Catholic Winter School in New Orleans at which the novelist was to give the entire series of his lectures. He was to be in New Orleans from February 24 to March 1. On the way, Crawford was booked for engagements in Memphis, Louisville, and Nashville. Pond had made the arrangements for Crawford's appearances very carefully: in each instance newspaper publicity preceded his arrival, and the papers printed a full report of the lecture on the day after Crawford's appearance. After each address, a literary, religious, or press club honored him at a reception.

Crawford's lectures at the Catholic Winter School in New Orleans constituted the high point of his entire tour. They repre-sented his most sustained success, for on four evenings he maintained and even increased the enthusiastic response of a highly critical audience. On the opening night he was introduced as "the greatest living American novelist."[27] Newspaper accounts of his performances support the comment made by the reporter for the *Daily Picayune* in an article written after the series was completed: "For five days Mr. Crawford has been in the city, lecturing night after night to the most cultivated and distinguished audiences, standing room being at a premium.... His leisure hours have all been taken up, the most distinguished social attentions being lavished upon him, and the best people vying with one another as to who should have the honor of claiming Mr. Crawford for an hour in their homes."[28] The Catholic clergy were especially lavish in their praises of his addresses.

New Orleans, moreover, was the only city visited by Crawford in which he had the opportunity to present his complete lecture course. He had originally planned four discourses: "Pope Leo XIII and the Vatican," "Early Italian Artists," "The Middle Ages in Rome," and "Modern Sicilian Life." In New Orleans he gave the first three lectures, but in place of "Modern Sicilian Life" he substituted by special request one called "Early Experiences in India and Mr. Isaacs." This last lecture which he had developed during the tour from a brief, informal talk for banquets and receptions into a lengthy address, became, with the account of Pope Leo XIII, his most popular subject. It is unlikely that the lecture on "Modern Sicilian Life" was given during the entire tour.

Crawford's New Orleans engagement represented a personal triumph achieved to a considerable extent through his own determination to succeed. He arrived in the city suffering from a severe cold, but he refused to postpone his lecture. After his second appearance, the *Daily Picayune* (February 27, 1898) reported that "Mr. Crawford was laboring under a severe attack of grippe and neuralgia." Regardless of his physical condition, Crawford finished the series at New Orleans; moved on to lecture in Corsicana and other cities in Texas; joined Major Pond in Kansas City; and spoke there on March 12. He was apparently still suffering from a bronchial infection, and he later told Pond that "he had had two hemorrhages . . . and that his left lung was very sore" but that "he intended to finish the tour no matter what the sacrifice, if it were possible."[29]

Years later, recalling the trip westward from Kansas City, Pond emphasized the novelist's cheerfulness and unfailing good humor; but in 1898 Crawford's letters sounded a rather gloomy note. From Colorado Springs, he wrote Mrs. Gardner:

> You have been here, I suppose, and you know what it is like. Just now it is bleak and desolate. . . . I am going steadily on my way, speaking every night, and I have done it so long now that things will probably go well to the end, as they generally do with indestructible people. A different city, a different hall, another audience every night—that is the round. It would be dreary if I had not a set purpose of doing it—but nothing bores one which one means to accomplish, and which is hard.[30]

The difference between the somewhat pessimistic outlook which he expressed in his private correspondence and the optimistic appearance that he presented to his business manager may have been due to the ill health which continued to plague him throughout the lecture tour.

From Colorado Springs, where Crawford spoke before a large audience, the two men continued their journey across the continent, the novelist lecturing wherever Pond had scheduled a performance. At Salt Lake City, the Roman Catholic bishop, four Mormon bishops, and clergymen of all the denominations represented in the city attended his lecture in the Methodist church. In his account of the performance, Pond revealed his astonishment at the inter-denominational character of Crawford's audience. The explanation, of course, lies in the basis of the novelist's immense popularity. Although in private life Crawford was a Catholic, his public career had never been closely associated with religion. So little publicity had ever been given to his religious affiliation that probably very few of his readers were even aware of it. Though the Catholic clergy supported his lectures and his subjects included Pope Leo XIII, his audiences came to hear him much more because of his contemporary fame as a great American novelist and because of a non-sectarian interest in the Pope than because of his private religious convictions. In a place so remote from the entertainment centers of the East as Salt Lake City, the visit of F. Marion Crawford was an event of great importance.

The experience at Salt Lake City was merely a prelude to the tremendous reception Crawford was to receive on the West Coast. His arrival in San Francisco from Ogden, Utah, was featured with great prominence by the two leading newspapers, the *Chronicle* and the *Call* on March 26. The former presented a full-column account illustrated with a large picture of the novelist, the story consisting mainly of a long sketch of Crawford's career. The article in the *Call* (March 26, 1898), set in double column width, began by stating, "There is wonderful vitality in Marion Crawford, whose name, as the writer of many successful novels, is known from one end of the Union to the other." The newspaper devoted the remainder of the story to Crawford's comments about his lecture tour, the West, and his method of writing; only a brief portion was biographical. Thereafter both papers printed long and detailed accounts of the novelist's lectures.

Crawford spoke three times to large audiences in the California Theater of San Francisco. His first lecture, delivered on March 28, was "Leo XIII and the Vatican." On the following evening he presented for his second engagement the expanded version of his own life-story which the San Francisco papers entitled the "Original Mr. Isaacs' Early Newspaper Experience in India." And on March

30, his final appearance, the title was reported as "Medieval Life in Italy." Thus Crawford, with the exception of the lecture on "Early Italian Artists," repeated the series that had been received with great enthusiasm in New Orleans. The order of his subjects in San Francisco suggests that Crawford himself rated the appeal of his lectures in this manner and makes it questionable whether he gave the lecture on "Early Italian Artists" more than a very few times during the entire tour.

The character of his audiences in San Francisco was typical of his experience elsewhere on the trip. Reviewing the lecture on "Pope Leo XIII," the *Chronicle* (March 29, 1898) noted the capacity crowd in attendance and added, "Doubtless the same people had sat many times at the feet of Crawford, the writer, and the fact that there were other notable, if less intellectual, attractions in town did not prevent the audience from being cultured and fashionable...." Taking cognizance of the fact that the Young Men's Institute, which sponsored his lecture, was a Catholic organization, the same paper observed that "the Institute, with broad liberality, had invited men of other faiths to act as vice-presidents. Besides well-known Catholics, Rabbi Nieto, Julius Kahn and Irving Scott were prominently placed." To support the contention that the occasion was a fashionable one, the reporter wrote that "Representative people occupied the boxes—the Frank Sullivans, the Casserlys, the De Youngs, the McDades. Representative men sat upon the stage...." The paper printed the guest list of the Forum Club which honored Crawford at the customary reception.

The remainder of Crawford's tour of the West Coast became a long succession of triumphs, marred only by his illness. Major Pond recalled that in San Francisco Crawford told him that the lung ailment which had been evident as they traveled west from Kansas City had become increasingly severe and that a physician had advised him to close the tour and return to New York. At the time Pond apparently counseled caution, pointing out the importance of health over money; for in his memoirs he wrote, "I cared nothing whatever as to the business part of it—that never entered my mind; but I assured Mr. Crawford that I would not be the means of his breaking down for a dozen fortunes."[31] Crawford's daughter, however, later remembered that the novelist wanted to interrupt the lectures but that Pond was unwilling to abandon the tour. For whatever reason, Crawford did continue the lecture tour speaking in southern California and then back up the coast to Seattle; Victoria, British Columbia; and Portland. At this point he turned back eastward to Helena, Montana; Winnipeg, Canada;

Fargo, North Dakota; and Duluth, Minnesota, where, according to Crawford, the tour ended on April 30, 1898.[32]

By sheer determination Crawford had fulfilled all of his engagements, and he had been successful. One of the most important factors which contributed to his outstanding success was the content of his lectures. As originally planned, four of them contained the general theme of Italian life and art in both the present and the past. Heard in their entirety, they could have constituted a coherent sequence which would have appealed to the interest and imagination of Americans at a time when American tourists in unprecedented numbers were traveling to Europe in search of culture. But it is doubtful that they were ever given as a complete course. The logical arrangement of his material would have placed the "Middle Ages in Rome" first, followed in order by "Early Italian Artists," "Modern Sicilian Life," and "Pope Leo XIII and the Vatican." This last lecture proved to be so outstanding that Crawford chose it above the others as his main attraction. Second in popularity, measured by newspaper accounts, was the lecture about Mr. Isaacs, which had begun as an informal talk about himself. Thus, except in such places as New Orleans and San Francisco where he was asked to give three or four performances, Crawford delivered the lecture on Pope Leo XIII; and, when he had the opportunity for a second appearance, he offered the expanded biographical account of his own experiences.

Despite the infrequency with which Crawford delivered the "Middle Ages in Rome," contemporary accounts are sufficiently complete to indicate the principal emphasis of the lecture.[33] He began it with an account of the desolation of the city during the time of the Rienzi. He placed great emphasis on the social conditions of the period which he contrasted with those of modern Rome. He briefly sketched the rise of the feudal barons and the establishment of the house of Colonna; described from firsthand knowledge several of the castles in and near Rome; and related in some detail the story of Vittoria Accoramboni. Crawford had a deep, personal interest in the career of Vittoria; for he had spent much of his boyhood in the "Villa Negroni" where Francesco Peretti and Vittoria lived after their marriage. The artistic monuments of the Middle Ages and the Renaissance he left to his next lecture.

Crawford's abandonment of the lecture on "Early Italian Artists" may explain his willingness to permit *Book Reviews* to publish lengthy excerpts from it while he was still lecturing. His main thesis was the superiority of the Italian Renaissance artists over modern workers. In *Book Reviews,* he stated his premise as follows: "Art is not dependent on the creations of genius alone. It is also the result of developing manual skill to the highest degree. Without genius, works of art might as well be turned out by machinery; without manual skill, genius could have no means of expression. As a matter of fact, in our own time, it is the presence of genius, without manual skill, or foolishly despising it, that has produced a sort of school called the impressionist."[34] The newspaper reporter for the *Daily Picayune* (February 26, 1898) probably conveyed the added forcefulness of Crawford when making the point orally: "He [Crawford] said, in opening, that art was, in a large degree, dependent upon manual-dexterity, although not wholly. Lacking the mechanical skill, genius cannot fully express its ideas. This is seen in the works of modern impressionist painters, in whose pictures the magnitude of the conception is often hopelessly in conflict with the inadequacy of the technical rendition thereof."

The painters of the Italian Renaissance, suggested Crawford, were superior to the modern Impressionists in their mechanical ability to draw and paint; and he asserted that the art of the Renaissance was "higher and nobler than that of to-day" because the artists were "men of universal learning and genius." "Nothing was merely for effect," he was quoted as saying; "their art seemed to compare itself with an ideal future. . . . Modern art is more theatrical. It may be said to compare itself with an ideal past, and to appeal to men's eyes." Crawford meant that the modern Impressionists sought to capture a reality that was of necessity in the past; but the Renaissance artists had endeavored to express an ideal or vision yet to be realized. The Impressionists represented the momentary scene; the Renaissance men expressed man's idea of moral perfection. From this frame of reference, Crawford examined the lives and work of a number of important Italian artists. Conservative as this criticism was, it nonetheless reflected at the turn of the century a widely respected and accepted point of view.

The comparison between the artists of the past and those of the present in the lecture on "Early Italian Artists" could have served not merely as the focal point of that lecture but also as a device for making a transition from Italian life of the early period to modern times. Logically, the next lecture in the series was that advertised as "Modern Sicilian Life." No full account of this lecture has been found; but, when Crawford was leaving New Orleans, a reporter asked him to comment on the Sicilian character and the Mafia. His reply probably included the basic points of the lecture he may never have delivered during the tour. "The Sicilians," remarked Crawford, "are the boldest, the strongest, the bravest and the most intelligent of any other Italians."[35] He pointed to the successful resistance of the Sicilians against the salt tax as an instance of their independence of character. The outstanding Sicilians he chose as examples were Crispi, Rudini, and Cardinal Rampolla. Although Crawford maintained that he did not know a great deal about the Mafia in Sicily, he defined it as "a sort of universal organized opposition to all government whatever, and for the sole advantage of Sicilians."[36]

In "Pope Leo XIII and the Vatican," the fourth lecture dealing with Italian life, Crawford continued his discussion of modern times, focusing attention on a great contemporary figure against a background of the past. It was a topic which he was well qualified to discuss because of his long residence in Italy, his friendship with officials of the Vatican, and his intensive study of Italian history. Moreover, the subject had been in his mind for considerable time. Almost two years before the lecture tour, he had published in the *Century Magazine* an article entitled "Pope Leo XIII and His Household." Crawford probably used this article as the basis for his analysis of "Pope Leo XIII and the Vatican," and in turn the lecture served as the essence of the chapter on "Leo the Thirteenth" in *Ave Roma Immortalis,* which he was completing during the lecture tour.

There can be little question that the address on "Pope Leo XIII and the Vatican" was the most carefully prepared, the best organized, and the most striking of the Italian series. In preparing for it, Crawford divided his material into three rather distinct topics. He began with a sketch of the political conditions in Europe during the nineteenth century, paying particular attention to the connections between European politics and the Catholic Church. He concluded this section of his address by establishing a contrast between the work of Pius IX and that of Leo XIII, suggesting that with the death of Pius IX an unprogressive era ended in Rome. Into this frame of reference, Crawford fitted the second portion of his lecture, which consisted largely of a biographical sketch of Pope Leo XIII and an elaborate description of the daily routine of the pontiff. If one can judge from newspaper accounts, it was this part of Crawford's speech that was most admired by his hearers.

The third and last section of the lecture contained an analysis of the Pope's official life with respect to both religious and diplomatic activities. Near the end of the lecture Crawford emphasized the Pope's disinclination to interfere with the consciences of American Catholics in the matter of voting. Stressir the Pope's efforts to formulate a reasoned defense of orderly society against radical political theories, Crawford concluded: "Leo XIII is at the head of a great body of human thought. He will not be there when the battle between anarchy and order is fought, but when the time comes the roads such men as he have planned are open and broad for the tread of many feet. The sword they forged is for use by many hands and they themselves in their graves have their share in the victories that humanize mankind."[37]

Crawford's audiences must have felt that they were listening to a man who could at one moment take them inside the Vatican to watch the Pope as he followed his daily routine and at the next moment enable them to grasp the significance of the pontiff's actions in historical perspective. As Crawford himself said, it was his most popular lecture.[38] Wherever he delivered it, the audience and the press responded in flattering terms. When he decided to use it for single engagements in preference to the other lectures, he undoubtedly made the best choice.

Second only to the address on the Pope in popularity and in frequency of delivery was the lecture on "Early Experiences in India and Mr. Isaacs." It appealed strongly to the thousands of Crawford's readers who were interested not only in the novels but also in the man who wrote them. Brief sketches of the novelist's career had appeared in various newspapers and periodicals, but never before had the autobiographical background of his first novel, *Mr. Isaacs,* been narrated in such detail as Crawford presented to his listeners during his lecture tour. In the lecture, he recounted the events which led to his journey to India, his experiences in Allahabad as editor of the *Indian Herald,* and the circumstances which prompted Sam Ward to suggest the writing of *Mr. Isaacs.* While discussing his adventures in India, Crawford described several unusual feats of Indian magic which he had witnessed, and he acknowledged that for portions of his novel he was indebted to the writings of Madame Blavatsky. His conclusion, which seemed fully evident from the content of the lecture, was that "there was very little fiction that was absolutely destitute of facts."[39]

V

The critical enthusiasm which his lectures received during his tour across the country must have been a source of great satisfaction to Crawford. A man of commanding presence, Crawford made a good impression when he stepped on the platform. As one reporter noted, "Personally Crawford is a handsome, impressive man. He is tall but so broad shouldered that he does not give the impression of height. He has strong, well-shaped hands. . . . His eyes are frank and pleasant, and his smile is ready and illuminating."[40] His delivery was not dramatic, yet it was often called eloquent in its simplicity and straightforwardness. The reviewer for the *Chronicle* (March 29, 1898) observed:

> He is not a magnetic speaker, for he is cool, unimpassioned and deliberate. But he has a fine presence, unstudied gestures, expressive hands, a good voice magnificently handled, an open face that changes expression with every sentence, and, above all, a stock of fine, pure English, and an elevated, though simple, style that places him high among lecturers. His sentences are perfectly formed and balanced, and there is not a single excrescence left unpolished. Yet he is never elocutionary. He is at all times a master of English prose, with a wide and deep vocabulary, and a faculty of vivid, terse description.

Crawford was an effective lecturer, a good talker, a superb story-teller but by no means a professional entertainer, cushion-thumper, or dramatic orator.

In a very real sense the praise that he received as a lecturer helped to wipe out the memory of the blunt remarks which the critics had made in 1892 about his readings and more recently their brutal treatment of his play, *Doctor Claudius*. Even more pleasing to Crawford must have been the realization that thousands had come to hear him lecture because they felt he was, as the San Francisco *Chronicle* said, "the first novelist of America."[41] From coast to coast his reception was a convincing demonstration of Crawford's immense popularity with the readers of fiction in America. His tour was indeed a personal triumph.

There were other results of the long trip across the continent. The financial returns were considerable; but of much greater consequence was the inference, which was inescapable to Crawford, that there was in America a large audience responsive to historical subjects—particularly to Italian historical subjects. During the past several years Crawford had become increasingly interested in Italian history, and the lecture tour showed him plainly that there was a market for additional literary effort in that direction. Crawford was beginning to tire of writing novels; and thus, by helping to channel his literary activities toward a new field, the lectures became a turning point in his career.

Crawford's achievements, however, were not reached without serious cost to himself. From his New Orleans appearances to the conclusion of the tour, he suffered from a lung ailment that became steadily worse; and, when he returned to Italy in May, 1898, his health had been permanently injured. Months later he wrote Major Pond that, if they ever again undertook such a tour, he would "take a patent reversible, india-rubber coffin which can be used as a bath, overcoat, or pulpit, and can be hermetically sealed so as to bring the lecturer home on ice from the point at which he dies!"[42] Despite his light tone, one surmises that Crawford knew he would never lecture again.

CHAPTER 8

Ventures into History

I

TO BE SUCCESSFUL, Crawford once wrote, the professional man of letters must possess "a sensitive and tactful appreciation of the public taste at a given time—an appreciation more than half unconscious, perhaps, but ... probably the only really indispensable element."[1] Few writers have exhibited this quality in a greater degree than Crawford. In the closing years of the nineteenth century, however, even the most insensitive author would have perceived that the taste of the reading public strongly favored literature dealing with some phase of history. The enormous popularity of Lew Wallace's *Ben Hur* (published in 1880 but not widely read until after 1882) as a novel and afterwards as a play set the pace for the historical novel dealing with religious themes. Anthony Hope's *The Prisoner of Zenda* (1894), also fabulously successful first as a novel and then as a play, established the pattern for the subsequent sword-and-cloak romances about European nobility framed in castles of long ago. Nor was the vogue of history confined exclusively to imaginative literature; there was a corresponding demand for non-fiction books about famous places and celebrated personages of the past.

The strength of Crawford's reaction to this popular enthusiasm for history is evidenced by the fact that, despite continual ill health, in two years (1898-1900) he published four works dealing with history: *Ave Roma Immortalis* (1898), *Via Crucis* (1899), *In the Palace of the King* (1900), and *The Rulers of the South* (1900); but it would be a mistake to assume that Crawford was merely catering to the contemporary taste. Actually, Crawford possessed a genuine interest in history; and, as he pursued his studies in Italian history, his interest intensified until the writing of novels became for him distinctly secondary to the preparation of the great historical work with which he intended to crown his literary career. This shift of emphasis from the contemporary scene to the past, from fiction to history, represents the most important aspect of the last decade of his life.

Despite illness and exhaustion from lecturing, Crawford resumed literary work shortly after his return to Italy in May, 1898. When the proof sheets of *Ave Roma Immortalis* began to arrive, he found that the seven persons he had employed to read them were unable to do the work. Crawford's manuscripts were usually written in a very fine but extremely neat autograph. Often a single page contained from nine to eleven hundred words, the total being indicated at the top of the page by small dots, one for each hundred words. Readers unaccustomed to Crawford's handwriting would have found it difficult to read under the best conditions, but the manuscript of *Ave Roma Immortalis*, which had been partly dictated and partly written on Crawford's knee in trains and in odd moments under hotel gas lights, was in very poor condition. Consequently, Crawford was forced to read most of the proof sheets himself, and it was not until October that the two volumes were ready. A month later, handsomely bound in red cloth and abundantly illustrated with maps, photographs, and drawings, the work was published by Macmillan.

Crawford in the meanwhile had virtually completed *Via Crucis* which he had begun while reading the chronicles of Rome in preparation for his lectures. Although the general subject matter of this novel owed something to Lew Wallace's *Ben Hur*, the choice of the title was probably influenced by the extraordinarily popular *Quo Vadis* by Henry Sienkiewicz. Crawford's novel of the twelfth-century crusade, like its predecessors, was permeated by the glamor of historical religious conflict and the affirmation of Christian belief. When the crusading adventures from England to Jerusalem have been completed, the hero, Gilbert Warde, has finally "learned and understood that the cause of God lies not buried among stones in any city, not even in the most holy city of all; for the place of Christ's suffering is in men's sinful hearts, and the glory of his resurrection is the saving of a soul from death to everlasting life, in refreshment and light and peace."[2] Despite the moral lesson which was explicitly stated at the end of the novel, Crawford would have argued that his purpose had been merely to amuse and that the instruction was only incidental.

After he completed *Via Crucis*, Crawford expected to work in the Vatican archives on a biography of Pope Leo XIII; and, as he wrote to Mrs. Gardner, "I have the Life of Christ before me, and I may go to the East this winter in my little boat and spend a long time in Jerusalem with the Franciscans.... Then there is Constantinople, and I may meet my illustrator there, and work with him for a month, on the old ground. I shall not mind the loneliness of another three thousand miles in the schooner."[3] None of these projects was ever completed. After making very slow progress with the life of Pope Leo XIII, Crawford eventually dropped it. As for his other plans, the journey to Jerusalem and the life of Christ never materialized; and his poor health in 1898 would not permit him to travel either to Constantinople or to America.

In the spring of 1899, the attacks of asthma from which Crawford suffered subsided enough for him to accept an offer to write a historical play. Early in October of the preceding year, Liebler and Company had produced an adaptation of Hall Caine's novel, *The Christian*. This play, in which Viola Allen played the leading role, proved to be an outstanding success, but as a member of the company later recalled, it became evident that

> eventually we'd want something sure-fire for Miss Allen to follow it with—something so spectacular—and expensive, of course—that it couldn't miss. . . . A little hasty research developed that, for sheer lavishness of background, the period of the free-for-all spending match at the Field of the Cloth of Gold was about the world's record—and it also gave us a crack at figures like Don John of Austria. A little thought—very little—suggested that great romancer, F. Marion Crawford, was the man to do that background picture.[4]

George C. Tyler, a director of the company, then approached Crawford about writing a play for Viola Allen which would rival the dramatic version of *Ben Hur* then scheduled for production in the fall of 1899. Tyler went to "Villa Crawford," negotiated the financial arrangements with Crawford, and acquainted him with the personalities of the cast which would act the play. After discussing the matter with Tyler and later with Viola Allen, Crawford decided that *In the Palace of the King*, which he had begun in the summer of 1897, would meet every requirement. Actually two works eventually resulted from these conferences, a play and a novel, both with the same title. As a novel, *In the Palace of the King* was deposited for copyright on January 13, 1900;[5] and a week later the copyright performance of the work as a play was given in London.

In some respects the relationship between the play and the novel is difficult to determine. After *In the Palace of the King* became a success on Broadway, Crawford was quoted in the New York *Daily Tribune* (January 26, 1901): "I do not believe in dramatization [of novels]; it is an artistic mistake. I think an author should not be hampered, in writing a book, by having to consider whether it will dramatize well." He added categorically that his play was "not a dramatization" of the novel, and he asserted that the "scenario" of the play was written before he composed a line of the book. Evidently Crawford desired to give the public an impression that he wrote a play and afterwards a novel and that the two works were independent of each other. Strictly speaking, the play may not be a dramatization of the written work of fiction; nevertheless, there is a close connection between them. With the exception of several of his earliest volumes, Crawford always worked from a detailed outline which he prepared in advance of the actual work of composition. The starting point, in the case of *In the Palace of the King*, was a story which Crawford devised to fulfill the requirements of Liebler and Company. As the first phase of composition, he prepared his customary detailed outline; by expanding it, he produced the scenario of the play and then the novel. The basic conception thus was the same for both works, although the scenario of the play did precede the actual composition of the novel; and, since the script of the play was prepared from the scenario, Crawford was correct in saying that the stage version was not a dramatization of the novel. What really distinguishes *In the Palace of the King* from Crawford's other works is the fact that both novel and play adhere strictly to the dramatic unities. Crawford believed firmly that the historical novel must be as dramatic as possible.

To insure that the dramatic version of *In the Palace of the King* should not repeat the failure of *Doctor Claudius*, Crawford spared neither trouble nor expense. The specific task of turning the scenario into the acting script was entrusted to Lorimer Stoddard, the talented son of Richard Henry Stoddard. In January, 1900, when Crawford came to the United States to arrange for the copyright of the novel, he discussed the play with Stoddard; and when Crawford returned to Italy in February he felt pleased with the selection of Stoddard as his assistant.

Doctor Claudius had been produced in New York without the advantages of trial performances in other cities. Neither Crawford nor Liebler and Company was willing to take such a risk with *In the Palace of the King;* and, as events proved, it was fortunate that they took this precaution. The initial performance was given at the dedication of the Richmond Theatre in North Adams, Massachusetts, on September 17, 1900. Although the audience received the piece enthusiastically, Tyler knew that extensive revisions would be necessary before the play could be presented in New York. After he was informed of the difficulties, Crawford left Italy and joined the company in the middle of October to supervise personally the alterations; and, until the end of November, he traveled with the company working with virtually no rest to get the script in satisfactory condition. Finally, the play opened at the Republic Theatre in New York City on December 31, 1900. The production was instantly popular; Viola Allen's reputation as a leading actress was greatly strengthened; and Crawford's long-cherished ambition to become a successful dramatist was realized.

In the final versions, the plots of both the novel and the play differ in no essential respects. In each Crawford presents a wide range of individualized, credible historical personages against a colorful background of royal pageantry during the reign of Philip II. The story, which is compressed into a single day's time, deals with the successful efforts of the heroine, Maria Dolores de Mendoza, assisted by her blind sister, Inez, to marry Don John of Austria, despite the intrigues of rival court factions. In the play, the episodes leading to the marriage are slightly altered to heighten the dramatic effect and to emphasize the role of Dolores (played by Viola Allen). The novel, though somewhat of a *tour de force* because Crawford had never been in Spain, is the best of Crawford's historical romances and certainly must be considered one of his most carefully written works. For action, suspense, subtle characterization, and effective use of period costume, both play and novel are in the best tradition of sword-and-cloak literature.

II

In the memoirs of his experiences with Liebler and Company, George C. Tyler remarked that "you didn't realize just how wonderful a person F. Marion Crawford was till you knew how sick he was."[6] Tyler added that Crawford "was a terrific and conscientious worker and yet all the time he was on the verge of collapse." After his lecture tour in 1897-98, Crawford never regained his full strength; but there were many times when Crawford believed there was notable improvement in his condition. Although his trouble was often called asthma, it was probably tuberculosis.

Poor health severely restricted his activities and forced him to remain in Italy longer than he had in previous years. His wife continued to spend much of her time away from "Villa Crawford." When he was there, he was usually too much occupied with his work or too ill, or unwilling, to participate in her social engagements. Crawford enjoyed the company of his children, particularly that of Eleanor and Clare; but he and his wife seldom saw each other. Adult companionship he found in two persons with whom he exchanged confidences during the last decade of his life. Both became associated with Crawford's ventures into history.

One such person was Vittoria Colonna, whom Crawford met a few months before he began to write *In the Palace of the King*. Her father was Prince Marcantonio Colonna, head of the most distinguished family in Rome. On her mother's side, she was descended from William Lock of Norbury Park, England. Her aunt, the Duchess Sforza (neé Vittoria Colonna), had been the "real-life" model for the Corona d'Astrardente of *Saracinesca*. Years later Vittoria Colonna, then the Duchess of Sermoneta, recalled the first time she saw Crawford:

His sister, Mrs. Winthrop Chanler . . . arranged to take me to the beautiful Villa Albani, and Crawford came to meet me there, his romantic nature and love of Roman history prompting him to make the acquaintance of a girl called Vittoria Colonna. I still remember the charm of that May afternoon . . . listening to the fascinating conversation of a type of man I had never met before in my short and sheltered life. A friendship sprang up between us that afternoon which lasted until his death. . . .[7]

Although she was much younger than he, she gradually began to occupy a position in his life somewhat analogous to that which Mrs. Gardner and, to a lesser degree, Mrs. Jones, had filled in America during the 1890's. With Vittoria Colonna, Crawford discussed his work almost as freely as he had with Mrs. Gardner. Vittoria Colonna, moreover, was in a position to assist him directly by using her influence to secure him access to her father's magnificent library. In May, 1900, for example, Crawford wrote her:

You spoke of some letters of the Admiral, Marcantonio, referring to the Battle of Lepanto, and you seemed to think it possible that there may be in your archives something from the hand of Don John of Austria. I wonder if your Father would allow a copy of these letters, or even one of them, to appear in my short history of Southern Italy and Sicily. Unfortunately I have not the advantage of knowing your Father. Is it too much to beg you to ask for me?[8]

The request was immediately granted; and, for the remainder of Crawford's life, she continued to help him obtain material for his history of Rome. They corresponded with great frequency, Crawford often writing her at intervals of a few days.

Of Crawford's other friend during these years, there is only scant information available beyond the comments Crawford made in his letters. Henry Brokman was born at Copenhagen, Denmark, May 10, 1868. Educated at the Academy of Copenhagen, he seems to have achieved recognition first by his pencil sketches and later by landscape painting. As a young man, he went to Italy; and, because he was fascinated by the brilliance of Mediterranean coloring, he remained most of his life in that vicinity. From Paris to Cairo he was known among artistic circles; but, although he exhibited in Frederick Kettel's New York studios, in the Royal Academy of Copenhagen, in the Academy of Munich, and in the Société Nationale des Beaux Arts at Paris, where he received a prize for his painting, *Le porte de Sorrente*, he never achieved widespread fame. Fourteen years younger than Crawford, Brokman survived his friend by many years. He died in 1933.

Although Crawford probably met Brokman shortly after returning to Italy in 1898, their association was not close until the winter of 1900 when Crawford, partly for reasons of health, decided to go to Sicily to write *The Rulers of the South*. He asked Brokman to illustrate the volumes. For a number of years Brokman and Crawford spent a large part of the summers together at Torre San Nicola. From there Crawford wrote Mrs. Gardner describing Brokman:

> My friend [Brokman] is with me, as he often is at this time of year. You probably did not know I had a friend! He is a Danish artist of great talent, about whom there has been much talk in Vienna and Paris and he cares for nothing but art and the sea, so we get on very well together. He was out sketching the other day and took the photograph I enclose—not for its artistic value but that you may have some little idea of the place I like best and in which I shall perhaps end my days. . . .
>
> Except Dante, I read little except Greek now, and chiefly the wonderful poetry of the vast Anthology. But please do not think me a pedant. I am no great scholar—it is too late—but I have at least the pleasure of reading easily and understanding. And I have it all to myself, for my friend has forgotten the little he ever learned of the language and thinks I am perfectly mad to go about with a score of Greek volumes—instead of learning Norse and studying the Heimskringle, which he says is the only poetry worth reading! So we disagree amiably—and he reads the news and tells me about motor car accidents and politics.[9]

Brokman and the tower, a romantic figure and a romantic place, were closely associated in Crawford's mind; he frequently coupled them in letters and, once, in a short story.[10] Possessing in common a fondness for the Mediterranean coasts, the open sea, and the stirring past of Italy, Crawford and Brokman strengthened their friendship by a sincere admiration for each other's art and by a tacit agreement never to interfere with the work each was pursuing. Few men knew Crawford as did Brokman; indeed, it may be said that he was the only close friend Crawford ever had among his own sex.

Throughout the winter and spring of 1900, Crawford devoted long hours to *The Rulers of the South;* and, when the work was finally completed early in August, he wrote a sincere dedication from Torre San Nicola: "To my friend Henry Brokman, to whose genius I am indebted for the drawings in this book, and whose companionship in Sicily and the South has lightened many labours." In writing the book, Crawford, as he said, wished "to give a simple and true account of the successive dominations by which Sicily and the south of Italy have sometimes prospered and sometimes suffered from the days of the Greek settlers down to the establishment of the house of Aragon."[11] However, his letter to Vittoria Colonna, asking permission to quote from the manuscripts of Don John of Austria, seems to indicate that Crawford originally intended to continue the narrative so far as the Battle of Lepanto (1571).[12] Instead, he virtually ended his history with the Peace of Cambrai (1529), and appended a chapter about the organization and activities of the Sicilian Mafia which he had already discussed in his novel, *Corleone.* The reason for inserting this concluding section, which disturbs the artistic unity of the book, appears to have been the popular interest—shared by Crawford—in the famous criminal society. As a history, *The Rulers of the South* is not a scholar's textbook; rather, like *Ave Roma Immortalis*, it is a beautifully written historical narrative designed to stimulate the intellectual curiosity of the general reader.

III

On February 7, 1901, Crawford wrote Mrs. Gardner from New York a brief resumé of his activities since the completion of *The Rulers of the South:* "I was here—but partly in the West [Chicago]—in the autumn [to revise the play, *In the Palace of the King*], and then ran back to Rome, to get my wife, who wished to come out. After ten days spent here, she is now gone to Washington to stay with her aunt [Mrs. Hobson]. She will return to Italy without me, early next month. I shall stay to finish some work—a new play."[13] The fact that Crawford would return to Italy merely to escort his wife back to the United States indicates that domestic tensions in the Crawford family were beginning to ease somewhat—an inference confirmed by Crawford's sister.[14]

In the same letter Crawford spoke of his immediate plans for literary work. He wrote: "The demon of work... is leading me to your favourite Venice. I am going to publish a little mediaeval

novel of Venetian life next autumn, and I hope to publish a
rather serious book—less dry than the Rulers of the South—on
three epochs in Venetian history in 1902." The play he mentioned
earlier, the novel of Venetian life, and the serious book were all
concerned with Italian history. The choice of his subjects reflected
the extent of his commitment to historical writing of one kind
or another.

The "new play" was *Francesca da Rimini.* In January, 1901,
while Viola Allen's performances of *In the Palace of the King*
were being applauded by both critics and audiences, Sarah Bernhardt requested Crawford to write a play for her. He was then
writing a historical novel which he planned to call "The Harvest
of the Sword." It was to deal, Crawford later remarked, "with
the closing scenes of that great struggle which was carried on
in Italy between the Papal party and the Imperialists, between
the Guelf and the Ghibelline";[15] that is, the story was to have
treated thirteenth-century Italian history and, more particularly,
Florentine history. In the novel Crawford intended to use the
story of Paolo and Francesca as simply one dramatic episode.
Instead, he expanded it into a play for the great French actress.
The other two literary projects mentioned in Crawford's letter
were also historical. The "little mediaeval novel of Venetian life"
appeared as *Marietta: A Maid of Venice.*[16] The "serious book"
on Venice eventually was called *Salve Venetia: Gleanings from
Venetian History,* but it was not to be published, as Crawford
hoped, in 1902.[17]

Early in the spring of 1901, Crawford returned to Italy; but
he did not go directly to Venice as he had planned; instead, he
remained at "Villa Crawford" to finish his play and to work on
his Florentine novel in his familiar tower-study which was described
by an acquaintance:

> There were whole volumes of closely written notes, giving the
> histories and genealogies of all the great families living in that
> city [Florence] during the times of which he will treat [that is,
> the thirteenth century]; there were numerous copies of old maps
> of the city, showing the roads and locating the important palaces
> and public buildings as they then existed, and extracts from records
> of those days, and even photographs of some of the paintings which
> have a place in Florentine annals. In addition to all this, Mr. Craw-
> ford said he had collected and read sixty books, many of them old
> and rare, which were written during the period or about it. "And
> I am not done yet," he added.[18]

Most of this research proved futile because "The Harvest of the
Sword" was never published and probably never finished. In June,

Crawford left Sorrento to go to Venice to meet Joseph Pennell, who had come to make the drawings for the history of Venice.

It was probably Sir Frederick Macmillan, not Crawford, who was responsible for the selection of Joseph Pennell as the artist to illustrate *Salve Venetia*. Pennell had established his reputation as a popular illustrator during the 1880's by his drawings for *Scribner's* and later for the *Century*. More recently he had worked for Macmillan on the *Highways and Byways* series. Early in 1901, Macmillan commissioned him to illustrate a second and more elaborate series which was to begin with Maurice Hewlett's *A Road in Tuscany* and to include Crawford's *Salve Venetia*. For this purpose Pennell went to Italy in the spring of 1901 and again in 1902, making sketches for Crawford's book in the summer and fall of both years. From the beginning of their association, they were mutually antagonistic. Crawford, who was probably disappointed that his friend Henry Brokman had not been employed as illustrator, was not inclined to be tactful; on the other hand, Pennell seems to have been contemptuous of expatriates and resentful of any lack of respect for his own art.[19]

The two men were together in Venice only a few days, for Crawford was suddenly called to London to discuss *Francesca da Rimini* with Sarah Bernhardt. After he had read the play to her, it was said that she became "most enthusiastic over it, walked the floor in excitement, saw situations, extemporized scenes,... accepted it on the spot and signed the contract for its production."[20] It was probably at her suggestion that he asked Marcel Schwob if he would undertake to prepare a French version of the play.[21] When Schwob, then in bad health and living on the island of Jersey, agreed tentatively to do the work, Crawford immediately brought the manuscript to him. Pierre Champion, the translator's friend and biographer, later published Schwob's reaction: "Le 29 juin, Marcel Schwob a lu 'la pièce qui est excellente et que j'ai grand plaisir à traduire. Ce sera un travail facile et que je ferai *bien....* Sa pièce est très belle, et je suis persuadé que Sarah la jouera. Ce serait un rôle admirable.' "[22] When it was finished, Crawford was delighted with the translation and part of its excellence he attributed to the fact that, as he said, "in writing the play for Sarah Bernhardt I was conscious that I was thinking in French half the time."[23] Crawford wrote a preface in French for Schwob's work when it was published in 1902.[24]

After giving the play to Schwob, Crawford returned to Italy where during the remainder of the summer he worked on *Marietta*. Although it does not belong to the sword-and-cloak type of historical novel (represented in Crawford's work by *In the Palace of*

the King), Marietta is a historical novel. Crawford claimed that
his story about the efforts of the Dalmatian waif, Zorzi Ballarin,
to establish himself as a glassmaker and to marry Marietta Bero-
viero, the daughter of his employer, was based upon an authentic
tradition, although he admitted that he had used a "novelist's
privilege" in altering the time sequence and in introducing fictitious
characters.[25] The leading figures belong to the artisan class, highly
respected citizens, but not, like the characters of *In the Palace of
the King,* members of the nobility. The principal setting, moreover,
is not the court, but an artist's workshop; in fact, *Marietta* suggests
comparison with *Marzio's Crucifix* rather than with the Spanish
romance. In the two novels of Italian life, Crawford firmly
grounded, with skilled craftsmanship, a plausible theme in a
setting which he knew from actual experience, and he interpreted
sensitive figures with whom he was in sympathy. *Marzio's Crucifix,*
possessing both an admirable fusion of symbol and plot and a
penetrating character-study, seems a better novel than the Venetian
romance. Although *Marietta* was very favorably reviewed by the
critics and sold well,[26] it represents the beginning of a decline
in the quality of Crawford's fiction. A few years later, this fact
was to become increasingly evident.

After he had corrected the proofs of *Marietta,* published by
Macmillan in the fall of 1901, Crawford made a brief visit to
New York and then returned to Italy where he began the novel
Cecilia. His writing, however, was interrupted in March, 1902,
when Sarah Bernhardt telegraphed Crawford to come to Paris
at once for immediate rehearsals of *Francesca da Rimini.* To
protect his copyrights, Crawford hastily ordered the printing of
twelve copies of his original English manuscript.[27]

Crawford remained in Paris until after the first performance
of *Francesca da Rimini* on April 22, 1902. Mme. Bernhardt, in the
title role, was supported by two capable French actors, Pierre
Magnier as Paolo Malatesta, and Edouard de Max as the deformed
husband, Giovanni. Sarah Bernhardt was acclaimed, as she probably would have been in almost any part, but the play itself
was only a qualified success.

The principal defect of the play was Crawford's preference
for historical accuracy over poetic tradition. The action of the
prologue of Crawford's play takes place in 1275 and deals with
Francesca's discovery on her wedding night of the deception which
has been practiced upon her. Fourteen years have elapsed when
the curtain rises again. Francesca, now a middle-aged woman,
has been deceiving her husband ever since the marriage; and her
paramour, Paolo, has also been unfaithful to his lawful wife. Thus,

instead of wronged innocence and ill-fated love, Crawford's audiences saw a drama of adultery which elicited sympathy for the injured husband. This treatment of the theme was consistent with Crawford's moralistic bias, but it did not make for a successful play about the Dante story. Sarah Bernhardt's biographer remarks that the role was not a sympathetic one.[28] Although after twenty-five performances, she transferred the play to the Garrick Theatre in London, critical reaction there merely intensified the unfavorable comments made about the Paris production. Crawford, however, continued to think well of his work.

After *Francesca da Rimini*, Crawford wrote no more plays dealing with historical subjects, and almost all of his subsequent fiction was concerned with contemporary life. He probably felt that the vogue of the historical novel and play had temporarily run its course. Since his main interest continued to focus upon his historical research, he paid less and less attention to the quality of his fiction. The Duchess of Sermoneta, who knew him well during these years, noted that Crawford referred to his novels "contemptuously as his 'pot boilers,' never wished me to read them, and . . . told me he did not even bother to correct the proofs."[29]

Cecilia: A Story of Modern Rome, which Crawford finished August 19, 1902, at Isola di S. Pietro, Isles of the Sirens, exhibits the weaknesses of his later novels. Upon his arrival in New York for his annual visit in the fall, Crawford was quoted by a reporter for the New York *Daily Tribune* (October 29, 1902):

> The young girl [Cecilia Palladio] is a modern heroine, who is under the impression that she has existed in a former state as the last of the vestal virgins, and she dreams about what she believes to have been her former existence. These dreams end by having a great deal of influence on her daily life. In this imaginary former state she had, of course, taken vows, as a modern nun would, and in her present and actual life she falls in love. Besides the dramatic situation in which she is placed by the story itself, there is the conflict going on within her all the time between these purely imaginary vows, which seem real, and the natural instinct of the living woman. Many of the characters are portraits of persons residing in Rome on the very spot where the vestal virgins are supposed to have lived.

Both the psychological conflict and the dramatic situation fail to be convincing. For credible motivation and characterization Crawford substituted "auto-suggestion," a mechanical plot, and characters who move like puppets on the end of a string. The compelling inference is that Crawford hastily concocted a melodrama with little consideration for its effect upon his ultimate literary reputation; nevertheless, the novel sold close to 100,000 copies.[30]

During the winter of 1902-03 Crawford engaged in a number of activities in New York. Early in December, he delivered an address at the opening of the exhibition of Italian books at the Grolier Club. His lecture, entitled "Italian Literature from the Thirteenth to the Seventeenth Century," was principally concerned with Dante, Petrarch, Boccaccio, and Boiardo. For some reason he failed to spend the Christmas holidays with Julia Ward Howe and Maud Elliott in Boston; instead, he wrote them a short note from New York promising to come later. He talked with Nellie Melba and went to the theater more often than he had in previous years. Crawford wrote the Duchess of Sermoneta: "Duse is acting here in d'Annunzio's plays and as a matter of duty I am going to them all, 'Gioconda,' 'Città morta' and 'Francesca.' The *literature* of them is beautiful but they are not dramatic and it is only Duse's popularity that keeps the audience tolerably quiet through the performance."[31]

Of his literary activities that winter, he wrote the Duchess: "I have just finished a modern English play, which is to be brought out next autumn in London by Martin Harvey and Miss Fay Davis. I wonder if you have ever seen either of them act. They are the best of the young—the *really* young actors. I spent most of yesterday afternoon with Fay Davis. She has great charm, is as fresh as a spring morning and perfectly unaffected."[32]

Martin Harvey, an English actor, had recently completed an engagement in New York as Count Skariatine in a dramatic version of Crawford's *A Cigarette-Maker's Romance*.[33] The novelette had been adapted for the stage by Charles Hannan and presented in London shortly after *In the Palace of the King* opened in New York.[34] Though he received a royalty for his rights to the story, Crawford had no direct connection with the production. Since Harvey, who specialized in the "character" role, had found the work admirably suited to his talents, he probably asked Crawford to write a similar piece for him. Miss N. de Silva, who played Vjera in *A Cigarette-Maker's Romance*, usually took the leading feminine role in Harvey's productions; but he may have desired to add Fay Davis to his company, and for this reason asked Crawford to create a role for her. Fay Davis, a Boston girl who had made her theatrical debut in London on November 5, 1895, as Zoë Nuggetson in R. C. Carton's *The Squire of Dames*, had also given "recitations." The play, however, which Crawford said he had written for Harvey and Fay Davis was never produced and never published. The only tangible literary result of Crawford's work during the winter of 1902-03 is the long short story, *Man Overboard!*[35] Although this story contains a part which conceivably could have been adapted for Harvey, it is very unlikely that it is a version of the lost play because there is no part for Fay Davis.

IV

Although Crawford had been working on his history of Venice since February, 1901, he had by no means finished it when he returned to Italy in the spring of 1903. While he continued his research in Venice during the summer, Charles Hall Garrett visited him. Later Garrett recorded his impressions:

> I found myself in the presence of a gracious man, who himself answered his electric bell; over six feet tall, broad-shouldered, with a slight stoop, large-limbed, athletically built, with a well-moulded head, a short, thick mustache, and closely cropped hair; smoking a brier pipe with a curved-bone mouth-piece. Preceding me with long strides across a large, sparsely furnished room, he politely insisted on my occupying an ample leather chair, while he overlapped a small straight-backed one, saying he preferred it, and toyed with a pen-staff on his desk, with which he has written all of his novels. On one side of the room were hung fencing-foils, and on the floor, in good order, lay Indian clubs and dumb-bells with which he exercises regularly, alternating with fencing with the best master of that art in the locality where he may be.[36]

By this time Crawford appears to have at least temporarily recovered his health, yet he was so sensitive about the subject that Garrett's reference to his "slight stoop" greatly annoyed him.

To Garrett, Crawford talked frankly about his studies for *Salve Venetia* and outlined the plan of the book. Garrett quoted Crawford as having said:

> I have read several hundred books, as well as many manuscripts, selected from thousands. Some histories of Venice comprise fifty volumes. I have not read modern ones, preferring to delve into the past. Most manuscript data is to be found in the Library of St. Marks and in the possession of the oldest families of Venice, but instituting a search of my own and keeping a sharp lookout on old-book sales, I unearthed many important tomes, as well as letters exchanged between ambassadors. Without attempting to write exhaustively on Venice, I have divided its history into three important periods, connecting them with short, comprehensive chapters, and prefacing the whole by one on early Venice—the oppression of those who were to become Venetians and raise the

most beautiful city in the world, by the Huns and Lombards who drove them from the mainland. The first of these periods is the fourteeenth century, dealing with the Great Conspiracies; the next the Renaissance, embracing the epoch of the development of its art and the wars of Emperors Charles VI. and Francis I.; the third deals with the eighteenth century, the decadence of Venice, the end of the Venetian Republic, and its final crushing by Napoleon I.[37]

These remarks indicate that in the past few months Crawford had made considerable progress on the history, but another year was to pass before the manuscript would be complete. Because of other demands upon his time, Crawford could hardly have been expected to work more rapidly than he did. The winter months were usually occupied with the annual journey to New York to assist with the affairs of the Macmillan Company, and at least two months during the summer were required for the composition of the yearly novel for the fall book-trade. Crawford seldom had uninterrupted time for historical research.

The novel which Crawford wrote before returning to New York in the autumn of 1903 was *The Heart of Rome: A Tale of the "Lost Water."* The story, which is certainly not one of Crawford's best, deals with the efforts of a young architect, Marino Malipieri, to find the "lost water" which flows beneath the foundations of an ancient Roman palace, the property of a noble family ruined by the Italian financial panic of 1888. When the water is finally located, the architect and the young girl whom he loves are trapped by the rising of the water in an underground cavern, which contains a hidden treasure. Their escape and subsequent marriage conclude the narrative. Even more than *Cecilia,* this novel appears to have been carelessly written and unduly "spun out," yet like the former, it sold well.[38]

During the following year, 1904, an event occurred which changed the direction of Crawford's historical work and to a marked degree influenced the course of his subsequent career. Accompanied by Horace Thompson Carpenter, an American painter and illustrator, Crawford left New York in the spring and returned to Rome. There he obtained permission for Carpenter, who had been engaged to illustrate the next two Crawford novels, to make sketches in the Colonna palace; and while the artist worked, Crawford talked to Professor Giuseppe Tomassetti, the archivist of the Colonna library. Tomassetti, who had been working in the archives for more than thirty years, had assembled a quantity of manuscripts, documents, and letters dealing with the history of Rome from the thirteenth to the sixteenth century. These he had previously offered to place at Crawford's disposal, but the latter had declined on the grounds that his literary reputation had been chiefly gained through fiction and that there were others better qualified to utilize the documents. Nevertheless, he was greatly tempted; and, when Tomassetti repeated his proposal a second time, Crawford accepted it eagerly.

Carpenter, who was present during Crawford's conversations with Tomassetti, later wrote an account of their discussions. Carpenter said that the final agreement between the two men was reached sometime afterwards on board the *Alda* while Crawford, his daughter, Clare, and the artist were sailing to Gaeta. After remarking that the contract "practically turns into Mr. Crawford's hands unused and undreamed of material of the greatest importance in the mediaeval history of Italy which is to gradually develop into a tangible record that will be of inestimable value," Carpenter continued:

> And it was at Porto D'Anzio a day or two prior to our call at Gaeta that Professor Tommasato [sic] had boarded the "Alda," and the privileges and rights of the entire material of the Colonna archives much of which had been classified under Professor Tommasato's learned direction had been transferred to Mr. Crawford. Our dinner under the awning of the "Alda's" deck that evening served to perfection by an immaculately uniformed, well trained crew—for the splendid looking fellows of that particular crew are wonders whether as sailors or attendants—will not soon be forgotten.[39]

To Carpenter it seemed a moment "full of significance and of more than ordinary interest."

For Crawford, it was centainly a moment of great importance. The plan gave him the opportunity to write a serious, or formal—not "romantic"—history of medieval Rome during the period embraced by the thirteenth and sixteenth centuries; and, although he could not as yet enter the Colonna archives, through Tomassetti he would have access to the material in them, and he would have the services of a trained assistant. With regard to the significance of Tomassetti's offer, Crawford said:

> Few people are aware of the wealth of material to be found in the Colonna archives and those who are aware of it have not obtained access. That is why there are so many noticeable gaps in the histories by Profs. Re and Gregorovius, which their authors have done their best to fill in by apocryphal data or by mere force of visualization. These archives were kept long before Martino V.

began to build that pile which is known today as the Palazzo Colonna. A particularly important break occurs in the published records dealing with the early part of the thirteenth century, when Orsini of the Guelphs and Colonna of the Ghibelline alternated in seizing power.

Then, again, very little is known concerning the administration of Branealeone degli Andalo, Count of Casalecchio, who was called to Rome by the Colonne to the great discomfiture of Innocent IV. . . . Moreover, the following period, up to the middle of the fifteenth century, embraces such episodes as the attempt by the Popes to establish a temporal kingdom, the death of Clement VII., the fall of the republic, down to the time that Oddo Colonna became Pontiff with the title of Martino V. . . .

Now this Oddo Colonna was a most assiduous collector of his family's chronicles. Many of the Colonne who followed him emulated his worthy example, until today the archives of his house, covering certain periods of mediaeval Rome, are entirely unequaled, even by the store in the library of the Vatican. Certainly the various Government repositories contain no such archives.[40]

Crawford fully realized that the work would, as he said, "mean many volumes and a labor of years, and entail most careful judgment in selection and preparation, so that the narrative, while complete in itself, shall also adequately supplement what has already been written." Indeed, Crawford thought that the history of Rome would comprise ten volumes; and from this time until his death, the project represented the "great dream" of his life,[41] the work upon which, he believed, his literary reputation would ultimately rest.

Crawford's acceptance of Tomassetti's offer thus represented a firm commitment to an enormous task to which Crawford looked forward with great eagerness. During the last few years he had become increasingly convinced that the study and interpretation of history was of far greater importance than the writing of fiction to please the taste of American and English readers for Italian romances. Historical scholarship might not be financially rewarding, but it possessed more permanent value than the work of the "public amuser." The decision of course did not mean that he would write no more novels, for Crawford knew that for years to come he would still be obliged to produce the yearly novel that provided the income necessary to maintain "Villa Crawford."

The commitment to Roman history exerted an immediate influence upon several of Crawford's projects. To clear the way for beginning work on it, he hastened to complete the Venetian history, and he abandoned all thought of writing the life of Pope Leo XIII. Although very little had been done by Crawford, this biography of the Pope had been in the background of his thoughts since the lecture tour in 1898. It had been planned as a single volume, but the documents which Count Eduardo Soderini, who was an intimate friend of the Pope's personal secretary, and the Vatican authorities assembled for Crawford's use were so extensive that the originally conceived biography became a mere episode. Referring to this material, Crawford said: "In reality three works are possible from it: the life of Pious IX and of his successor [Leo XIII], and an elaborate historical work covering with marvelous detail the Church and political history as well as the intimate chronicles of the Vatican during their administrations."[42] Clearly Tomassetti's proposition forced Crawford to make a choice between the subjects afforded by the Vatican documents and by the history of Rome. The former could be handled relatively quickly, but Crawford's choice indicates that he felt the latter to be more significant and congenial.

V

During the summer of 1904, Crawford accomplished more than his usual amount of writing. In addition to completing *Salve Venetia* he wrote *Whosoever Shall Offend*[43] and began *Fair Margaret*.[44] These were the two novels for which Carpenter had come to Italy to make sketches. Carpenter, who admired Crawford, remained for most of the summer as a guest at "Villa Crawford." The visit of Marcel Schwob, however, was less pleasant. At Crawford's urging, Schwob arrived about the middle of June, accompanied by his Chinese servant and Flip, a Pekingese dog; but, although Schwob remained for a month, he was unhappy. The climate at Sorrento did not improve Schwob's health; he complained of having to dress formally for dinner; and he was irritated because he could not understand Italian. He wrote Mme. Schwob:

Elle ["Villa Crawford"] est admirablement située sur le sommet de la falaise surplombant la mer—l'air y est exquis. Mais on est loin de tout absolument. Voilà pourquoi je n'y pourrais pas rester. Car je ne verrais jamais rien, ni Naples, ni Pompéi. Madame Crawford est très aimable, les enfants charmants . . . [sic] J'ai une grande bibliothèque à ma portée—deux chambres dans l'une desquelles Ting couche sur un lit de camp. Seulement, comme je te le dis, c'est la vie de "château," plus ou moins, et je n'aime guère cela... *[sic]* j'ai très peur de m'ennuyer. Tout est réglé ici à l'heure et à la minute.[45]

Lacy Collison-Morley related an incident which happened during Schwob's visit: "Crawford liked to argue after dinner and would at times get somewhat heated, for he could not bear to be beaten. One night when dinner was on the terrace, Schwob, seeing it was wiser to desist, remarked as he looked across the Bay at the glowing cone, 'Vesuvius is very lively to-night.' "[46] Unfortunately, Schwob's health and irritability became steadily worse; and although Crawford provided every comfort, the Frenchman was eager to depart.

While Schwob was visiting at "Villa Crawford," there was no opportunity for Crawford to cruise in the *Alda*. After Schwob left, the illness of three of Crawford's children continued to prevent the customary summer excursions on the Mediterranean. For two months Crawford and his wife nursed Eleanor, Harold, and Bertram through attacks of typhoid fever. Crawford himself lost weight from anxiety and lack of sleep. Nevertheless, there were long periods when Crawford could work uninterruptedly in his tower study; and, by the time he returned to New York in October, 1904, he would probably have described himself as more historian than novelist.

CHAPTER *9*

Storyteller to a Generation

I

IF CRAWFORD had lived ten years after he made his decision to become a historian, he might have achieved substantial recognition in the field. His grasp of detail, his ability to organize, and his narrative skill would have greatly assisted him; and his unique position, which could be described either as that of an American Italian or an Italian American, gave him at the same time the proper balance of involvement and detachment. Crawford had wisely abandoned the religious materials offered him by the Vatican in favor of the subject that had challenged him since his boyhood—Rome. For the first time in years, he could work enthusiastically. The future looked so bright that he could have repeated the comment which he made when he first considered turning to history, "Life looks so short that I am beginning to doubt whether I can cut my patterns out of it."[1] As it turned out, the four years that remained to him were not long enough for Crawford to write the novels that were an economic necessity and at the same time to publish the results of his historical research.

Before Crawford could devote any sustained effort to his projects with Professor Tomassetti, the yearly novel had to be completed and business affairs with the Macmillan Company in New York settled. Probably by the time that Crawford left America in the spring of 1905, he had finished *Fair Margaret* which was to be the novel for that year. Since it would not be published until November, he could devote the summer and a large part of the winter to his studies before he would be required to write another novel for 1906. For this reason and because of ill health, Crawford did not come to the United States during the winter of 1905-06; instead, he worked in Rome. There the Duchess of Sermoneta often secured advantages for him that would have otherwise been difficult to obtain. In December, 1905, he wrote her:

Following up our conversation of last night, I write to ask you whether you will very kindly transmit my request to your Father. The position is this: Professor Tomassetti and I are working together at a History of Rome, and it would be a great advantage to me if the Prince would authorize him to let me occasionally come in the morning and use the table in the *library not in the archives—* for my work, as well as the printed books of reference on the shelves. I should certainly not interrupt the Professor's own work, but it would make a difference, and a great one, if I could be near him now and then, for I often lose time through lack of an indication which he could give me in one word. The use of the books would also be very valuable to me, as I of course cannot bring all I need to Rome for the winter. It would be understood that I should not touch anything in the *archives,* and Tomassetti would be responsible for me. Indeed, this all comes to this,—that he, Tomassetti, may be allowed to use his discretion in letting me come in.[2]

The attention he gave to what was essentially a simple request that could have been made directly to Prince Colonna indicates the care Crawford took to insure that no unfortunate incident prejudiced his standing in the archives.

Early in 1906, however, Crawford turned his attention to the novel that he knew he must write that year. By March 6, he had already completed *Arethusa,* a historical romance set in Constantinople and dedicated to his daughter, Eleanor. When he found that he could sell the serial rights to this novel for release in 1907,[3] he felt obliged to write and substitute another novel for publication in 1906. *A Lady of Rome,* accordingly, was completed at Torre San Nicola on August 18, 1906. Although the initial printing of 22,000 copies for the London edition alone would indicate Macmillan's faith in the salability of the work, the critics discovered in it evidence of their "waning appreciation" of Crawford's later work. In an effort to commend the novel, the writer for *The Times Literary Supplement* (October 26, 1906) asserted that it "recalls more than one of his early books in theme as well as manner" and continued: "The old virtues are discovered; the pictures are neatly pencilled; local fidelity is everywhere conspicuous; Rome, with its society, its habits, its churches, its language is portrayed with picturesque accuracy." But the same reviewer concluded that, despite these virtues, when the climax "coincides with an opportune death ... and leads to the normal reward of long-separated lovers, what illusion there was is irretrievably shattered."

Because of the severity of his attacks of asthma, Crawford was unable to make his customary voyage to America in 1906. He spent his second consecutive winter in Rome (1906-07), working on the history, writing a new novel, *The Primadonna,* and occasionally making short trips to Sorrento. His letter to Julia Ward Howe in April, 1907, leaves no doubt of his condition as well as his desire to go to Boston once more: "It is very kind of you to put me up, and I shall be quite comfortable *downstairs*—indeed I much prefer that room as I am very wheezy and going up to my room several times in the day would be rather troublesome."[4]

II

In April, 1907, Crawford came to the United States for the last time. Very likely he realized that the time remaining to him was not long. Certainly his actions suggest an effort to accomplish quickly the unfinished business of his American experiences in Boston as well as to arrange matters with his publishers in New York so that he would not be required to return each year. With the Macmillan Company Crawford negotiated a contract whereby he would write three or four novels to be held by the firm and issued at stated intervals; the agreement thus permitted Crawford to pursue his historical research uninterrupted by the task of writing the yearly novel. Meanwhile, he had made arrangements to go to Boston.

Places in the United States had never meant very much to Crawford, but Boston had certain realities as well as memories that he did not deny. He wanted to see Julia Ward Howe, who was soon to celebrate her eighty-eighth birthday; but his main object in going to Boston was to see Mrs. Gardner once more. When he arrived, Julia Ward Howe wrote in her diary that he still possessed all of his former charm and appeared greatly improved in health since she last saw him; but Laura Richards, his cousin, noted that he "looked fragile, sunken, like a person with lung disease."[5] Despite Crawford's entreaties that his visit be kept secret, it was soon known to many; but, when former acquaintances endeavored to see him, he refused to meet them.

The day following his arrival, Crawford walked through Fenway Court with Mrs. Gardner. In the last few years she had ceased to answer his letters; but, as Crawford admired her art collection and praised her taste, their friendship became strong again. At fifty-three Crawford still felt the charm which Mrs. Gardner, even at the age of sixty-seven, continued to exert over his intellect and emotions. This was their last meeting. As Crawford went away, intending to express his reaction adequately in a letter, he could only say that he had a "wonderful impression, quite indescribable,"[6] and add: "What I *cared* for more, and shall remember with different feelings, is to have seen you happy in your very own surroundings, and not displeased to let an old ghost like me wander through them beside you. If you ever haunt the Palazzo Isabella in a future age, I shall be much honoured if I am asked to haunt with you now and then!" He corrected a mistake in her catalogue and offered to read the proof of subsequent editions for her. A few weeks later he tried again to record his impressions of Fenway Court:

About your Palazzo di Venezia—well, I was first preoccupied with yourself, after the long silence for which I am at a loss to account. Never mind that—we have met again, and it looks as if we should write to each other often. I hope so. And I saw you in your very ownest surroundings, in the place you have made for yourself after your own heart—and in which I shall probably always think of you now.

It is a good place, well dreamed, and well realized after dreaming—so well, indeed, that I could not notice half of what I saw, for the simple reason that I knew it was there and could be taken for granted as safely as if the palace were really in Venice. . . .

When I began to think about the impression it left me—to think objectively, as one does about such things—I believe the dominant thought was for the *sobriety* of taste that distinguishes your work from that of some professionals. Mere pleasing prettiness can be noisy, eccentric and even meretricious—or become prettier than ever by kicking over the traces—but nothing really noble can be anything but sober—and perhaps a little melancholy. . . .

Your place is grave and calm—as a Venetian Senator! In more than one of the great rooms I had the sensation of being in Italy, in an old palace, when the chairs and looking glasses are covered for the summer. It was so real that I felt no curiosity to verify details—that was the oddest part of it. . . .

Then too, when I shut my eyes and see it again, I feel that I should not wish anything to be different. *Negative* approval is much more far-reaching than positive admiration, where minor things are concerned—what does not jar *must* be right, if one has grown up with what is good. So do not be hard on me for not howling praises of everything. I would rather feel about it as I do, than have any other recollection of it all. It is so altogether yours, the form of your thought, that you and it are one—like light and air—you are at peace with it and ever newly refreshed by it. At least, that is the way it strikes me.

Of the pictures and other things, I have nothing to say—unless it be that they, too, seem *at peace*—the great masterpieces of that formidable life that has gone out forever. You know their immense value and, besides, the value they have for yourself from the battle fought in getting them. So now, I have *said!*[7]

Crawford felt that he had to say something, yet the sense of finality that came to him upon seeing her in new and different surroundings and upon realizing that so far as he could see in the future and very likely forever there would henceforth be only letters between them produced emotions in Crawford that made expression unusually difficult if not actually painful. He knew that he was really not writing about the collection at Fenway Court which meant little to him; instead, he was recording the end of one phase of their relationship that had been and still remained meaningful to him.

III

The final arrangements which Crawford made with the Macmillan Company in New York proved to be the beginning of a productive year in Crawford's career. With the advice of George Brett, president of Macmillan, Crawford decided to postpone publication of the already completed second volume, *The Primadonna,* of the planned singer trilogy until after he had finished the third volume, *The Diva's Ruby,* in 1908.[8] Meanwhile, he would write for the Christmas trade of 1907 another novel— *The Little City of Hope.* As events proved, Crawford actually wrote a third novel, *The Undesirable Governess,* during 1907.

His immediate plans were to sail for England on May 31, remain there for a month, and reach Sorrento about July 3, 1907. A week after his arrival, his wife and children were to leave for their vacation in the Tyrol; and Crawford, accompanied by Brokman, expected to cruise in the *Alda* to Sicily and Africa and then in the eastern Mediterranean until the fall gales made sailing unpleasant. He carried out his intentions, except that instead of sailing, he and Brokman spent most of their time at Torre San Nicola. There in the embrasure of a huge window overlooking the sea, Crawford wrote *The Diva's Ruby* and *The Little City of Hope.*

As he worked, Crawford may well have recalled the splendor of Mrs. Gardner's Venetian palace and compared it to the simplicity of his lonely tower. Evidently he wished her to know something of his surroundings, for he wrote her: "The tower is a place of silence and here I hear no sound through the big west window but the ripple of the sea—or the booming smash of the breakers on the rocks in a northwest gale. The walls and the vault of my room are whitewashed.... The floor is stone, with a piece of brown carpet where I write, and the table is of deal! There is a distinct lack of luxury about it all, though I have everything I want."[9]

In *Fair Margaret, The Primadonna,* and *The Diva's Ruby,* which comprise the "singer trilogy," Crawford returned to the fictional patterns he had skillfully employed in the 1880's and 1890's. The readers of this new series may have recalled the linked novels of the *Saracinesca* and *Ralston* groups, the cosmopolitan or international atmosphere of *Mr. Isaacs, Doctor Claudius,* and *Paul Patoff,* as well as the character of the ubiquitous Paul Griggs. These characteristics are conspicuous in the singer trilogy. Moreover, the unfolding of the story through the exploitation of secondary characters follows the technique which Crawford established in the Italian novels. Thus, the plotting of *The Primadonna* and *The Diva's Ruby,* appears strikingly similar to the structure of *Sant' Ilario* and *Don Orsino.* To make the parallel complete, the unity of *Fair Margaret* resembles that of *Saracinesca.* In both the earlier and the later series, Crawford began with a limited number of characters and a single action in the first volume; then in the two subsequent novels, he expanded both by developing the "histories" of additional or minor figures. Unfortunately, the result of this practice was not so successful in the singer trilogy as it had been in his earlier work.

Crawford insisted that the three novels of the later group comprised "really all one story, from Margaret Donne's beginnings to her marriage."[10] In *Fair Margaret* he traced the progress of her operatic career from her early experiences through her debut in a Paris opera house. At the end of *The Primadonna,* she has become a great singer and decided "to try" an engagement with a wealthy Greek. During the final volume, Margaret changes her mind and decides to marry instead Rufus Van Torp, an American financier. Thus, in one sense the trilogy is "all one story." On the other hand, the unity of action and the development of the heroine's character are virtually destroyed by Crawford's technique. Despite his theories of fiction, Crawford clearly presented in *Fair Margaret* a social problem—what is the effect of a stage career upon a woman's personality and upon her social position? Implicitly, he promises to show the reader what changes take place in a sensitive, refined, and gifted girl who possesses musical ambitions. One aspect of the question is, of course, the attitude of men toward such a woman. In the two succeeding novels, however, Crawford lost his grasp upon the issues and upon Margaret's career; he presented instead a murder story in *The Primadonna* and a jewel robbery in *The Diva's Ruby*. These novels, it is true, are skillfully unified, but in them Margaret Donne often becomes a secondary character. The lengthy treatment of Van Torp's affairs and the episodes dealing with the ruby seem extraneous. Not only do they make the novels appear padded, but they destroy the significance of the initial themes; and for this reason Margaret Donne is not a fictional personality vividly realized or remembered by the reader.

Referring to the singer trilogy, Crawford once remarked to Mrs. Gardner: "Of course, there is fiction in the stories, but there is more truth and many of the scenes are taken, whole, from life. I have seen and known a great deal of all those people from the *professional* side, which society never sees."[11] Indeed, Crawford had known intimately a number of singers and actresses, especially Sarah Bernhardt and Nellie Melba; and Margaret Donne's character appears to be a mixed portrait of these women; but at times Crawford may have ascribed some of their peculiarities to minor figures. The connection between life and fiction is definitely suggested by Crawford's correspondence with the Duchess of Sermoneta in 1908. In one letter the Duchess, who had met Melba at a dinner party, described the great soprano as "rather a poseuse." Crawford replied:

I am very sorry you did [meet Melba at dinner], for if you had any illusion about the great artist you lost it, and you were moved to say a very cruel thing which was not like you. Why do people give "artistic dinners" and ask the Almanach de Gotha to dine with "Who's Who"? Calvé once said to me that "it takes three generations of peasants to make a voice," and she wound up by striking her knee with her solid fist and crying out at the top of her lungs: "Ah moi, je suis paysanne, par exemple!" And once, in America I think, I was talking to Sarah Bernhardt after luncheon when she took out a rouge box and puff and proceeded to dab herself with colour. I asked her why she did it, especially as she was looking very well that day. She laughed and answered: "Mon petit, c'est mon mètier!" Whereupon the society people present were dreadfully shocked. But what else do you expect? And what can you *exact* from people brought up as you cannot imagine? *They* are professional singers, musicians, actresses, perhaps painters, literary men;—*you* are—well, a professional princess! It is their ideal of joy to be asked to meet you on a footing of equality with *them*. They do their best to imitate you for an hour, and the result is pitifully funny. I am a professional, too. It is not an effort for me to eat nicely, and keep my elbows off the table because I happen to have been born among people who had good manners—but that is mere chance, since much greater than I, like Dickens and Zola, were not.[12]

The incidents and manners to which Crawford refers are strikingly paralleled by those which Margaret Donne encountered in the home of Madame Bonanni in *Fair Margaret*.

In the same letter, Crawford continued: "I have known M[elba] close on sixteen years; I never knew her do a mean or unkind thing, and I have known of her doing a good many very generous ones, and some few things that took real courage and decision. One was when the lights went out in the theatre at San Francisco in the earthquake, and she stopped the panic, for she kept singing all the time." This episode in Melba's life Crawford utilized in the first chapter of *The Primadonna*. But the most obvious use of an actual event for fictional purposes in this novel occurs when Paul Griggs, moved by thoughts of his own sad past, writes in the singer's autographbook. This scene is almost identical to that described by Melba in her memoirs. Almost the only difference is the substitution of Crawford for Griggs and Melba for Margaret Donne.[13]

Finally, a week before Crawford wrote the letter in which he discussed the manners of artists, he had explained to the Duchess of Sermoneta that Melba had been "hurt by my 'Soprano,' taking it to herself, whereas nothing could have been further from my thought than to dissect an old acquaintance."[14] Crawford added that after a long talk they had "made it up nicely." The fact remains, nevertheless, that Melba recognized the relation between the fiction of Crawford's novels and the realities of her own life; and there can be little doubt that Crawford, even in his last novels, continued to turn real life into romance. What he seems to have lost, however, was the ability, or the inclination, to shape the living actuality into a fictional whole.

Since Crawford had already decided not to publish *The Diva's Ruby* until the following year, he remained at Torre San Nicola long enough to write a Christmas story called *The Little City of Hope*. Before beginning its composition, however, he described the plot to Mrs. Gardner just as years earlier he had written to her about *Mr. Isaacs, Doctor Claudius,* and *A Roman Singer*: "It is about an exiled man and his only child, and with little bits of colored paper and odds and ends, and glue, they make a model of their own city, where they hope to be some day again, working at it in the evening when the man has done his work, and they call it the City of hope, and at last, on Christmas tide, the hope is fulfilled, and they are where they would be, in their own home. The thought pleases me."[15] The title and the basic idea for this story had been given to Crawford many years before by his sister, Annie von Rabé; the details and actual composition were, of course, the work of Crawford himself. After the Macmillan Company published the novel in November, 1907, and it became a popular success, Crawford generously gave his sister a share of the profits.[16]

Crawford's next novel—the third he had written since leaving the United States at the end of May, 1907—affords a similar instance of his utilization of someone else's ideas. Encouraged by Crawford, the Duchess of Sermoneta had written a short story, "The Stormy Night," about one of the balloon ascents which she had made, and in January, 1907, Crawford had sent her a detailed criticism of her work.[17] Shortly after finishing *The Little City of Hope,* he devised a plot for a novel which would incorporate her story; and, when he received her manuscript and permission to use it, he wrote: "The baby [her story] arrived safely by post... and only needs to be put into the right surroundings to present a very fine appearance. In fact it only needs a little nourishment. It is to be called 'The Undesirable Governess,' whose mad father turns up in the lunatic asylum, making your invention the climax that brings everything all right."[18] Although Crawford had finished the work by Christmas, it was not published until after his death.[19]

IV

Early in October, Crawford had returned to Sorrento where, despite illness, he had finished *The Undesirable Governess.* Shortly after Christmas, he wrote Mrs. Gardner: "I have only had bronchitis myself, with painful asthma, but when one has been hit in the lungs even that is serious. I still have to be carried upstairs."[20] Very probably, Crawford never walked upstairs again. By February, when his health had improved, he wrote more cheerfully:

> Altogether things are looking better than they did a month ago. My daughter Clare is up and goes out, after a long and tedious illness.... Eleanor's wedding is put off till after Easter.... As for me, I am busy, as usual, and amongst other things I am again coaching my son Bertie in Greek plays....
>
> Do not worry about my being carried up stairs, for I only submit to it now because the doctor thinks it is a useless strain on my breathing, and I can walk pretty well on a level and go up mild hills well enough. But stairs bother me a little, and there are always lots of men about to carry me in this delightful country where one can have 'people,' in a fine plural, instead of labour-saving machines, and steam heat, and cold storage, and the nasty atmosphere of Progress with a capital *P.*[21]

The concerns of his children and the composition of another novel detained Crawford at Sorrento until the end of April, 1908. He knew that Harold, his elder son, was not making good grades at Harvard and he was worried about his other son's chances of passing the entrance examinations at Oxford. Eleanor's marriage, on the day after Easter to a young Italian nobleman, Pietro Rocca, gave Crawford immense satisfaction; and Clare, who rapidly recovered from her illness, became her father's most cherished companion. To finish his new novel, *Stradella,* before the coming of good sailing weather would permit him to travel again, Crawford was working steadily, often so long as sixteen hours a day. To Mrs. Gardner, he wrote: "There is little time for reading and what there is I give to old friends, mostly classics now. If I live much longer, I daresay I shall take up my Sanskrit again—long forgotten! But the Greeks appeal to me most, and there are things I read over and over again in the Anthology and Pindar. It is quite wrong, of course, for I ought to be reading mediaeval history for my Rome—but that is work and the other is play, though it is harder!"[22] Writing the novel took him away from his historical work, but Crawford knew that it had to be done. *Stradella* represented the fourth novel he had finished since he left the United States in May, 1907.[23] With it out of the way, Crawford hoped to return to his historical studies.

Weeks passed before Crawford was able to resume work on the history of Rome. Late in April he suffered a relapse, and the attacks of asthma began again. In May, he spent a few days at Torre San Nicola; and then, upon the advice of his physicians, he sailed for England and Scotland where he remained all summer. There he may have actually begun to write the first volume of his history. His breathing improved greatly; and, when he returned to Sorrento in September, he could walk up low hills with only an occasional halt. "It *feels* like magic," he declared, "after all these years of helplessness—five or six, at least—since I was able to move easily."[24]

In the fall of 1908 Crawford went for the last time to Torre San Nicola still hoping that he would eventually recover. From there he wrote: "My remaining girl, Clare, is here with me—a companion and a consolation for many things. She is the only one of my children who is gifted as well as good looking, and she has a heart of grace, too, which is rare. Happily she is very fond of me, and [we] spend delightful hours together in this solitude, taking long walks in the hills and dining by the light of the moon on the huge terrace at the top of the tower. *Walks* yes!"[25] Unfortunately, his improvement proved only temporary. Early in

November, he began to have a low fever which was aggravated by slight heart attacks.

Although Crawford realized that he was slowly dying, he remained cheerful and patient. He burned every letter he had received, including those from Mrs. Gardner; destroyed his manuscript notes and "bits of paper"; and kept only the manuscripts of his completed books and plays, as he said, "to show that I really wrote them!"[26] For years he had instructed Mrs. Gardner to address him in care of his publishers, but now he said: "Let me hear when you can—or will. I think none would care if you wrote straight here now and then—not that it is any quicker, but mysteries are useless."[27] Certainly Crawford knew that, even if he lived long enough to finish the history, he would always be a semi-invalid.

Despite his suffering, he joked about his appearance. To the Duchess of Sermoneta, he wrote: "In appearance I look like the Camel just after he has passed through the Eye of the Needle. As a study of bones (I love your energy in going to the life school, and I envy it!) my outward man would perhaps find more favour in your eyes than at any previous moment of our acquaintance. 'Che bello scheletro!' my doctor says every time he examines my carcass to see if there is any earthly reason why this fever should go on."[28] To his daughter, Clare, he remarked that his heart felt as if it had sunk into his waistcoat pocket.[29] In the time of his greatest suffering, Crawford was patient and resigned.

Despite his illness, he continued to work. During the winter of 1908-09, he completed the only volume of the history of Rome which he was ever to write[30] and his last novel, *The White Sister*.[31] By January, 1909, *The White Sister* was ready for Macmillan; and Crawford expected that a play based upon the novel would be produced in February. He was disappointed when he learned that the production had been postponed until the fall.

Of all Crawford's library of fiction, *The White Sister* represents his most extensive utilization of Catholic themes and Catholic settings. With a wealth of color and emotional conflict, he traced the life of a young girl Angela Chiaromonte who, under a misapprehension, enters the Convent of the White Sisters of Santa Giovanni d'Aza only to face the tragically inherent consequences of her act. At the beginning of the novel, Angela, supposedly the daughter of a wealthy Italian nobleman, is ejected from her home and social position by the disclosure that she is a penniless, illegitimate foundling. At this moment the Italian government sends her lover, Giovanni Severi, on an ill-fated expedition to

Massowah. After his death has been reported, Angela becomes persuaded that if one helps others, "God will help you."[32] She enters the convent, takes the vows, and eventually becomes Sister Giovanni, the most skillful surgical nurse of the order.

Several years later, after she has learned that she was defrauded of her good name and fortune, Angela decides to serve as a nurse in a leper colony. Before she leaves the convent, however, Giovanni Severi, long believed to be dead, suddenly returns to claim her former promise. Torn between her spiritual vows and her earthly love, Angela resolves to remain true to the Church. Her position becomes even more difficult when Giovanni, who has been injured by the explosion of a powder magazine, refuses to permit an amputation which would save his life unless she relents. At this crisis, the nun's perplexities are resolved by the priest, Ippolito Saracinesca, who promises to obtain a release for Angela from her religious vows.

If, in the final chapter of *The White Sister*, Crawford appears to have made an artistic mistake—as at least one contemporary Catholic reviewer asserted[33]—by resolving Angela's dilemma through the intervention of a priest, one must remember that Crawford's theory of the novel favored a happy ending. For the nun to have agreed, heedless of her vows, to leave the convent with her lover would have been unthinkable to a novelist of Crawford's beliefs. The obvious alternative was, of course, a tragic conclusion, permitting Angela to remain a nun and allowing Giovanni to die. As a matter of fact, this was the resolution of the plot which Viola Allen, Lillian Gish, and Helen Hayes employed with telling effect in both the stage production and in the two motion picture versions of the novel. Indeed, it is highly probable that Crawford himself considered using the unhappy conclusion for the work. The governing factor for Crawford was almost always his estimate of his readers' preferences, and in this instance a "sensitive and tactful appreciation of the public taste" may well have inspired the happy denouement.

While Crawford was writing the final chapters of *The White Sister*, the Messina earthquake of December 28, 1908, focused world interest upon this Italian city of approximately 150,000 population. When the extent of the disaster began to be apparent— estimates of the dead varied from 77,000 to 120,000 (the figure Crawford accepted)—committees in Italy, England, Germany, and the United States were hastily organized to dispatch relief supplies to the stricken areas; and various news agencies appealed to writers living in Italy for first-hand reports. Crawford received a number of offers for articles; and, because several of them were too attractive to be refused, he began to collect materials for a comprehensive account of the disaster. To the New York *World,* Crawford cabled a long account of the disaster based upon the reports sent him by his son-in-law, Pietro Rocca, who had been among the first to reach Messina after the earthquake. Crawford also began a series of articles about the tragedy for the *Outlook,* and the first installment, "The Greatest Disaster in History," appeared in this magazine in March, 1909. It may have been the last piece of literary work that Crawford ever completed.

V

During the brief time of life that remained to him, Crawford worked when he was able, trying to complete the Messina articles and perhaps to work on the history of Rome. He suffered so severely from asthma that he could sleep only when held or tied to a chair. He had hoped to come to America for Julia Ward Howe's ninetieth birthday celebration in May, but a journey of this sort was obviously impossible. His physicians advised him to take a "cure" at Nauheim; and during the first week in April, it seemed as if he might eventually be able to travel that far. Indeed, the fever left him, but his family soon became aware that there was no real improvement in his condition. On the morning of April 9, Crawford suffered a heart attack and a few hours later he died. In Boston on April 10, Julia Ward Howe wrote in her diary the simple fact: "Today brings the sad news of Marion Crawford's death at Sorrento." Then, as if looking back into the past, the ninety year old woman added, "Poor, dear Marion! The end in his case comes early." The next day, Easter Sunday, she stood at the chancel of the Church of the Disciples and spoke briefly about Crawford. What Mrs. Gardner at Fenway Court felt or thought about his death, she kept to herself; but even had she wished to comment, there was scarcely anyone in his family to whom she could have revealed her feelings.

The funeral took place the day after Easter. The sailors from the *Alda* carried his casket covered by a large cross of lilies from "Villa Crawford" to the little church of Sorrento. After the services there, the funeral cortege, led by a group of priests, moved along the street named for him, the Corso Marion-Crawford, through the village of Sant' Agnello, to the cemetery on the plateau above the town. The entire population of Sorrento and Sant' Agnello either walked in the procession or watched it from sidewalks and balconies draped in mourning. At the cemetery, a chant was sung and orations delivered by Italian dignitaries. Later a monument was erected to his memory.

Crawford died believing that he had not lived to complete the work that would have made him remembered by posterity. From that point of view the energy and months of work which had already gone into the history of Rome were wasted effort cheated of fruition by the disease that killed him. Crawford seems never to have considered the fact that the odds were overwhelming that, even had he completed the ten-volume history of Rome, he would still have always been identified with his novels. No history, no matter how authoritative, or how well written, could have erased or effectively dimmed Crawford's accomplishment that by almost any standard had been phenomenal. In a writing career of twenty-seven years, which was much shorter than that of Howells or James, he had produced forty-four novels that at a very conservative estimate had sold more than two million copies; and, regardless of the lasting artistic value of his work, he had served as storyteller to an entire generation. He had identified himself so closely with the books he had written that, to hundreds of thousands of readers throughout America and England and in Europe, the name Marion Crawford was synonymous with their idea of the romance and charm of Italy. If a very few sneered and if others spread gossip, to most he was always the "magnificent Marion Crawford." He had indeed astonished them all by making a mark that was not exceeded or even equaled in the nineteenth century; and, despite his own tendency to undervalue his fiction, he had made a permanent contribution to American literature.

CHAPTER *10*

Appraisal

I

D URING the 1890's and the first decade of the twentieth
century, any educated man conversant with literary matters
in this country would probably have named F. Marion Crawford,
William Dean Howells, and Samuel Langhorne Clemens as the
leading professional men of letters in the United States. By virtue
of his prominence for many years as editor of the *Atlantic Monthly*,
as literary columnist of the "Editor's Study" and of the "Editor's
Easy Chair," and as author of an impressive succession of novels,
plays, poems, travel sketches, and miscellaneous pieces, Howells'
preeminence was fully established; and Mark Twain's seemingly
inexhaustible flow of humor, satire, and social comment made
him not only an admired but also a much loved and venerated
figure.

As a practitioner of the profession of letters, Crawford could
have felt comfortable in their presence. His claim to inclusion in
such excellent company would have been based upon his forty-four
novels, thirty-two articles, four plays, three volumes of history,
two books of travel, an important book of criticism, and twenty
miscellaneous pieces. From the time he began to write until his
death in 1909, the best literary journals in both America and
England were full of what he wrote and what was written about
him. There was scarcely a month during his entire career that
something new from his pen was not available for his admirers
to read. During his lifetime three collected editions of his works
were published, a mark of recognition not accorded to Howells
whose writings have never been issued in this manner. On the
level of popular appeal and the versatility of his talent, Crawford
stood on an equal footing with Howells and in certain respects
even possessed a slight edge. Aside from divergences in their
approach to literature and in the artistic quality of their work,
the major difference between Crawford and Howells lies in the
powerful and direct influence which Howells exerted upon his

contemporaries and the best writers of the younger generation. In Crawford's experience, there was no parallel to this relationship.

Crawford, of course, was scarcely in a position to exercise the kind of influence that made Howells the dominant figure that he was before 1900. The latter's connection with the *Atlantic Monthly* between 1871 and 1881 amounted to control of the most important single publication outlet in the country, and it established his position of leadership before Crawford even considered entering the field. It was fortunate for Crawford that he had no desire to compete on this level. Whereas Howells possessed an uncommon talent for making friends and avoiding enemies, Crawford was never able to establish friendships among his literary colleagues; and what friends he enjoyed were almost all women whose relationships to him were without exception personal. Even if his temperament and personality had not hindered him from exerting a personal influence over his fellow writers, the fact that Crawford lived in a foreign country from which he had to commute across the Atlantic to his place of business would have made the kind of power attained by Howells almost an impossibility. A sensitive, idealistic introvert, Crawford operated alone. His ear was ever attuned to changes in public taste. He considered himself a practitioner of letters; he was neither a teacher nor a proselytizer; and he never exhibited the slightest desire to develop a following among younger writers.

II

Regardless of the variety of his literary activities, Crawford's major contribution, as well as his principal occupation, was the creation of a large shelf of entertaining and compelling novels. From first to last, fiction was his craft and the basis of his fame. "He always had a story to tell and he knew how to tell,"[1] wrote a contemporary critic as he reviewed Crawford's last novel and looked back over his fiction; and, as if to restate the matter, the writer then added, "He was a born story-teller, and, what is more rare, a trained one." The comments agree with what Crawford would have wanted his critics to say, for he liked to think of himself as a modern and Western counterpart of the Oriental story-teller who sat in the bazaar and earned his living by his ability to hold the interest of his listeners. The story—the moving ribbon of action, the continual answer to what happened—was the basis of Crawford's art.

Crawford never seems to have been aware that the ribbon of action could move so rapidly that it would become a source of weakness in his fiction. Nowhere is the validity of this observation more apparent than in the novels often grouped together as the Saracinesca series. In the opening trilogy, which comprises *Saracinesca, Sant' Ilario,* and *Don Orsino,* Crawford's desire to chronicle the impact of changing political and social events upon the members of an Italian family resulted in a concentration upon character, a faithful adherence to the realities of the Italian background, and at the same time a minimum of incident. As a result of these factors, Crawford achieved in this trilogy a balance and interdependence of character, of realistic detail, and of incident. These novels, together with *Katharine Lauderdale* and *The Ralstons,* which exhibit the same qualities in somewhat less degree, represent the peak of his artistic achievement. In writing the remainder of the Saracinesca series, however, Crawford no longer felt the constricting influence of theme and allowed his inventiveness free rein. Consequently, by subordinating character and Italian coloring to multiple incidents in the plot, Crawford gave additional evidence of his skill as an inventor of incident but failed to reach the artistic level of the earlier trilogy.

In his own day there was a tendency among critics to give a kind of unity to Crawford's work by appraising him as primarily a novelist of Italian life. A statistical analysis of his fiction does not substantiate this view, for he actually employed Italian settings in less than half of his work. With respect to setting, his novels may be classified as follows: twenty-one novels in Italy; seven in America; three in Germany; two in England; two in Turkey; one each in France, Switzerland, Spain, India, Arabia, and Persia; and three predominantly in no single country. These figures demonstrate that, measured by such an objective or external criterion as setting, Crawford was far more an international novelist than he was an interpreter of Italy. Yet those who sought to show that Crawford's huge shelf of fiction, diverse as it seemingly appeared, was nevertheless cut from the same tree were essentially correct.

The basic unity, however, came not from without but from within the novels themselves—or, rather, from within Crawford himself. They are a projection of Crawford's personality, his tastes, his ideals, his dreams, his hopes, his fears, and his disappointments. Seen from this standpoint, the important fact is not so much that he wrote novels with settings in eleven different countries but that, excluding his historical novels, the characters, incidents, and plots of virtually every novel he wrote derived from his own experiences in these countries. The reason that Italy, America, and Germany account for the settings of three-fourths of his work is simply that he lived the major portion of his life in these countries. The great appearance of variety and the consequent absence of sameness in his work offer a striking testimony to the amazing richness of his life.

The essential wholeness of Crawford's vast body of fiction and its inseparable connection with his own life is nowhere better seen than in his creation of an entire fictional society that spreads out over Europe and America in sixteen novels beginning with his first work, *Mr. Isaacs,* and ending with his last, *The White Sister.* Although the four novels primarily concerned with the Saracinesca family *(Saracinesca, Sant' Ilario, Don Orsino,* and *Corleone)* lie at the heart of this cycle, it also includes other Italian novels *(Taquisara, Casa Braccio, Pietro Ghisleri,* and *A Lady of Rome),* American novels *(Katharine Lauderdale* and *The Ralstons),* and novels that take place in several countries *(Paul Patoff, Fair Margaret, The Primadonna,* and *The Diva's Ruby).* In each of these novels, Crawford presented what was in every respect a complete story; but, by making a minor character in one novel become a major character in another, he gave his readers a feeling of participation with him as storyteller and with his characters as actors that carried over from one novel to another. The most prominent utilization of this device occurs in the novels of the Saracinesca family, but members of the family also appear in other novels, notably *A Lady of Rome* and *The White Sister.* Conspicuous among the numerous characters who take roles in more than one novel are Ugo del Ferice, Count Spicca, Pietro Ghisleri, Gianforte Campodonico, Donna Tullia Mayer, Walter Crowdie, and Anatase Gouache; but, of all these linking characters, by far the most important is Paul Griggs.

Crawford's method of composing his novels required the creation of a central or near-central character representing himself who functioned as a frame of reference or sounding board for the development of the action. In his first novel Crawford named this fictional representative of himself Paul Griggs and in private correspondence specifically identified himself with this character. In most of his subsequent fiction he gave his own spokesman other names, but in 1887 with *Paul Patoff* he re-introduced Paul Griggs. In the middle years of the 1890's he wrote three novels in which Paul Griggs once more played a role. In the first two of these, *Katharine Lauderdale* (1894) and *The Ralstons* (1895), Paul Griggs occupies a minor position; but, by mentioning "the strange story of Griggs' life"[2] and leaving one of the threads of the plot plainly unresolved, Crawford sought to arouse the curiosity of his readers in the novel that was to feature Paul Griggs as hero. In *Casa Braccio* (1895), one of the longest novels

Crawford ever wrote, he presented Griggs's story. After *Casa Braccio,* he made no further mention of Griggs until 1908 when Crawford gave him a part in *The Primadonna* (1908) and in *The Diva's Ruby* (1908).

The character of Paul Griggs thus in effect helps to bind together what would otherwise be widely separated parts of Crawford's total output of fiction. A novel set in India *(Mr. Isaacs)* and one set in Constantinople *(Paul Patoff)* are effectively joined to the body of Crawford's Italian and American novels. Moreover, by associating in a single volume *(Casa Braccio)* Walter Crowdie and Paul Griggs of his American novels with members of the Campodonico family and Pietro Ghisleri of the Italian series, Crawford effectively linked two other large segments of his work. Finally, by introducing Paul Griggs into the singer trilogy he tied it into the previous groups. In other words, the repeated appearances of Paul Griggs and other important characters constituted the major fictional device by which Crawford brought almost half of his novels together as one huge artistic canvas.

As Crawford's acknowledged fictional equivalent, Paul Griggs serves also to demonstrate the close relationship between the experiences of Crawford's own life and those of the characters in his novels; nevertheless, the novels in which Paul Griggs plays an important role *(Mr. Isaacs, Paul Patoff, and Casa Braccio)* are scarcely more autobiographical than many of his other volumes. Crawford's use of his own life in his fiction, however, cannot be explained merely on the basis of a method of composition which required his own participation in each novel as he wrote it. In a very real sense Crawford would have agreed with Thomas Wolfe's statement that "a man must use the material and experience of his own life if he is to create anything that has substantial value."[3] On his part, Crawford never desired to confine himself to realities, and he never hesitated to invent incidents that had no relation to his own life for the sake of creating a more exciting and compelling story. Yet it is true that Crawford's novels were a projection of his own personality, and they did take their particular quality from his own experiences. His biography thus furnishes an indispensable commentary upon his novels.

III

Crawford's novels, which admirably suited the tastes of a generation of readers, were written according to a theory which may not have been entirely original with him but to which he assuredly gave classic expression. In advocating the claims of the

literature of entertainment, Crawford was joined by such critics
as Brander Matthews and Hamilton Wright Mabie and by such
able and popular literary practitioners as Robert Louis Stevenson,
Louise de la Ramée (Ouida), Henry Rider Haggard, Winston
Churchill, Stanley J. Weyman, Agnes Repplier, and many others.
Crawford spoke for them all, and during the 1890's he argued
powerfully in their behalf against the claims of the already
entrenched Realism of William Dean Howells and the incipient
Naturalism of Stephen Crane.

In the light of the developments in the theory and practice
of fiction since Crawford's lifetime, his theory seems rather the
product of a value-system that was rapidly becoming outmoded
than the work of a man who was opening new areas for literary
exploration. Crawford's approach was comprehensible only in
terms of a tradition that accepted without questioning the rationality and the moral responsibility of man. Neither Realism nor
Naturalism exhibited any necessary connection with Christian
humanism. Realism, whose strongest advocate and acknowledged
leader in America was an agnostic, was in the strictest sense
confined to a technique; nevertheless, the literary practice of
Realism led very smoothly into the literary techniques of Naturalism, the basic philosophical premises of which must be regarded
as antagonistic to the prevailing notions of Christian belief in
Crawford's day. With the exception of Crawford's theory, the only
other literary theory which received any vogue in the 1890's and
which granted man the ability to improve himself by discriminating
between right and wrong principles of conduct was that of
Henry James.

Since the critical tenets of both Crawford and Henry James
were based upon similar beliefs about the nature of man and his
relation to the universe, it seems strange that the two theories
had very little in common. The answer of course lies in the very
widely different ideas which Crawford and James held about
the nature of the novelist's art. Above all else, Crawford believed
in a rapidly moving narrative of events and in the dramatization
of ideal conduct against a backdrop of realistic settings. He
was well aware that his plots were often melodramatic, but so
long as the melodramatic incident was in itself possible and
momentarily believable—and many of his incidents were based
upon his own experiences—he was often willing to sacrifice
psychological motivation and the minute analysis of character to
attain excitement and suspense. For Crawford, the story was the
thing; the great requirement, motion. On the other hand, Crawford
saw Henry James's work as the turning of consciousness back

upon consciousness; and, regardless of the ethical result of such a process, he could not accept it as the proper ingredient of fiction. Without mentioning Henry James by name, Crawford may have had the former's fiction in mind when he wrote in *The White Sister:*

> An accomplished psychologist would easily fill a volume with the history of Angela's soul from the day on which she learned the bad news till the morning when she made her profession and took the final vows of her order in the little convent church. But one great objection to psychological analysis in novels seems to be that the writer never gets beyond analysing what he believes that he himself would have felt if placed in the "situation" he has invented for his hero or heroine. Thus analysed, Angela Chiaromonte would not have known herself, any more than those who knew her best, such as Madame Bernard and her aunt the Princess, would have recognised her. I shall not try to "factorise" the result represented by her state of mind from time to time; still less shall I employ a mathematical process to prove that the ratio of dx to dy is twice x, the change in Angela at any moment of her moral growth.[4]

Crawford's gloss upon this passage makes his criteria and his critical position clear: "What has happened must be logical, just because it has happened; if we do not understand the logic, that may or may not be the worse for us, but the facts remain." Crawford preferred the reader to understand the logic, but failing that understanding, he wished the facts of the action to be crystal clear. In the critical argument with Henry James, however, Crawford appears to have lost, largely because of James's marvelous comprehension of the esthetic problems of fiction and because his concept of the novel could very easily be emptied of its assumptions about the moral responsibility and rationality of man and conveniently merged with the psychology of Sigmund Freud and the literary preferences of James Joyce. So far as the masters of fiction in the twentieth century are concerned, Crawford spoke with prophetic insight when he exclaimed: "The old fashioned novel is really dead, and nothing can revive it nor make anybody care for it again."[5] Yet with certain changes necessitated by different social and moral standards, literature written according to the theory of entertainment has continued to flourish ever since Crawford's day.

Although Crawford's literary reputation will probably always rest upon his contributions in the novel and in literary criticism, during his lifetime he was also recognized as an acceptable playwright, as a very successful lecturer, and as a promising historian. Like many a successful novelist, Crawford tended to believe that a novelist's abilities to write effective dialogue and to capture the dramatic incident were talents that qualified him to write plays. After the failure of *Doctor Claudius* convincingly demonstrated the uncertainties and problems of playwriting, Crawford wrote *In the Palace of the King* more to silence his critics than to continue as a dramatist. Later his *Francesca da Rimini,* which he wrote mainly to please Sarah Bernhardt, proved only a qualified success; and he did not live long enough to witness the acclaim given Viola Allen in the dramatization of *The White Sister* or to enjoy the motion picture versions which starred Lillian Gish and Ronald Coleman in 1923 and a decade later Helen Hayes and Clark Gable. Compared to his record as a novelist, Crawford's efforts to write plays were not brilliant; however, he had the good sense to try his fortune in the theater only upon rare occasions.

Because of a combination of factors, Crawford was more successful as a lecturer than he was as a dramatist. His magnificent physique, his aristocratic bearing, and his cultivated manners gave him a commanding presence on the platform. His fame as a world traveler and as a romantic American novelist living abroad brought thousands to the lecture hall merely to see him; and his Italian subject matter held a strong appeal for a generation of Americans to whom Italy was the seat of culture and romance. The combination of all these circumstances and the quality of his performance enabled him to compete on even ground with such other distinguished American men of letters as William Dean Howells, Samuel Langhorne Clemens, and George Washington Cable. Had not his poor health precluded additional public speaking engagements, Crawford would almost certainly have repeated the successful lecture tour of 1897-98.

The quick response of American audiences to the lectures dealing with Italian subjects helped to strengthen Crawford's desire to write about Italian history. Although his volumes about Rome, Sicily, and Venice represented the products of his interest in Italian history, Crawford made almost no perceptible progress with the vast multi-volume history of Rome in the Middle Ages—the project that occupied his most serious attention during the last years of his life. In part at least, this decision to write history may have been an error in judgment; for, by making his novel writing seem less important to him than it had been, his interest in historical research tended to foster a decline in the quality of his later fiction.

IV

An appraisal of F. Marion Crawford's contribution to American letters should begin with recognition of the important fact that, although his position and experience were almost unique in the century and certainly foreign to most Americans, he was nevertheless very much the product of a value-system which dominated America (and England) throughout his lifetime. In fact, the combination of these two elements accounts for his extraordinary appeal to his generation and for his ultimate standing in literary history. To understand them is to comprehend the peculiar literary phenomenon that Marion Crawford exemplified in his life and in his books.

Throughout the nineteenth century, American artists and, toward the end of the period, American tourists in ever increasing numbers persistently sought out Italy as the land in which a man might most nearly satisfy or realize his craving for the good life. For such men as Horatio Greenough, Hiram Powers, Thomas Crawford, and Henry James, it was a conscious search, a deliberate choice of a sojourn in a foreign land; and even if they became expatriates, at least they had first reached maturity within an American frame of reference. The fact that F. Marion Crawford was born there, that he knew Italy before he knew America, that it was "home" and not foreign to him made the difference that separated him from the cultural voyagers of his time. The difference, of course, manifested itself in his measurement of America by Italy, instead of Italy by America; in his lack of understanding of American practices; and in his lifelong preference for things Italian over things American. Even more subtly, his birth and boyhood in Italy tended to accentuate his aristocratic ideas about the nature of the good life. Finally, his long residence in Italy prepared him—as no other American before him—to embody in fiction for American and English readers their own dreams of the culture of Italy.

Had Crawford been a rebel against the accepted value-system of his time, his contribution would certainly have been far otherwise than it was. He was not a rebel. Indeed, to a far greater extent than Clemens, Howells, and James, who at times had serious doubts about the values of the official American culture, Crawford found satisfying the ideals and standards accepted by the leaders of the American genteel tradition. From these concepts he never considered withholding allegiance. Unlike Howells and James, Crawford never questioned the value or the desirability of embodying the ideal in literature; and he consistently emphasized the need for universality and affirmed the beauty of the moral. The same generation that acclaimed Longfellow at his death as the most popular poet in the world also applauded Crawford at the bookstores as its most consistently popular novelist. Indeed, the coincidence of Crawford's moral and literary ideals and beliefs with those of the majority of decent, church-going, middle-class readers of the late nineteenth century goes far to explain his appeal to Americans. Like Longfellow, whose eulogy he helped Sam Ward to write for the *Atlantic Monthly,* Crawford vindicated in an ideal world of far-away Italy the eternal verities that his American readers knew were equally as valid in Kansas City as in the Isles of the Sirens.

A great deal of Crawford's writing directly reflected his response to the women whom he admired and loved. In Mrs. Jones's phrase, he was to a very marked degree "a woman's man."[6] Throughout his life he was extremely susceptible to feminine charm, sympathy, and approval. He sought their companionship and pressed his confidences upon them. In addition to his mother, Louisa Terry, and his cousin, Maud Elliott, Crawford responded emotionally to such women as Lily Conrad, Mrs. Gardner, Bessie Berdan, Mrs. Jones, Nellie Melba, Sarah Bernhardt, and Vittoria Colonna. They represented to him splendid examples of femininity that he turned into the almost perfect heroines of his novels. He put each one upon a pedestal; and, when one fell from it, she broke his heart and saddened the years of life that remained to him. Yet Crawford never lost faith in his ideal of womanhood, and he continued to embody his concept in his novels. He refused to challenge Robert Grant's dissection of the frightening pragmatism of Selma White in *Unleavened Bread,* and he willingly resigned to William Dean Howells the exposure of the unladylike forwardness of Marcia Gaylord in *A Modern Instance.* For his part Crawford would continue to portray women whose love was true and whose manners were above reproach. In theory and in practice he affirmed his conviction that all men and women were interested in love "either for its present reality, or for the memories that soften the coldly vivid recollection of an active past, and shed a tender light in the dark places of bygone struggles, or because the hope of it brightens and gladdens the path of future dreams."[7] Crawford had experienced all of these phases; and, by illustrating them in his fiction and by adopting the ideals if not the practicalities of his generation, he affirmed his readers' faith, if not in their own goodness, at least in their own potential for goodness.

It was in fact the remarkable consonance of Crawford's beliefs with the aspirations of his generation that made him in the eyes of most Americans a major writer. His cosmopolitan outlook and consequent freedom from provincialism, his apparent conversancy with the cultures of the West and the East, his insistence upon Christian principles in the conduct of life, and his affirmation of the ideal in art made him seem to exemplify the qualities which Americans associated with the ideal life. To many of his admirers, he represented the life of art, culture, and the spirit at its best.

Howells is the most convenient measure of Crawford's position. In their emphasis upon the importance of discipline, self-realization, and Christian ethics and morality in the conduct of life, the principles of both men coincided; and in their insistence upon truth and reality as the base of all good fiction, both men were in substantial agreement. Howells, however, eventually became convinced that American literature must concern itself with peculiarly American institutions—specifically, American political, social, economic, and ethical problems. This conviction effectively separated Howells from the intellectual and ethical tradition in which he had begun his literary career and from the theory and practice of fiction represented by F. Marion Crawford. Even if he had desired to write in accordance with Howells' notions, Crawford's lack of familiarity with American attitudes and problems would have barred him from success. The literary practices advocated by Howells gave enormous support to the Naturalists and their followers in the twentieth century. It would be ridiculous to assert that Crawford has been a powerful influence upon the major writers of twentieth-century America. Yet the thousands of novels written in the present century according to the guide lines expressed by Crawford furnish compelling evidence that literature of the type he wrote remains a vital part of our culture.

Notes and References

Chapter One

1. For accounts of the Ward family, see John Ward, *A Memoir of Lieut.-Colonel Samuel Ward* (New York, 1875); [Mrs.] Maud Howe Elliott, *Uncle Sam Ward and His Circle* (New York, 1938); and [Mrs.] Louise Hall Tharp, *Three Saints and a Sinner* (Boston, 1956).

2. [Mrs.] Maud Howe Elliott, *My Cousin, F. Marion Crawford* (New York, 1934), p. 1.

3. Letter from Louisa (Ward) Crawford Terry to Jane Campbell Crawford, January 6, 1863, in the Houghton Library of Harvard University; manuscript material in this library, which will be referred to hereafter as HL, has been used with the permission of the Director, William A. Jackson.

4. Louisa Terry to Jane and Mary Crawford, December 8, 1863, HL.

5. Louisa Terry to Jane Crawford, May 9, 1864, HL.

6. *Ibid.*, July 9, 1864.

7. Elliott, *My Cousin*, p. 17.

8. Sometime after 1869 Lily married the Marchese Theodoli; she was often ill, and Louisa Terry frequently mentioned in her letters visits to the suffering Lily. Mrs. Elliott recalled her as the "golden lily" and said Crawford fell in love with her when he was fifteen and "never fell out." See Elliott, *My Cousin*, p. 57.

9. Francis Marion Crawford, *A Tale of a Lonely Parish*, in *The Complete Works of F. Marion Crawford* (authorized ed.; New York [1883-1904]), p. 10; unless otherwise stated, all references to Crawford's novels presume this edition of his works. Years after this novel was published, Crawford remarked in an interview recorded by Robert Bridges that "I lifted that little village bodily out of my memory and put it into my story, even to the extent of certain real names and localities."—Robert Bridges, "F. Marion Crawford: A Conversation," *McClure's Magazine*, IV (March, 1895), 321. "Billingsfield, Essex," appears to be a fictional name for Hatfield Broad Oak, Essex; the church at Billingsfield suggests St. Mary's church at Hatfield; and "Billingsfield Hall" may owe something to the nearby Barrington Hall, since there are certain parallels between their histories. See D. W. Coller, *The People's History of Essex* (Chelmsford, 1861), pp. 318-21. There is likewise reason to indicate that the fictional hero, John Short, who was preparing for Trinity, was based upon Crawford himself; Short's "boyish fancy" for Mary Goddard may recall Crawford's affection for Lily Conrad. For several interesting anecdotes of Crawford's life at Hatfield Broad Oak, see Mrs. Hugh [Mary Crawford] Fraser, *A Diplomatist's Wife in Many Lands* (2 vols.; London, 1911), I, 122-23.

10. Samuel Ward to Louisa Terry, January 18, 1872, HL.

11. *Ibid.*, February 10, 1872.

12. See Elliott, *My Cousin*, pp. 32-36.

13. Louisa Terry to Samuel Ward, September 16, 1872, quoted in Elliott, *My Cousin*, p. 37. Since almost all of the letters quoted by Mrs. Elliott are available in the Houghton Library, quotations have been made from

these originals; letters published by Mrs. Elliott but not in the Houghton Library have been cited to her book.

14. Crawford as quoted in "Marion Crawford, Novelist, Is Dead," New York *Times*, April 10, 1909.

15. Louisa Terry to Luther Terry, August 7, 1874, HL.

16. Julia Ward Howe to Louisa Terry, January 31, 1867, HL; see also Julia Ward Howe to Annie Ward Mailliard, [November] 10 and 16 [1866].

17. Louisa Terry to Luther Terry, July 8, 1877, HL.

18. *Ibid.*, September, 1874.

19. *Ibid.*, February 22, 1875.

20. Crawford to Louisa Terry, December 8, 1875, HL.

21. *Ibid.*, March 16, 1876.

22. *Ibid.*, April 9 [1876].

23. *Greifenstein*, p. 6.

24. Louisa Terry to Crawford, May 24, 1877, HL.

25. Louisa Terry to Luther Terry, June 17, 1877, HL.

26. *Ibid.*, July 8, 1877.

27. *Ibid.*, July 18, 1877.

28. The pertinent chapters are as follows: *Katharine Lauderdale*, I-III, XVIII, XXII-XXIII; *The Ralstons*, I-II, XIX.

29. Elliott, *My Cousin*, p. 42.

Chapter Two

1. Luther Terry to Louisa Terry, July 28, 1877, and Annie Mailliard to Louisa Terry, August 25, 1877, HL.

2. Crawford to Maud Howe, July 29, 1879, HL.

3. Crawford as quoted in "A Hero of the East," New York *Daily Tribune*, January 18, 1898.

4. Crawford to Louisa Terry, September 2, 1879, HL.

5. Jacob died in 1921 after spending his last years in poverty. Most of his immense fortune he is said to have spent proving his innocence of charges of fraud in connection with the sale of the "Imperial Diamond" to the Nizam of Hyderabad.

6. Crawford is quoted in Francis Whiting Halsey, ed., *Authors of Our Day in Their Homes* (New York, 1902), p. 231.

7. Crawford to Margaret Terry, September 18, 1882; the letter is published in Mrs. Winthrop Chanler, *Roman Spring: Memoirs* (Boston, 1934), pp. 131-44; a photostat of the original is in the Isabella Stewart Gardner Museum, Boston, Massachusetts. Norman Douglas, in *Looking Back* (New York, 1933), pp. 403-4, expresses a point of view contrary to what is maintained here; Douglas calls Crawford "a rabid Catholic." On the other hand, Samuel Prescott Hall, who knew Crawford well, has commented: "I am sure he was not a 'rabid' Catholic—he was too polished a man of the world to obtrude or press his opinions, and one might know him for months without knowing his faith; and he freely granted the right of each to his own opinion."—letter to John Pilkington, Jr., June 11, 1951.

8. Maurice Francis Egan, "Some American Novels," *The American Catholic Quarterly Review*, XVII (July, 1892), 624-25.

9. Crawford, "The Press in India," New York *Daily Tribune*, March 11, 1883.

10. *Ibid.*

11. Samuel Ward to Julia Ward Howe, October 27, 1880, HL. Ward added that five of Crawford's staff quit the paper with him.

12. Beverly Smith, "All-Time Champ of the Lobbyists," *The Saturday Evening Post*, CCXXIII (December 23, 1950), 24.

13. Julia Ward Howe to Samuel Ward, May 30, 1881, published in Elliott, *My Cousin*, p. 86.

14. For an account of the lecture, see Boston *Evening Transcript*, May 11, 1881. Crawford had written it in March. He was pleased at its reception and wrote Uncle Sam that he had made money and that Longfellow and Holmes were present for it.

15. Crawford to Samuel Ward, May 11, 1881, Library of Congress.

16. *Ibid.*, August 28, 1881.

17. *Ibid.*, August 20, 1881.

18. *Ibid.*, August 23, 1881.

19. *Ibid.*, September 25, 1881, HL.

20. *Ibid.*, September 30, 1881.

21. Crawford to Louisa Terry, January 3, 1882, HL.

22. *Ibid.*, March 26, 1882. For Crawford's article, "False Taste in Art," see *The North American Review*, CXXXV (July, 1882), 89-98. Crawford helped Sam Ward to write "Days with Longfellow," *The North American Review*, CXXXIV (May, 1882), 456-66.

23. Crawford to Samuel Ward, January 27, 1882, HL.

24. Crawford to Louisa Terry, November 23, 1881, HL.

25. *Ibid.*, December 8, 1881.

26. *Ibid.*, January 3, 1882.

27. Crawford to Samuel Ward, February 11, 1882, Library of Congress.

28. *Ibid.*

29. *Ibid.*, February 14, 1882, HL.

30. Samuel Ward to Julia Ward Howe, March 23, 1882, HL.

31. Crawford to Louisa Terry, March 26, 1882, HL.

32. *Ibid.*

33. Fragment of letter from Crawford to Mrs. Isabella Stewart Gardner in the Isabella Stewart Gardner Museum, Boston, Massachusetts; manuscript material from the museum has been used with permission of the Director, George L. Stout. Unless otherwise noted, Crawford's letters to Mrs. Gardner should be assumed as included in the museum collection; other material from the collection has been identified by the letters GM.

34. Crawford to Louisa Terry, January 3, 1882.

Chapter Three

1. Crawford quoted by Bridges, "F. Marion Crawford," p. 320.

2. Crawford to Samuel Ward, August 22, 1882, HL.

3. Crawford to A. Bence Jones, February 7, 1883, GM.

4. Bridges, "F. Marion Crawford," p. 320.

5. Crawford to Samuel Ward, April 27, 1882, HL.

6. Crawford to Mrs. Gardner, date missing, but probably written about May 18; the italics are Crawford's.

7. Bridges, "F. Marion Crawford," p. 320.

8. Crawford to Samuel Ward, June 15, 1882, HL.

9. *Ibid.*, June 22, 1882.

10. Mrs. Gardner retained the original telegram which is now in the

Gardner Museum. Crawford's reply to his uncle's telegram betrays the tension which had been increasing at the Gardners' home: "There was rejoicing in all the coasts of Beverly at your telegram announcing the definite accepting of Isaacs.... I had succeeded in working myself into a state of suspense about the book and my kind hostess was as much interested as I."—*Ibid.*, August 22, 1882.

11. *Ibid.*, June 11, 1882, HL.
12. *Ibid.*, July 6, 1882.
13. *Ibid.*, July 26, 1882.
14. *Ibid.*, August 12, 1882.
15. *Ibid.*, August 22, 1882.
16. Crawford to Mrs. Gardner, fragment.
17. Crawford to Samuel Ward, September 25, 1882, HL.
18. Crawford to Mrs. Gardner, fragment.
19. Crawford to Samuel Ward, September 30, 1881, typescript, HL.
20. Crawford to Mrs. Gardner, fragment.
21. See letter from Crawford to Louisa Terry, February 23, 1883, HL.
22. Crawford to Samuel Ward, September 25, 1882, HL. Ward was inclined to feel hurt when Crawford seemed to prefer Mrs. Gardner's company and advice to his uncle's. Ward spoke of the matter directly in a letter to Louisa Terry (September 12, 1882, HL): "When I came up from down town [New York] and proposed that he [Crawford] should start on Saturday morning the secret flew out that his kind hostess Mrs. Gardner was to be in Boston for the day ... and he wanted to consult her about 'Mr. Isaacs and other matters' [and] it would be his only opportunity of seeing her and he thought it best upon the whole to go to Newport and there finish his novel. All this might have just as well been said first as last, and I should not have had to chew the cud of regret that my unvarying kindness should not have made him loth to leave me alone. But *place aux dames* and her influence over him is less noxious than those of others might be and we are in the 19th Century and I regard her as an ally whom I cannot replace."
23. George G. Brett to Crawford, January 20, 1883, GM.
24. Crawford to Samuel Ward, February 22, 1883, HL.
25. See letters from Samuel Ward to Louisa Terry, January 9, 1883, and February 11, 1883, HL.
26. Crawford to Samuel Ward, February 22, 1883, HL.
27. Samuel Ward to Louisa Terry, February 11, 1883, and Crawford to Samuel Ward, February 22, 1883, HL.
28. *Ibid.*
29. Samuel Ward to Louisa Terry, January 18, 1883, HL.
30. Crawford to Mrs. Gardner, fragment pasted into the inside cover of Mrs. Gardner's copy of *A Roman Singer*, GM; the first ellipsis in the text quoted appears in the manuscript; the second represents the break between the fragmentary parts of the letter. The only episode of importance which Crawford later added to the summary he wrote for Mrs. Gardner was the Baroness' infatuation for Nino, which ends with her suicide midway in the novel; and when the book is read today, this obviously contrived episode appears as a flaw. Crawford modeled her character after a woman in Italy whom he had thoroughly detested.
31. Crawford to Samuel Ward, February 22, 1883, HL.
32. *Ibid.*
33. Crawford to Louisa Terry, February 23, 1883, HL.

34. *Ibid.*
35. *Ibid.*
36. *Ibid.*
37. *Ibid.*, December 21, 1882.
38. Crawford to Samuel Ward, February 22, 1883, and to Louisa Terry, February 23, 1883, HL.
39. *Ibid.*
40. Crawford to Mrs. Gardner, fragment.
41. *Ibid.*
42. *Ibid.*
43. Crawford to Louisa Terry, April 6, 1883, HL.
44. *Ibid.*, April 27, 1883.
45. Crawford to Maud Howe, May 17, 1883, HL.

Chapter Four

1. Crawford to Louisa Terry, May 17, 1883, HL.
2. See Crawford's letter to Maud Howe, July 31, 1883, HL.; *To Leeward* was published by Houghton, Mifflin and Company in Boston and New York in December, 1883, although the title page of what appears to be the first edition bears the date 1884. The English edition (two volumes) was published in London, 1883, by Chapman and Hall.
3. *To Leeward*, pp. 50-51.
4. It began as a serial in *The Atlantic Monthly*, LII (July, 1883) and continued through LIII (June, 1884). The novel was published in 1884 by Houghton, Mifflin and Company in Boston and New York and by Macmillan in London.
5. Crawford to Maud Howe, July 31, 1883, HL.
6. *To Leeward*, pp. 68-70. Although considerably altered, the account of the shipwreck in Chapter X may be a fictional treatment of Crawford's experience off the coast of Bermuda when coming to America from Italy in 1881.
7. *Ibid.*, p. 71.
8. *Ibid.*, p. 193.
9. *Ibid.*, pp. 390-91.
10. *Ibid.*, p. 396.
11. Crawford to Louisa Terry, September 3, 1883, HL.
12. Crawford to Samuel Ward, October 25, 1883, HL.
13. Crawford to Louisa Terry, November 4, 1883, HL.
14. Samuel Ward to Julia Ward Howe, January 1, 1884, HL.
15. Crawford to Louisa Terry, February 15, 1884, HL.
16. *Ibid.*, February 29, 1884.
17. *Ibid.*
18. Crawford to Julia Ward Howe, July 31, 1884, quoted in Elliott, *My Cousin*, p. 181.
19. Crawford to Louisa Terry, July 5, 1884, HL.
20. The archbishop in Constantinople refused to grant a license unless Bessie signed a promise to rear her children in the Catholic faith. The Berdans objected to this condition, but eventually were reconciled to it by Bessie and Crawford. See letter from Crawford to Louisa Terry, September 20, 1884, HL.
21. Elizabeth Berdan Crawford to Mary Kimball Berdan [January 24,

1885], quoted in "Glimpses of Life in Nine Capitals," typescript by Mrs. Hiram [Mary Kimball] Berdan, owned by Signora Eleanor Marion-Crawford Rocca, Sorrento, Italy; hereafter cited as Berdan memoirs.

22. In this instance Crawford utilized his recent American experience for the setting, added a love story, and invented a slight plot. The technique strongly reminds one of the composition of *Mr. Isaacs*.

23. Crawford to Maud Howe, July 31, 1884, HL.

24. See *An American Politician*, Chap. XXIII; Crawford uses the phrases *party spirit* and *party system* almost interchangeably.

25. *Ibid.*, p. 59.

26. *Ibid.*, p. 338.

27. Throughout Crawford's novels, one finds remarks upon contemporary political movements; for representative examples of his attitude see *Marzio's Crucifix*, pp. 67, 125, 207; *A Lady of Rome*, pp. 353-58; and *The White Sister*, pp. 238-39.

28. The manuscript, now in the Yale Library, bears the following note in Crawford's handwriting: "Rome, December, 1884. With the exception of the first chapter, written at Sorrento in 1883, in August, this book was written by me in thirty-two days, from November 3rd to December 4th inclusive."

Chapter Five

1. Elizabeth Crawford to Mary K. Berdan, January 25, 1885, quoted in Berdan memoirs.

2. Entry in journal of Mary K. Berdan, July 23, 1885, Berdan memoirs.

3. Crawford to Louisa Terry, November 20, 1885, HL.

4. *Ibid.*, January 8, 1886.

5. *Ibid.*, February 22, 1886. The American edition of *Saracinesca* was published in 1887 by Macmillan in New York. It was issued simultaneously by Blackwood in Edinburgh. The work had already been serialized in *Blackwood's Edinburgh Magazine*, CXXXIX-CXLI (May, 1886-April, 1887).

6. Crawford to Louisa Terry, December 23, 1885, HL.

7. *Ibid.*, February 19, 1886.

8. *Ibid.*, March 2, 1886. Despite Crawford's announcement of the new family name, it was not legally changed in the United States until 1902, when Crawford petitioned the Supreme Court of New York on behalf of his children for authority to use the name, Marion-Crawford; for a record of the court action, see "Legal Notices," New York *Times*, March 25, 1902.

9. Entry dated May 3, 1886, Berdan memoirs.

10. After it appeared as a serial in *Macmillan's Magazine*, LVI (May-October, 1887), *With the Immortals* was published by Macmillan in 1888 simultaneously in New York and London. *Paul Patoff* first was published as a serial in *The Atlantic Monthly*, LIX-LX (January-December, 1887) and in 1887 it was published by Houghton, Mifflin and Company in Boston and New York and by Macmillan in London.

11. Louisa Terry to Margaret Terry Chanler, July 13, 1887, HL.

12. Mother Marion-Crawford to John Pilkington, Jr., April 12, 1951. The list does not include Crawford's two personal servants nor the crews of his three boats and later, his yacht.

13. Louisa Terry to Annie Mailliard, June 21, 1887, copy furnished by Miss Rosalind Richards, Gardiner, Maine.

14. Elliott, *My Cousin*, p. 204.

15. See Bridges, "F. Marion Crawford," p. 321. *Marzio's Crucifix* appeared serially in *The English Illustrated Magazine* during the summer of 1887; before it was published as a book in London and in New York by Macmillan, Crawford added two chapters to the work.

16. *American Fiction: An Historical and Critical Survey* (New York, 1936), p. 389.

17. Early in June, 1887, Crawford received a request from the Committee of Arrangements for the celebration of the Constitutional Centenary in Philadelphia to write a poem for the occasion. Crawford was supposed to compose an ode that could be set to music and used as a national hymn. Honored by the request, Crawford began to write with enthusiasm and after a month's work completed it. "A National Hymn" was recited at the centenary celebration in September, 1887.

18. For an account of Crawford's first visit to San Nicola, see Mrs. Hugh [Mary Crawford] Fraser, *Italian Yesterdays* (2 vols.; New York, 1913), I, 56-58. Many of the details in the present account were furnished by Mother Marion-Crawford, April 12, 1951. See also Elliott, *My Cousin*, pp. 225-26.

19. *Sant' Ilario* was issued as a serial in *The English Illustrated Magazine*, VI (October, 1888, through September, 1889). It was published by Macmillan simultaneously in London (3 vols.) and New York (1 vol.) in August, 1889. A second edition in one volume was published in London in November, 1889.

20. Louisa Terry to Maud Elliott, April 30, 1888, copy furnished by Miss Rosalind Richards, Gardiner, Maine.

21. Louisa Terry to Margaret Chanler, June 23, 1888, HL.

22. *My Cousin*, p. 91.

23. Louisa Terry to Margaret Chanler, January 27, 1889, HL.

24. Although the novel was almost certainly written at this time, its publication was postponed twice before it finally appeared as a serial in *Longman's Magazine*, XVIII and XIX (May, 1891, through April, 1892). After it was published by Macmillan in both England and America early in April, 1892, *Publisher's Weekly* announced that the entire first edition was sold on the day of publication, and on May 28, 1892, the same magazine advertised a "3rd edition now ready." Critical reaction was varied, but most reviewers treated it as a revealing comment upon Crawford's own life and career.

25. *Greifenstein* was published in 1889 by Macmillan simultaneously in London and New York.

26. It appeared as a serial in *The English Illustrated Magazine*, VIII (October, 1890, through September, 1891). In September, 1891, the novel was issued in three volumes by Macmillan in London and in one volume in New York.

27. *Khaled*, p. 3.

28. Luther Terry to Margaret Chanler, May 26, 1891, HL.

29. *Don Orsino* first appeared as a serial in *Macmillan's Magazine*, LXV-LXVII (January through December, 1892); and in *The Atlantic Monthly*, LXIX-LXX (January through December, 1892); and in November, 1892, it was published simultaneously by Macmillan in New York and London. Like the other volumes in the trilogy, it enjoyed a tremendous popularity.

30. See *Saracinesca*, pp. 12, 450.

31. *Ibid.*, p. 18.

32. *Ibid.*, p. 450.

33. *An American Politician,* pp. 327-28.

34. *Don Orsino,* p. 448.

35. *Ibid.*

36. *Saracinesca,* p. 2.

37. Mother Marion-Crawford to John Pilkington, Jr., April 12, 1951.

38. On February 6, 1885, Crawford attended a notable entertainment given at the Orsini palazzo in Rome. Before the affair took place his wife wrote her mother: "To-night the ball of balls given by the Princess Orsini takes place. There are over two thousand invitations given and she opens forty salons." And two weeks later she wrote again: "I quite forgot to tell you about the Orsini ball. I never saw or dreamed of anything so beautiful in the way of a ball. There were about one thousand five hundred people there, and the whole thing looked like a great picture painted by a great master. Prince Orsini was very kind to me, gave me his arm and took me through each room so as to show me each thing in turn. The Orsini arms are a bear, so during the cotillion, a very large stuffed bear was brought in, carrying a large box full of flowers. How I wish you could have been there to see it, dear Mama, for everyone says it will be an historical ball." These letters, dated February 6 and 19, 1885, are quoted in the Berdan memoirs. Crawford used the Orsini ball as the basis of his description of the Frangipani ball in *Saracinesca.* For additional examples of Crawford's use of his own experiences in this novel, see Elliott, *My Cousin,* pp. 236-39.

39. James Rennell Rodd, *Social and Diplomatic Memories: 1884-1893* (London: Edward Arnold and Co., 1922), p. 251.

40. *Ibid.,* p. 252.

Chapter Six

1. *The Letters of Henry James,* ed. Percy Lubbock (2 vols.; New York, 1920), I, 104; although Crawford's name was omitted by Lubbock, there can be no question about his identity.

2. *Under Pressure* (New York, 1892). The dedication, signed April, 1892, follows: "To F. Marion Crawford.... May it be a grateful tribute to your friendly incitement to write and to your assurances that my modest essay was not deprived of interest. Lily Theodoli."

3. Elliott, *My Cousin,* p. 232.

4. *Ibid.*

5. Crawford to Mrs. Gardner, fragment, probably written in either October, 1892, or March, 1893.

6. Crawford to Maud Elliott, November 17, 1892, HL.

7. *Ibid.,* November 20, 1892.

8. *Ibid.,* November 26, 1892.

9. Crawford to Mrs. Gardner, fragment, probably written in either October, 1892, or March, 1893.

10. New York *Daily Tribune,* November 18, 1892. Only one novel was serialized. *Pietro Ghisleri* appeared in the New York *Tribune* from March to July, 1893, and during the same year it was published by Macmillan simultaneously in New York (one volume) and London (three volumes). Crawford released the manuscript of *The Children of the King* to Macmillan immediately after arriving in this country, and the novel was published simultaneously in New York and London in February, 1893.

11. "New Novels," *The Athenaeum,* July 22, 1893, p. 125.

12. New York *Times,* December 11, 1892.
13. New York *Daily Tribune,* February 21, 1893.
14. *The Novel: What It Is* (New York, 1893), pp. 7-8.
15. *Ibid.,* pp. 8-9.
16. *Ibid.,* p. 11.
17. *Paul Patoff,* p. 107.
18. *The Three Fates,* p. 166.
19. *The Novel: What It Is,* p. 82.
20. *Ibid.,* p. 12.
21. *Ibid.,* p. 14.
22. *Ibid.,* pp. 16-18.
23. *Ibid.,* p. 19. In the passage immediately following, Crawford tried to clarify further his meaning by saying: "Wordsworth tried the moral lesson and spoiled some of his best work with botany and the Bible. A good many smaller men than he have tried the same thing since, and have failed. Perhaps 'Cain' and 'Manfred' have taught the human heart more wisdom than 'Matthew' or the unfortunate 'idiot boy' over whom Byron was so mercilessly merry. And yet Byron probably never meant to teach any one anything in particular, and Wordsworth meant to teach everybody, including and beginning with himself."
24. *Ibid.,* p. 23.
25. *Ibid.,* p. 39 .
26. William Dean Howells, *Criticism and Fiction* (New York, 1891), p. 149.
27. *The Novel:What It Is,* p. 40.
28. *Ibid.,* p. 41.
29. *With the Immortals,* p. 78.
30. *Saracinesca,* p. 6.
31. *Paul Patoff,* p. 105.
32. *The Three Fates,* p. 39. For similar expression of this idea in Crawford's works, see *Adam Johnstone's Son,* pp. 279-80; *A Rose of Yesterday,* pp. 113-14; and *Whosoever Shall Offend,* p. 332.
33. *The Novel: What It Is,* pp. 90-91.
34. *Ibid.,* p. 45.
35. *Ibid.,* pp. 45-46.
36. *Ibid.,* p. 81.
37. *Ibid.*
38. *Ibid.,* p. 80.
39. *Criticism and Fiction,* pp. 10-12.
40. *The Novel: What It Is,* pp. 64-65.
41. *Ibid.,* pp. 54-56.
42. *Ibid.,* p. 53.
43. *Ibid.,* pp. 76-77.
44. Throughout *The Novel: What It Is,* Crawford made an analogy between the play and the novel. For example, he wrote (pp. 49-50): "It may fairly be claimed that humanity has, within the past hundred years, found a way of carrying a theatre in its pocket; and so long as humanity remains what it is, it will delight in taking out its pocket-stage and watching the antics of the actors, who are so like itself and yet so much more interesting. Perhaps that is, after all, the best answer to the question, 'What is a novel?' It is, or ought to be, a pocket-stage. Scenery, light, shade, the actors themselves, are made of words, and nothing but words, more or less cleverly put together. A play is good in proportion as it represents the more dramatic, passionate, romantic, or humorous sides of real life. A novel is excellent

according to the degree in which it produces the illusions of a good play—but it must not be forgotten that the play is the thing, and that illusion is eminently necessary to success." Later (p. 57) he declared: "What am I, a novel-writer, trying to do? I am trying, with such limited means as I have at my disposal, to make little pocket-theatres out of words. I am trying to be architect, scene-painter, upholsterer, dramatist and stage-manager, all at once. Is it any wonder if we novelists do not succeed as well as we could wish, when we try to be masters of so many trades?"

45. *Ibid.*, pp. 86-87.

46. *Ibid.*, p. 22.

47. In addition to writing *Marion Darche*, Crawford was also contemplating collaboration with Brander Matthews upon a dramatization of *Marzio's Crucifix*.

48. Crawford to Mrs. Gardner [July, 1893].

49. *Ibid.*, June 13, 1893. He was going to Constantinople to refresh his memory before writing two articles about that city; see "Constantinople," *Scribner's Magazine*, XIV (December, 1893), 714-32, and XV (January, 1894), 3-22. In October, 1895, the articles were published in book form by Charles Scribner's Sons.

50. Crawford to Mrs. Gardner, June 13, 1893.

51. *Ibid.* [August 14, 1893].

52. For details of the Berdan case, see *Cases Decided in the Court of Claims*, XXV (1889-1890), 355-89, and XXVI (1890-1891), 48-82. A review of the entire case appears in *United States Reports*, 156 (1894), 552-74. A private bill for the purpose mentioned here was actually passed by Congress and approved March 2, 1899; see *The Statutes at Large of the United States of America* (Washington, D.C., 1899), 1549. Very likely it was a similar bill that Crawford was endeavoring to get through Congress in 1893-94.

53. *Katharine Lauderdale* and *The Ralstons* were published simultaneously in New York and London by the Macmillan Company in 1894 and 1895 respectively.

54. Crawford to Mrs. Gardner, October 9, 1893.

55. *Ibid.*

56. *Ibid.* November 25 [1893].

57. *Ibid.* [November 26, 1893].

58. There is a notable parallel between the character and experience of Jack Ralston and Crawford himself. In addition, the character of Jack Ralston's mother resembles that of Louisa Terry. Mrs. Gardner may have contributed something to the character of Katharine Ralston.

59. *The Ralstons*, p. 313.

60. *Ibid.*, p. 334.

61. In this manner the *Ralston* and *Saracinesca* novels and *Casa Braccio* were linked with *Pietro Ghisleri* and subsequently with such novels as *Taquisara, Corleone,* and even *The White Sister;* and if the presence of Paul Griggs is regarded as the criterion of the related novel, this list could be extended considerably.

62. Crawford to Mrs. Gardner, January 31, 1894.

63. *Ibid.*, February 25, 1894. On March 30, 1894, he wrote her: "Somebody wrote a book called the 'Three Miss Kings' which kills the title I had chosen." His ultimate choice was of course a quotation from Shakespeare's *A Midsummer Night's Dream*. The novel was published by Macmillan simultaneously in New York and London, 1894, after serialization in *The Century Magazine*, XLVIII, n.s. 26 (July through September, 1894).

64. A copy of Crawford's translation of Notovich's book exists in the Library of Congress, but it is likely that this was deposited for copyright purposes and never actually published. Crawford's articles on mysticism were originally intended as the introduction to it. For the review of *Marcella,* see "Two Opinions of Mrs. Humphry Ward's 'Marcella,'" *Book Reviews,* I (April, 1894), 273-76. The first "opinion" was written by Crawford, the second, by Hamilton W. Mabie. For the essays on mysticism, see "A Modern View of Mysticism," *Book Reviews,* II (June, July, and August, 1894), 49-57, 109-15, and 149-53 respectively. The two articles for the *Century* were "Coasting by Sorrento and Amalfi" and "Washington as a Spectacle," *The Century Magazine,* XLVIII, n.s. 26 (July and August, 1894), 325-36 and 482-95 respectively. The travel sketch was "Bar Harbor," *Scribner's Magazine,* XVI (September, 1894), 268-84; it was subsequently published in book form, July 11, 1896, by Charles Scribner's Sons. The first edition has become a rare Crawford item, since of 1,000 copies printed, a fourth were destroyed by accident. A typescript of this work, said to have been made by Mrs. Mary Cadwalader Jones, with corrections in Crawford's autograph, is in the Henry E. Huntington Library, San Marino, California.

65. *The Ralstons,* p. 313.

66. Photostat copy in Houghton Library. Beginning January 29, 1893, Crawford wrote several letters to Miss Lauderdale.

67. Crawford to Mrs. Gardner, April 27 [1894]. The sequence to which Crawford referred consisted of *Marion Darche, Katharine Lauderdale, The Ralstons,* and *Love in Idleness.*

68. See Elizabeth Christophers Hobson, *Recollections of a Happy Life* (New York and London, 1916), pp. 49-56.

69. *Casa Braccio,* pp. 265-67.

70. *Ibid.,* p. 324.

71. *Ibid.*

72 Crawford to Mrs. Gardner, May 10, 1894.

73. *Ibid.,* May 13, 1894.

74. *Ibid.,* October 1, 1898.

75. Nellie Melba, *Melodies and Memories* (New York, 1926), pp. 130-31.

76. *The Primadonna* (New York, 1908), pp. 93-94.

77. Crawford to Mrs. Gardner, June 17, 1894.

78. Crawford was still correcting the proof when he left for Sorrento. The copyright was not deposited until September 19, 1894; and although there exists a copy dated "1894," the novel was not actually published until November, 1895, by Macmillan in New York and London (two volumes). Meanwhile it had appeared in *The Century,* XLIX and L, n.s. 27 and 28 (November, 1894, through October, 1895).

Chapter Seven

1. *Adam Johnstone's Son,* p. 5.

2. Mrs. Crawford and the children did not accompany him. On August 8, Louisa Terry wrote Maud Elliott (HL) that Crawford had gone to Schinznach for three weeks. She added, "Bessie is having rather a gay summer with Neapolitan acquaintances. On one of these very recent moonlight nights she drove with a large party over the hills to Pagliano where they all supped sumptuously . . . and reentered her own gate only at 4 o'clock in the morning."

3. *The Century Magazine*, LI, n.s. 29 (January, 1896), 322-40.

4. Crawford to Mrs. Gardner, November 24, 1895.

5. See "Pope Leo XIII. and His Household," *The Century Magazine*, LI, n.s. 29 (February, 1896), 590-603; "St. Peter's," *The Century Magazine*, LII, n.s. 30 (July, 1896), 323-39; and "The Vatican," *The Century Magazine*, LII, n.s. 30 (August, 1896), 577-88. Eventually, these articles became the basis for several of Crawford's lectures and later were incorporated with only slight changes in *Ave Roma Immortalis*.

6. After appearing as a serial in *The Century Magazine*, LIII, n.s. 31 (November, 1896, through February, 1897), *A Rose of Yesterday* was published by Macmillan in London and New York in 1897.

7. Although the copyright was deposited May 26, 1896, *Corleone* was not published by Macmillan in New York and London (two volumes) until late in October or early in November, 1897. Meanwhile, it appeared as a serial in *Munsey's Magazine*, XVI-XVIII (February, 1897, through February, 1898).

8. *A Rose of Yesterday*, p. 206.

9. "Some Novels of the Year," *The Atlantic Monthly*, LXXXIII (January, 1899), 130.

10. Crawford to Mrs. Gardner, October 1, 1895.

11. Mrs. Jones's comment is contained in the typescript notes of an interview between Mrs. Elliott and Mrs. Jones, HL. She also remarked upon Crawford's dislike of many people in New York. Crawford was a frequent guest in her home in New York and at her summer cottage in Bar Harbor.

12. Crawford to Mrs. Gardner, July 20, 1895.

13. *Ibid.*, November 15, 1895.

14. Letters to John Pilkington, Jr., June 11 and 16, 1951.

15. Douglas, *Looking Back*, p. 404.

16. Crawford to Mrs. Gardner, December 29, 1894.

17. Margaret Chanler to Luther Terry, May 12, 1896, HL.

18. Crawford to Mrs. Gardner, May 18, 1896.

19. *Ibid.*

20. *Ibid.*, January 26, 1897.

21. Crawford to Mrs. Gardner, March 1, 1897.

22. *Ibid.*

23. *Ibid.*, August 13, 1897.

24. *Ibid.*

25. See "Ave Roma Immortalis," *The Academy and Literature*, LIV (November 19, 1898), 287; and "Immortal Rome," *The Spectator*, LXXXI (December 17, 1898), 912-13. Among the better reviews are "Ave Roma Immortalis," *The Athenaeum*, 1898, 2 (December 17, 1898), 858-59; "Mr. Crawford's Ave Roma," *The Atlantic Monthly*, LXXXIII (February, 1899), 275-81; and Josiah Renwick Smith, "The Romance of Rome," *The Dial* [Chicago], XXV (December 1, 1898), 390-91.

26. J[ames] B[urton] Pond, *Eccentricities of Genius: Memories of Famous Men and Women of the Platform and Stage* (New York, 1900), p. 457.

27. New Orleans *Daily Picayune*, February 25, 1898.

28. *Ibid.*, March 1, 1898.

29. Pond, *Eccentricities of Genius*, p. 462.

30. Crawford to Mrs. Gardner, March 15, 1898.

31. Pond, *Eccentricities of Genius*, p. 462.

32. See New York *Tribune*, May 8, 1898.

33. See New Orleans *Daily Picayune*, February 27, 1898, and San Francisco *Chronicle*, March 31, 1898.

34. "The Early Italian Artists," *Book Reviews*, V (February, 1898), 255.

35. New Orleans *Daily Picayune*, March 1, 1898.

36. *Ibid.* Later Crawford included a chapter on the Mafia in his book on Sicily; see *The Rulers of the South: Sicily, Calabria, Malta* (2 vols.; New York and London, 1900), II, 363-85.

37. San Francisco *Chronicle*, March 29, 1898; compare *Ave Roma Immortalis*, II, 267.

38. See New York *Tribune*, February 1, 1898.

39. New Orleans *Daily Picayune*, March 1, 1898.

40. San Francisco *Chronicle*, March 26, 1898.

41. March 26, 1898.

42. Pond, *Eccentricities of Genius*, p. 464.

Chapter Eight

1. Crawford to John Phillips Street, November 22, 1892, HL.

2. *Via Crucis*, p. 396. The novel was serialized in *The Century Magazine*, LVII-LVIII, n.s. 35-36 (November, 1898, through October, 1899). In November, 1899, it was published by Macmillan in New York and London. A publisher's advertisement in the New York *Times Saturday Review*, January 20, 1900, p. 48, reads as follows: "Eight editions of 5,000 each were exhausted in as many weeks after publication, and that the one now on sale is the fifty-third thousand of *Via Crucis*." In March, 1900, a writer in the *Bookman* observed that *Via Crucis* was in its "seventieth thousand."— See "Chronicle and Comment," *The Bookman*, XI (March, 1900), 7-8.

3. Crawford to Mrs. Gardner, October 2, 1898.

4. George C. Tyler, "Not That It Matters," *The Saturday Evening Post*, CCVI (February 10, 1934), 16.

5. It appeared as a serial in *Munsey's Magazine*, XXIII and XXIV (April, 1900, through January, 1901), and was published in book form by Macmillan in New York and London later in October, 1900.

6. Tyler, "Not That It Matters," p. 17.

7. Vittoria Colonna, Duchess of Sermoneta, *Things Past* (New York, 1929), p. 108.

8. Crawford to the Duchess of Sermoneta, May 25, 1900, quoted in *Things Past*, p. 110.

9. Crawford to Mrs. Gardner, July 24, 1907.

10. "For the Blood Is the Life," *Collier's*, XXXVI (December 16, 1905), 17-20. It was reprinted in Crawford's *Wandering Ghosts* (New York, 1911), pp. 167-94. In the story, Brokman appears as Holger and the tower, which is accurately described, forms the background.

11. *The Rulers of the South*, p. 25.

12. See above, p. 158.

13. Crawford to Mrs. Gardner, February 7, 1901.

14. Interview with Mrs. Winthrop Chanler, April 11, 1951.

15. Crawford as quoted in *Authors of Our Day in Their Homes*, ed. Halsey, p. 233.

16. Published by Macmillan in New York and London, 1901.

17. It was published in two volumes by Macmillan in New York and London, 1905.

18. Letter from Leigh Mitchell Hodges quoted in "The Lounger," *The Critic*, XXXVIII (April, 1901), 303.

19. Pennell published his comments about Crawford in the article, "Adventures of an Illustrator: VI–With Hewlett and Crawford in Italy," *The Century Magazine*, CIV, n.s. 82 (June, 1922), 293-300, and again in his autobiography, *The Adventures of an Illustrator* (Boston, 1925), p. 285.

20. Mrs. Hugh Fraser, quoted in "Shakespearean Revivals," newspaper clipping, March 30, 1902, Theatre Collection, HL.

21. See Louis Verneuil, *The Fabulous Life of Sarah Bernhardt*, translated by Ernest Boyd (New York and London, 1942), pp. 228-29.

22. Pierre Champion, *Marcel Schwob et son temps* (Paris, 1927), p. 157.

23. Crawford to the Duchess of Sermoneta, December 8, 1902, quoted in *Things Past*, p. 112.

24. See Marcel Schwob, *Francesca da Rimini* (Paris, 1902).

25. "Note" at conclusion of *Marietta*, p. 458.

26. Reviewers said that *Marietta* touched perfection in its kind; see "New Novels," *The Athenaeum*, 1901, 2 (November 23, 1901), 695; "Novel Notes," *The Bookman* [London], XXI (December, 1901), 98; and "Novel Notes," *The Bookman*, XV (April, 1902), 198. For the first printing in October, 1901, Macmillan in London printed 20,000 copies, and two months later an additional 15,000 were required–Publisher's statement. Although figures are not available, the American sale was probably larger than the English.

27. *Francesca da Rimini: A Play in Four Acts* (New York, 1902).

28. Verneuil, *Life of Sarah Bernhardt*, pp. 239-40.

29. *Things Past*, p. 109.

30. Publisher's statement. It was published in New York and London, October, 1902, by Macmillan. The character of Cecilia may have been suggested by the personality of Gladys Marie Deacon to whom Crawford was very much attracted in 1902. The daughter of Mrs. Edward Parkman Deacon, Gladys Deacon later became the Duchess of Marlborough.

31. Crawford to the Duchess of Sermoneta, December 8, 1902, quoted in *Things Past*, p. 112.

32. *Ibid.*, p. 114.

33. Harvey gave the first performance of the work in New York at the Herald Square Theatre, November 12, 1902. Too short a play to be given by itself, Harvey normally presented it in conjunction with another play. For a review of the performance, see "Martin Harvey's Double Bill," New York *Times*, November 14, 1902.

34. *A Cigarette-Maker's Romance* was first produced at the Court Theatre, London, February 11, 1901.

35. F[rancis] Marion Crawford, *Man Overboard!* (New York: The Macmillan Company, 1903). The copyright was deposited March 7, 1903, and the work was published in May. The story also appeared in *The Strand Magazine*, XXV (June, 1903), 664-76.

36. Charles Hall Garrett, "A Talk with Marion Crawford," *The Lamp*, XXVII (October, 1903), 216.

37. *Ibid.*

38. Published October, 1903, by Macmillan in New York and London, *The Heart of Rome* sold more than 40,000 copies in America by 1904; and in England 24,500 copies were made of the first printing.

39. Carpenter's letter was published in "The Lounger," *The Critic*, XLVIII (June, 1906), 483-84.

40. Crawford quoted by Walter Littlefield, "F. Marion Crawford Returned from Italy," New York *Times*, October 30, 1904, p. 21.
41. Mother Marion-Crawford to John Pilkington, Jr., April 12, 1951.
42. Crawford quoted by Littlefield, "F. Marion Crawford Returned from Italy," p. 21.
43. Published October, 1904, by Macmillan in New York and London.
44. Published November, 1905, by Macmillan in New York; in London it was issued as *Soprano: A Portrait*.
45. Schwob's letter quoted by Champion, *Marcel Schwob*, p. 223.
46. L[acy] Collison-Morley, "A Romantic American at Home–Marion Crawford," *The Nineteenth Century*, CXLI (June, 1947), 307.

Chapter Nine

1. Crawford to Mrs. Gardner, October 2, 1898.
2. Crawford to the Duchess of Sermoneta, December 15, 1905, quoted in *Things Past*, p. 115.
3. *Arethusa* was serialized in *The American Magazine*, LXIII-LXIV (January through September, 1907), before being published in book form by Macmillan in New York and London, 1907.
4. Crawford to Julia Ward Howe, April 22, 1907, HL.
5. Laura Richards [Mrs. Charles Wiggins], quoted by Elliott, *My Cousin*, p. 294.
6. Crawford to Mrs. Gardner [May 22, 1907].
7. *Ibid.*, June 12, 1907.
8. Macmillan published *The Primadonna* in New York and London, May, 1908, and *The Diva's Ruby* in New York and London, October, 1908. A month later the three novels of the trilogy were bound alike and sold as a set. Crawford promised Melba to dedicate the third volume to her.
9. Crawford to Mrs. Gardner, September 1, 1907.
10. *Ibid.*
11. *Ibid.*, November 29, 1908.
12. Crawford to the Duchess of Sermoneta, July 10 [1908], quoted in *Things Past*, pp. 120-21.
13. See above, Chapter VI, pp. 128-29, and *The Primadonna*, pp. 92-94.
14. Crawford to the Duchess of Sermoneta, July 1, 1908.
15. Crawford to Mrs. Gardner, September 1, 1907.
16. Crawford to Maud Elliott, January 5, 1908, HL.
17. See the Duchess of Sermoneta, *Things Past*, pp. 117-19.
18. Crawford to the Duchess of Sermoneta [November, 1907], quoted in *Things Past*, p. 119.
19. *The Undesirable Governess* was published by Macmillan, April, 1910, in New York and London. It had already appeared as a serial under the title "The New Governess," in *The Pall Mall Magazine*, XLIV (July through October, 1909).
20. Crawford to Mrs. Gardner, December 31, 1907.
21. *Ibid.*, February 11, 1908.
22. *Ibid.*, April 23, 1908.
23. *Stradella* appeared as a serial in *The Delineator*, LXXII-LXXIV (September, 1908, through September, 1909) before being published by Macmillan in London and New York, 1909.

24. Crawford to Mrs. Gardner, October 4, 1908.
25. *Ibid.*
26. *Ibid.*, October 4, 1908.
27. *Ibid.*, November 29, 1908.
28. Crawford to the Duchess of Sermoneta [c. January, 1909], quoted in *Things Past*, p. 122.
29. Mother Marion-Crawford to John Pilkington, Jr., April 12, 1951.
30. The volume was never published.
31. Published by Macmillan simultaneously in New York and London, May, 1909.
32. *The White Sister*, p. 103.
33. See "New Books," *The Catholic World*, LXXXIX (August, 1909), 690.

Chapter Ten

1. "Crawford's Last Novel," *The Independent*, LXVI (May 6, 1909), 982.
2. *The Ralstons*, p. 313.
3. Thomas Wolfe, *The Story of a Novel* (New York, 1946), p. 21.
4. *The White Sister*, pp. 112-13.
5. See above, Chapter VII, p. 137.
6. See above, Chapter VII, p. 134.
7. *The Novel: What It Is*, p. 43.

Selected Bibliography

PRIMARY SOURCES

A Note on Manuscript Sources and Bibliography

Letters and other manuscript material written either by Crawford or about him are included in the following collections at the Houghton Library of Harvard University: manuscripts presented by Mrs. Winthrop Chanler, Genesco, New York; papers presented by the children of Laura E. Richards; and the documents presented by Miss Rosalind Richards, Gardiner, Maine. Additional letters, manuscripts, and other documents relating to Crawford are owned by the Isabella Stewart Gardner Museum, Boston, Massachusetts; the Library of Congress; the New York Public Library; and Lawrence Terry, Concord, Massachusetts. Manuscripts of Crawford's novels are held by the Library of Congress, Harvard University, Yale University, Princeton University, University of Pennsylvania, and John Pilkington, Jr.

The following bibliography of Crawford's published works and secondary materials about him represents a selection of the most important items. For a fuller bibliographical treatment see Jacob Blanck, comp., *Bibliography of American Literature* (New Haven, Connecticut: Yale University Press, 1957), II, 341-63; and John Pilkington, Jr., "A Crawford Bibliography," *University of Mississippi Studies in English,* IV (1963), 1-20.

Published Works

A. *Fiction*

The bibliography listed below represents first editions; where the publisher's name is not mentioned, the Macmillan Company should be assumed.

Mr. Isaacs: A Tale of Modern India. New York, 1882. Issued simultaneously in London.

Doctor Claudius: A True Story. New York, 1883. Issued simultaneously in London.

To Leeward. London: Chapman and Hall, 1883, 2 vols. Issued in Boston and New York: Hougton, Mifflin and Company, 1884.

A Roman Singer. Boston and New York: Houghton, Mifflin and Company, 1884. Issued simultaneously in London, 2 vols.

An American Politician: A Novel. Boston and New York; Houghton, Mifflin and Company, 1885. Issued simultaneously in London: Chapman and Hall, 2 vols.

Zoroaster. New York, 1885. Issued simultaneously in London, 2 vols.

A Tale of a Lonely Parish. New York, 1886. Issued simultaneously in London, 2 vols.

Saracinesca. New York, 1887. Issued simultaneously in Edinburgh: Blackwood, 3 vols.

Marzio's Crucifix. New York, 1887. Issued simultaneously in London, 2 vols.

Paul Patoff. Boston and New York: Houghton, Mifflin and Company, 1887. Issued simultaneously in London, 3 vols.

With the Immortals. New York, 1888. Issued simultaneously in London, 2 vols.

Greifenstein. New York, 1889. Issued simultaneously in London, 3 vols.

Sant' Ilario. New York, 1889. Issued simultaneously in London, 3 vols.

A Cigarette-Maker's Romance. New York, 1890. Issued simultaneously in London, 2 vols.

Khaled: A Tale of Arabia. New York, 1891. Issued simultaneously in London, 2 vols.

The Witch of Prague: A Fantastic Tale. New York, 1891. Issued simultaneously in London, 3 vols.

The Three Fates. New York, 1892. Issued simultaneously in London, 3 vols.

Don Orsino. New York, 1892. Issued simultaneously in London, 3 vols.

The Children of the King: A Tale of Southern Italy. New York and London, 1893.

Pietro Ghisleri. New York, 1893. Issued simultaneously in London, 3 vols.

Marion Darche: A Story without Comment. New York, 1893. Issued simultaneously in London, 2 vols.

Love in Idleness: A Tale of Bar Harbour. New York and London, 1894.

Katharine Lauderdale. New York and London, 1894, 2 vols.

The Ralstons. New York and London, 1895, 2 vols.

Casa Braccio. New York and London, 1894 [1895], 2 vols.

Adam Johnstone's Son. New York and London, 1896.

Taquisara. New York and London, 1896, 2 vols.

Corleone: A Tale of Sicily. New York and London, 1896 [1897], 2 vols.

A Rose of Yesterday. New York and London, 1897.

Via Crucis. New York and London, 1899.

In the Palace of the King: A Love Story of Old Madrid. New York and London, 1900.

Marietta: A Maid of Venice. New York and London, 1901.

Cecilia: A Story of Modern Rome. New York and London, 1902.

The Heart of Rome: A Tale of the "Lost Water." New York and London, 1903.

Whosoever Shall Offend. New York and London, 1904.

Fair Margaret: A Portrait. New York, 1905. Issued in London (1905) as *Soprano: A Portrait.*

A Lady of Rome. New York and London, 1906.

Arethusa. New York and London, 1907.

The Little City of Hope: A Christmas Story. New York, 1907. Issued simultaneously in London.

The Primadonna: A Sequel to "Fair Margaret." New York, 1908. Issued in London (1908) as *The Primadonna: A Sequel to 'Soprano.'*

The Diva's Ruby: A Sequel to "Primadonna" and "Fair Margaret." New York, 1908. Issued in London (1908) as *The Diva's Ruby: A Sequel to 'Soprano' and 'Primadonna.'*

The White Sister. New York, 1909. Issued simultaneously in London.

Stradella: An Old Italian Love Tale. New York, 1909. Issued simultaneously in London.

The Undesirable Governess. New York, 1910. Issued simultaneously in London.

Wandering Ghosts. New York, 1911. Issued simultaneously in London as *Uncanny Tales.*

B. *Plays*

Francesca da Rimini: A Play in Four Acts. New York, 1902.

The White Sister: A Romantic Drama in Three Acts. With Walter Hackett, [New York] Dramatists Play Service, Inc., 1937.

Selected Bibliography

C. *Non-Fiction*

The Novel: What It Is. New York and London, 1893.
Constantinople. New York: Charles Scribner's Sons, 1895. Issued simultaneously in London.
Bar Harbor. New York: Charles Scribner's Sons, 1896.
Ave Roma Immortalis: Studies from the Chronicles of Rome. New York and London, 1898, 2 vols.
The Rulers of the South: Sicily, Calabria, Malta. New York and London, 1900, 2 vols.
Salve Venetia: Gleanings from Venetian History. New York and London, 1905, 2 vols.

D. *Articles in Newspapers and Periodicals*

"False Taste in Art," *North American Review,* CXXXV (July, 1882), 89-98.
"What Is a Novel?" *The Forum,* XIV (January, 1893), 591-99.
"Emotional Tension and the Modern Novel," *The Forum,* XIV (February, 1893), 735-42.
"Two Opinions of Mrs. Humphry Ward's 'Marcella' " [Part I], *Book Reviews,* I (April, 1894), 273-76.
"A Modern View of Mysticism," *Book Reviews,* II (June, 1894), 49-57.
"A Modern View of Mysticism. II," *Book Reviews,* II (July, 1894), 109-15.
"Coasting by Sorrento and Amalfi," *The Century Magazine,* XLVIII, n.s. 26 (July, 1894), 325-36.
"A Modern View of Mysticism. III," *Book Reviews,* II (August, 1894), 149-53.
"Washington as a Spectacle," *The Century Magazine,* XLVIII, n.s. 26 (August, 1894), 482-95.
"Bar Harbor," *Scribner's Magazine,* XVI (September, 1894), 268-84.
"A Kaleidoscope of Rome," *The Century Magazine,* LI, n.s. 29 (January, 1896), 322-40.
"Pope Leo XIII. and His Household," *The Century Magazine,* LI, n.s. 29 (February, 1896), 590-603.
"St. Peter's," *The Century Magazine,* LII, n.s. 30 (July, 1896), 323-39.
"The Vatican," *The Century Magazine,* LII, n.s. 30 (August, 1896), 577-88.
"The Early Italian Artists," *Book Reviews,* V (February, 1898), 255-60.
"The Romance of Rome," *Frank Leslie's Popular Monthly,* XLVII (April, 1899), 580-92.
"Leo the Thirteenth," *The Outlook,* LXI (April 1, 1899), 772-80.
"Vatican and Quirinal," *The Independent,* LIII (February 14, 1901), 361-62.
"The Greatest Disaster of History: First Paper," *The Outlook,* XCI (March 27, 1909), 673-90.

SECONDARY SOURCES

In the selection of references for this portion of the bibliography, newspaper articles, although cited fully in the notes to the text, have been for the most part omitted. In the choice of the other items included here, the objective has been to provide a representative sampling of materials about Crawford published during his lifetime and the most important studies of his life and work since his death.

"About Novels," Boston *Evening Transcript*, December 19, 1892. Interesting material not only as a report of Crawford's public readings but also as an early expression of his theory of the novel.

BRIDGES, ROBERT. "F. Marion Crawford: A Conversation," *McClure's Magazine*, IV (March, 1895), 316-23. Contains valuable information about Crawford's literary career and method of writing novels.

BROOKS, VAN WYCK. *The Dream of Arcadia: American Writers and Artists in Italy, 1760-1915*. New York: E. P. Dutton and Co., Inc., 1958. Includes a well-written but not very penetrating chapter about Crawford's life in Italy.

CHAMPION, PIERRE. *Marcel Schwob et son temps*. Paris: Bernard Grasset, 1927. Provides information about Crawford's *Francesca da Rimini*.

CHANLER, MRS. WINTHROP. *Roman Spring: Memoirs*. Boston: Little, Brown, and Company, 1934. A very important source of information about Crawford's life and personality; also valuable for insights into his family and friends.

COLLISON-MORLEY, L[ACY]. "A Romantic American at Home—Marion Crawford," *The Nineteenth Century*, CXLI (June, 1947), 302-8. Based 'largely upon already published sources, this article contains little that is new and merely continues the romantic view of Crawford accepted by the public during his lifetime.

COLONNA, VITTORIA, Duchess of Sermoneta. *Things Past*. New York: D. Appleton and Company, 1929. Perhaps the most valuable single source for material about Crawford's life after 1900; reprints letters showing his interest in historical research.

COOPER, FREDERIC TABER. "Francis Marion Crawford—An Estimate," *The Bookman*, XXIX (May, 1909), 283-92. A thoughtful criticism of Crawford's work by a contemporary critic; important to the student interested in Crawford's contribution to the American novel.

————. "Representative American Story-Tellers: Francis Marion Crawford," *The Bookman*, XXVI (October, 1907), 126-36.

————. *Some American Story Tellers*. New York: Henry Holt and Company, 1911. Discusses Crawford's work in Chapter I.

DOUGLAS, NORMAN. *Looking Back*. New York: Harcourt, Brace and Company, 1933. Includes several unflattering anecdotes about Crawford.

ELLIOTT, MAUD HOWE. "Glimpses of Marion Crawford," *The Commonweal*, XX (August 24, 1934), 401-3. Excerpts from *My Cousin* but includes other material.

————. *My Cousin: F. Marion Crawford*. New York: The Macmillan Company, 1934. The chief value lies in the letters which Mrs. Elliott publishes; but where scholarly accuracy is important, the text should be compared with the original letters now in the Houghton Library of Harvard. What gives her book its special significance is the fact that she knew Crawford during the early years of his literary career.

————. *Uncle Sam Ward and His Circle*. New York: The Macmillan Company, 1938. A much more scholarly book than *My Cousin*. Provides a wealth of information about the Ward, Crawford, and Terry families.

FRASER, MRS. HUGH. *A Diplomatist's Wife in Many Lands*. London: Hutchinson and Co., 1911, 2 vols. Mrs. Fraser, who was Crawford's sister, includes several anecdotes about Crawford's early life, but her volumes are chiefly valuable for information about the kind of social and literary milieu in which he lived.

————. *Italian Yesterdays*. New York: Dodd, Mead and Company, 1913, 2

Selected Bibliography

vols. The comment made in the preceding entry applies here with even more pertinence.

FRASER, MARY CRAWFORD [Mrs. Hugh]. "Notes of a Romantic Life: The Italian Days of Francis Marion Crawford, and the Intimate Side of His Character," *Collier's*, XLV (April 23, 1910), 22-24. A flattering account of Crawford's life and personality.

GALE, ROBERT, ed. " 'My Dear Uncle'—Three Letters from Francis Marion Crawford to Samuel Ward," *Studi Americani*, V (1959), 325-38. Prints for the first time three letters which contain biographical information about Crawford in 1883 and 1884.

GARRETT, CHARLES HALL. "A Talk with Marion Crawford," *The Lamp*, XXVII (October, 1903), 216-18. Contains an account of Crawford's historical research.

HALSEY, FRANCIS WHITING, ed. *Authors of Our Day in Their Homes*. New York: James Pott and Company, 1902. Describes "Villa Crawford" in Chapter XVII.

HARKINS, E[DWARD] F[RANCIS]. *Little Pilgrimages among the Men Who Have Written Famous Books*. Boston: L. C. Page and Company, 1902. Discusses Crawford on pp. 169-83.

KNIGHT, GRANT C. *The Critical Period in American Literature*. Chapel Hill, North Carolina: University of North Carolina Press, 1951. Sees Crawford's *The Novel: What It Is* as "a classic presentation of the romanticist's dialectics" and presents a brief but accurate summary of Crawford's literary theories.

LITTLEFIELD, WALTER. "F. Marion Crawford Returned from Italy Chats Entertainingly about His New Novel and Other Things," *The New York Times*, October 30, 1904, pp. 21-22. An important newspaper article because of Crawford's remarks about his literary projects.

MELBA, NELLIE. *Melodies and Memories*. New York: George H. Doran Company, 1926. Contains an account of her friendship with Crawford.

OUIDA [LOUISE DE LA RAMÉE] "The Italian Novels of Marion Crawford," *The Nineteenth Century*, XLII (November, 1897), 719-33. A thoughtful and widely discussed critical essay which she reprinted in her *Critical Studies* (Chapter III, pp. 85-111).

PENNELL, JOSEPH. *The Adventures of an Illustrator Mostly in Following His Authors in America and Europe*. Boston: Little, Brown, and Company, 1925. Pennell's dislike of Crawford is evident in the account of their meeting in Italy; Chapter XXXI includes some information about the relationship between author and illustrator.

————. "Adventures of an Illustrator: VI—With Hewlett and Crawford in Italy," *The Century Magazine*, CIV, n.s. 82 (June, 1922), 293-300.

PILKINGTON, JOHN, JR. "A Crawford Bibliography," *University of Mississippi Studies in English*, IV (1963), 1-20. Although not exhaustive, a more complete bibliography than in the present study.

————. "F. Marion Crawford: Italy in Fiction," *American Quarterly*, VI (Spring, 1954), 59-65. An evaluation of Crawford's use of Italy in his fiction.

————. "F. Marion Crawford's Lecture Tour, 1897-1898," *University of Mississippi Studies in English*, I (1960), 66-85. A detailed study of Crawford's lectures under the managership of Major James Burton Pond.

————. "The Genesis of *Mr. Isaacs*," *University of Mississippi Studies in English*, II (1961), 29-39. An account of the circumstances of the writing of Crawford's first novel.

PILKINGTON, JOHN, JR. "A Novelist and His Public," *University of Mississippi Studies in English*, III (1962), 79-89. An analysis of the influence of the reading public upon Crawford's literary career.

POND, J[AMES] B[URTON]. *Eccentricities of Genius: Memories of Famous Men and Women of the Platform and Stage*. New York: G. W. Dillingham Company, 1900. Contains Pond's estimate of Crawford's lecture tour in 1897-98.

QUINN, ARTHUR HOBSON. *American Fiction: An Historical and Critical Survey*. New York and London: D. Appleton-Century Company, 1936. Despite some inaccuracies, Quinn's analysis of Crawford's contribution to the American novel remains an excellent survey of the totality of his work.

RICHARDS, LAURA E., and ELLIOTT, MAUD HOWE. *Julia Ward Howe: 1819-1910*. Boston: Houghton Mifflin Company, 1916. 2 vols. Of value chiefly for background material about Crawford and his family.

SCHWOB, MARCEL. *Francesca da Rimini*. Paris: Librairie Charpentier et Fasquelle, 1902. Contains Crawford's preface to Schwob's translation of *Francesca da Rimini* into French.

SMITH, BEVERLY. "All-Time Champ of the Lobbyists," *The Saturday Evening Post*, CCXXIII (December 23, 1950), 24, 53-55. Although the focus of this article is on Sam Ward, it also includes a good deal of material relevant to Crawford.

THARP, LOUISE HALL. *Three Saints and a Sinner*. Boston: Little, Brown and Company, 1956. Although Mrs. Tharp's book is primarily a biographical account of the Ward sisters and Sam Ward, there is material of interest to the student of Crawford's life and literary work.

TYLER, GEORGE C. "Not That It Matters," *The Saturday Evening Post*, CCVI (February 10, 1934), 16-17, 32, 34, 38. An important article for information about Crawford's play, *In the Palace of the King*.

VEDDER, HENRY C. *American Writers of To-Day*. New York and Boston: Silver, Burdett and Company, 1895. A full treatment of Crawford's work at a time when his reputation was very high.

WALPOLE, HUGH. "The Stories of Francis Marion Crawford," *The Yale Review*, XII (July, 1923), 673-91. A valuable essay on Crawford's work by a sympathetic yet critical admirer.

WHARTON, EDITH. "The Three Francescas," *The North American Review*, CLXXV (July, 1902), 17-30. Compares Crawford's play about Francesca with those by Stephen Phillips and Gabriele D'Annunzio.

Index